D1270833

The Long Term Missing

The Long Term Missing

Hope and Help for Families

Silvia Pettem

ROWMAN & LITTLEFIELD
Lanham • Boulder • New York • London

Published by Rowman & Littlefield
A wholly owned subsidiary of The Rowman & Littlefield Publishing Group, Inc.
4501 Forbes Boulevard, Suite 200, Lanham, Maryland 20706
www.rowman.com

Unit A, Whitacre Mews, 26-34 Stannary Street, London SE11 4AB

Copyright © 2017 by Silvia Pettem

All rights reserved. No part of this book may be reproduced in any form or by any
electronic or mechanical means, including information storage and retrieval systems,
without written permission from the publisher, except by a reviewer who may quote
passages in a review.

British Library Cataloguing in Publication Information Available

Library of Congress Cataloging-in-Publication Data Available
ISBN 9781442256804 (cloth : alk. paper)
ISBN 9781442256811 (electronic)

♾™ The paper used in this publication meets the minimum requirements of American
National Standard for Information Sciences—Permanence of Paper for Printed Library
Materials, ANSI/NISO Z39.48-1992.

Printed in the United States of America

*To all who bring home the missing
and identify the unknown*

Contents

List of Illustrations   xi

Foreword   xiii

Acknowledgments   xvii

1 Why Finding the Missing Is Important   **1**
Provides Resolution for Families   2
    Gina and Her Dad: Returned Identities   2
Aids in Arrest and Conviction of Criminals   5
    Lisa Kay Kelly and Her Killer   6
Gives Dignity and Justice to the Victims   8
    Retired Sheriff Is "Our Girl's" Best Advocate   8

2 Categories of Long-Term Missing Adults   **15**
Suspicious Circumstances   16
    Jeanne Overstreet   16
Adults at Risk/ Endangered   17
Voluntary Disappearances   19
    Ellenor Hacker   21
    Brenda Heist   22
Natural or Accidental Death Most Likely   23
    Alaskan Adventurers Find Answers for Families   24
Undetermined   26
    Gloria Jean Baird   26
    John William Gates   27

3 Children: Helping to Bring Them Home   **31**
Runaways   32
Abductions   34

Elizabeth Smart   36
Polly Klass   37
Lost, Injured, or Otherwise Missing Children   37
Marie Ann Blee: Someone Knows What Happened   39
Critically Missing Young Adults   43
NCMEC: Behind the Scenes   43
Forensic Imaging Team   44
Project ALERT®   44
Biometrics Team   45
Forensic Services Unit   45
Carol Schweitzer: A Privilege to Speak for the Children   46
The Case of Curtis Huntzinger   48

4 Proactive Police   **51**
CSO Beth Buchholtz: Making a Difference in Her Community   51
Names for the Unknown   51
Prevention and Best Practices   53
Matching the Missing and the Unidentified   54
Detective Stuart Somershoe: A Voice for the Victims   57
Missing and Unidentified Persons Unit   58
Long-Term Missing Persons   59
Jane Doe 92-1169   61
Shannon: Once Lost and Now Found   62
Trooper Brian F. Gross and the Westmoreland County Girls   64
Back in Time   65
Fast-Forward to the Present   67
Exhumation   68
Identification   70

5 Civilian Searchers   **73**
David and Rosemary: Face of a Friend   73
College Days   74
Pursuing the Search   76
Finally, the Family   77
Victim Advocates and Dedicated Individuals   78
Janet Franson: Doing God's Work   79
Jody Ewing: All Iowa All the Time   82
Civilian Search Teams   86
Colorado Forensic Canines: Human Remains Detection   86

6 Celeste's Sister Sara: Found Alive in Mexico   **91**
Growing Up in Colorado   91
The Downward Spiral   93
Functioning Amid Dysfunction   93

An Unlikely Club   94
Thinking Like an Investigator   95
Meanwhile, South of the Border   96
Bringing Sara Home   97
    Road Trip   98
    Mission Accomplished   99

7 NamUs: An Investigative Tool   101
How Law Enforcement Uses NamUs   101
    Paul Daniel Kirchhoff: The Man on the Train   102
Melissa Gregory: Representing a Region   107
How Families Use NamUs   109
    Look Up a Missing Person's Case   110
    Enter a Missing Person's Case   111
    Give More Information   112
    Track a Missing Person's Case   112
    Print a Poster   112
    Learn About Additional Resources   113
    Search the Unidentified Persons Database   113
Paula E. Beverly: Found by Her Sisters   114

8 Become Your Long-Term Missing Person's Advocate   117
Communicate with Law Enforcement   118
Get the Case into NamUs and Give DNA   120
Missing Persons Day Events   122
    Michigan   123
    New York City, New York   125
    Orange County, California   125
    Arizona   126
    Colorado   131
Support Groups   132
    Missouri Missing   132
    Families of Homicide Victims and Missing Persons
        (FOHVAMP)   132
    NCMEC's Team Hope   133
When Is It Time to Go to the Media?   134
    Print and Broadcast Media   134
    Social Networking   136
Do I Need a Private Investigator?   138

9 Gather Information, Document, and Do the Research   141
People Searches   142
Ruling Out Proof of Death   145
Published Records   147

Public Records   148
    Federal Public Records   149
    State Public Records   150
    Local/County Recorded Documents   152
    Police and Sheriff Records   153
    Coroner and Medical Examiner Records   154
    Probate Court Records   154
Newspapers and Obituaries   154
    New People to Interview   157

10 Pitfalls and Legalities   **159**
Psychics: A Pitfall to Avoid   159
Don't Go Negative   160
Legal Action   160
    Legal Presumption of Death   161
    Civil Lawsuits   163

11 Retrospect: Inside a (Previously) Cold Case   **167**
Blue Earth Jane Doe   168
    Prairies of Minnesota   168
    A Teenager Leaves Texas   169
    The Unidentified Woman   170
An Unlikely Confession   173
Jane Doe Gets an Advocate   177
    Changes in the Twenty-First Century   177
    Deb Anderson Moves the Case Forward   179
    Identification as Michelle Yvette Busha   181

12 Final Words   **183**
John and Jane Does Can Be Anywhere   183
    Independence Pass John Doe   184
    Little Miss Nobody   187
Missing in the Military   189
    Clay Bonnyman Evans and His Grandfather   189
    The Vacant Chair   191
Once Lost, Now Found   192
    Corporal Athol Goodwin Kirkland   193
    Carol Ann Cole   193
    Wilma, Shannon, and Dorothy   194

Notes   197

Bibliography   219

Index   229

About the Author   241

List of Illustrations

Figure 1.1	Linda and Rick Herren	3
Figure 1.2	Lisa Kay Kelly's Gravestone	7
Figure 1.3	Sheriff Blythe Bloemendaal	12
Figure 2.1	John William Gates and Family	27
Figure 3.1	Ed Smart and John Walsh	37
Figure 3.2	Paul and Ramona Blee	39
Figure 4.1	Phoenix Investigative Team	63
Figure 4.2	Cherub Garden, Heritage Sun West Cemetery	65
Figure 4.3	Westmoreland County Gravestones	69
Figure 4.4	"Jane Doe 1967"	71
Figure 5.1	David Egerton and Rosemary Ulrich	74
Figure 5.2	Lost and Missing in Indian Country	80
Figure 5.3	Colorado Forensic Canines	88
Figure 6.1	"Sara" and Celeste with Their Brother	92
Figure 6.2	Tijuana, Mexico Border	96
Figure 7.1	Paul Daniel Kirchhoff's Grave Marker	106
Figure 7.2	NamUs Logo	108
Figure 7.3	Paula E. Beverly's Niche Cover	115
Figure 8.1	Registration, Missing in Arizona Day Event	127
Figure 8.2	Family and Detectives, Missing in Arizona Day Event	128
Figure 8.3	Displays, Missing in Arizona Day Event	130
Figure 9.1	Microfilm Scanner and Computer	157
Figure 11.1	Crime Scene, "Blue Earth Jane Doe"	171
Figure 11.2	Exhumation, "Blue Earth Jane Doe"	180

Figure 12.1 Evergreen Cemetery, Leadville, Colorado   184
Figure 12.2 "Little Miss Nobody" Gravestone   186
Figure 12.3 Wilma June Nissen Gravestone   195
Figure 12.4 Shannon Michelle Aumock Gravestone   195
Figure 12.5 Dorothy Gay Howard Gravestone   196

Foreword

Summers in Arizona are brutal. As my partner and I drove to Rosa's home in south Phoenix, the temperature had already soared to more than 100 degrees. The heat just made our task more dolorous. There is no easy way to tell a mother her son is dead. It's horrific and is something I have had to do numerous times as a missing person detective.

Rosa's adult son had been missing for twelve years. We, in the Phoenix Police Department, had long suspected that he had been murdered, but this was only confirmed when we received a lab report matching the DNA profile of her son to skeletal remains found in a neighboring county.

I had called ahead to make sure Rosa was home. She answered the door with a mixture of anticipation and dread and then ushered us into her small living room where we sat down.

"There's no easy way to say this," I began. Rosa's hands began shaking and her tears started flowing. I continued, telling her what I knew about her son's death years before. I finished, saying, "I'm so very sorry to give you this news."

And, through her tears, she said, "No, this is better. It's better to finally know, to finally have an answer."

The number of missing and unidentified persons in the United States is staggering. At any given time, more than 80,000 people are reported missing. On top of that, there are an estimated 40,000 unidentified bodies lying in morgues, graveyards, or yet undiscovered. That's the population of a small city. No wonder the National Institute of Justice has described the situation as "the nation's silent mass disaster."

But numbers are . . . just numbers. When you try to codify what that means in human terms, you encounter pain on an unimaginable scale. Families of the missing suffer in a world of "not knowing." As human beings, we deal with death in very different ways. We have enacted rituals, processes, and prayers to help us navigate the pain of losing those we love. Each of us finds a path through the grief when someone dies. That is how we survive, how we continue.

Families of the missing, however, are denied this process. Imagine, if you will, your mother leaving to run some errands and never returning. Or your brother's car being found abandoned in the desert, with no sign of him. Or your child walking to school and disappearing along the way. Imagine the fear and uncertainty, the inability to sleep, the growing panic. Imagine that feeling continuing for days, months, years, even decades. Imagine going through every birthday, every holiday, all the anniversaries, and never having an answer.

Thankfully, most of us will never know what that is like. It is a nightmare no one should have to experience.

In my years investigating missing person cases, I have encountered hundreds of families who are living this nightmare. I am humbled by their courage and strength in facing what would destroy most of us. These families have entered an uncharted, frightening territory that, until now, had no guidebook or map. Where do you look when a loved one is missing? Who do you turn to? How should you act? What is going on? The most common question asked is: What should I do?

The book you hold in your hands fills a much-needed gap. Along with inspiration and hope, it offers answers to these questions.

If you have read Silvia Pettem's other books on the topic (*Someone's Daughter: In Search of Justice for Jane Doe* and *Cold Case Research: Resources for Unidentified, Missing, and Cold Homicide Cases*), you know that she has a great passion for the subject of missing and unidentified persons. In *Someone's Daughter*, Silvia was swept away by the half-century-old mystery of a Jane Doe homicide victim, buried in a Boulder, Colorado, cemetery. That book documents Silvia's journey from local historian to full-fledged criminal investigator in resurrecting the case, aiding in the identification of the victim, and fleshing out the life of the probable killer. *Someone's Daughter* reads like a fictional mystery-thriller but is even more remarkable because all of it is true.

In working the "Boulder Jane Doe" case, Silvia learned many valuable lessons and then shared them in the law enforcement textbook *Cold Case Research*. The book is filled with educational case studies and detailed instructions on gathering and documenting the historical evidence that becomes the foundation for cold cases. It is a book I frequently reference while working my missing person cases.

In *The Long Term Missing: Hope and Help for Families*, Silvia goes one step further, offering sound advice and guidance to family members who have missing loved ones. Within this book, you will discover and learn how to use available tools and resources, including the databases of the NamUs System that has revolutionized the search for the missing and the unknown. You may be surprised at the numerous services offered by the National Center for Missing & Exploited Children® (NCMEC). Before the final pages, family members will know where to search and will understand the importance of preserving medical and dental records, photographs, and fingerprints. If you have not yet contributed a DNA sample in your loved one's missing person case, you will surely do so after reading this book.

In addition to outlining specific tasks a family should undertake, Silvia will introduce you to others who have experienced the terrible limbo that is a missing person case. In these pages, you will meet Gina Hoogendoorn and be inspired by her quest to find her father who was lost in a boating accident in 1997 in Wyoming. You will find hope in the story of Celeste Shaw, who located her sister alive in Mexico, eight years after her disappearance. You will get to know some of the large networks of like-minded individuals (law enforcement, medical examiners, victim advocates, and others) who are tirelessly working to identify the thousands of nameless dead in this country. One of these is Deb Anderson, who never gave up on identifying "Blue Earth Jane Doe" and returning her home. We must always remember that every unidentified person is a missing person to someone out there.

Having a loved one go missing is a confusing and terrifying situation. Families experience loss, fear, uncertainty, and despair. As the old saying goes, knowledge is power, and in these pages, you will find knowledge to empower yourselves. You will be taught how to navigate the unknown territory you have entered. You will recognize what realistically can and should be done in a case. Best of all, you will become your long-term missing person's advocate, not only to law enforcement but to the rest of the world.

And, maybe—hopefully—you will find resolution and answers.

Detective Stuart Somershoe
Missing and Unidentified Persons Unit
Phoenix Police Department

Acknowledgments

Former British prime minister Winston Churchill once wrote, "Writing a book is an adventure. To begin with, it is a toy and an amusement. Then it becomes a mistress, then it becomes a master, then it becomes a tyrant. The last phase is that just as you are about to be reconciled to your servitude, you kill the monster, and fling him about to the public."

Churchill neglected to say that writing a book, at least one like this, is also group effort. I could not have done it without input from the many people whose stories appear on the following pages. Like an extended family, each fits like a piece of a puzzle into the daunting task that has become our mutual goal—bringing home the missing and identifying the unknown.

Gina Hoogendoorn's inspiring story, in chapter 1, of how Gene and Sandy Ralston recovered Gina's father's remains, motivated me to seek out the experiences of other family members. Meanwhile, Investigator Cheryl Moore explained how identifying Lisa Kay Kelly led to her killer, and former sheriff Blythe Bloemendaal told me that giving Wilma June Nissen's name to "Our Girl" was one of the happiest times of his life.

In my research for chapter 2, Robert Gates got me intrigued with the mystery of his missing grandfather. Roland Halpern kept me up to date in the search for his missing uncle, and Stephanie LaPoint presented the case of her missing mother. I'm grateful for their contributions. I also spent an enjoyable afternoon with the late Kevin A. McGregor, who told me of his (and Marc Millican's) amazing discovery a half century after the crash of a Northwest Airliner in Alaska. Mike Grimm and Chriss Lyon had put me in contact with the adventurer. And thanks to Valerie van Heest for reviewing the airplane-crash portion of my manuscript.

Chapter 3 is about children. Dorothy Holmes Brown kindly corresponded with me about her brother Freddie, abducted as a toddler. Longtime friends Paul and Ramona Blee shared the long road they have traveled, following the disappearance of their daughter Marie. And Carol Schweitzer, Senior Forensic Case Specialist at the National Center for Missing & Exploited Children® (NCMEC), took the time to answer my many questions about the role of NCMEC in helping to bring children home. With enthusiasm and compassion, she also opened my eyes to the many resources that NCMEC has to offer. Thanks also go to NCMEC's Media Relations Manager Ashley Iodice for facilitating our correspondence.

Three law enforcement professionals are profiled in chapter 4. I wish to thank Community Service Officer Beth Buchholtz, Trooper Brian F. Gross, and Detective Stuart Somershoe for providing an inside look into their specialized fields and for discussing a few of their many accomplishments, including Detective Somershoe's identification of a former Jane Doe as Shannon Michelle Aumock. Thanks go, too, to Paty Rodriguez at the Heritage Sun West Cemetery in El Mirage, Arizona, for explaining her role in Shannon's burial.

Chapter 5 reveals the power of civilian searchers. David Egerton helped to solve the twenty-year mystery of his missing classmate and friend, Rosemary Ulrich. Thanks go, too, to Melinde Byrne, who put me in contact with David. Janet Franson and Jody Ewing both are victim advocates; Janet works with the Native American population, and Jody keeps track of cold cases in Iowa. In addition, I enjoyed learning about human remains detection through the eyes of handlers (and their dogs) in the organization, Colorado Forensic Canines. Thanks to Bonnie Guzman, Kim Sadar, and Morgan Wolf for allowing me to tag along on several of their searches in Colorado.

Detective Ron Lopez put me in contact with Celeste Shaw, whose eight years of searching for her sister culminated in bringing her home, alive, from Tijuana, Mexico. I greatly appreciated the time Celeste spent with me, over long lunches and continued correspondence, to really fill me in on her own family's experiences, as shown in chapter 6. Officer Kevin Brosnahan, from the US Consulate, facilitated a dramatic turning point in the story.

In chapter 7, George Kirchhoff graciously related his family's experiences following the disappearance of his son Paul. As in Celeste's sister's investigation, Detective Lopez's use of the NamUs System figured prominently into the discovery of Paul's remains. Now retired, Detective Lopez has set the bar for others who work to bring home the missing. I also appreciated NamUs Regional Administrator Melissa Gregory's behind-the-scenes look at NamUs, an important investigative tool, and Stephanie Clack for revealing the power of NamUs for family members. Becoming a missing person's advocate falls on the shoulders of civilians and law enforcement alike.

Chapter 8 includes an explanation of how Lesha Johanneck's and Alyssa Hillman's Facebook page led to the identity of "Grateful Doe" as Jason Callahan. Thanks also go to Sergeant Sarah Krebs who answered my questions on the Missing in Michigan Day event, to Elmo Nevayaktewa who gave me a parent's perspective at the Missing in Arizona Day event, and to others who invest their time, money, and expertise to bring missing-day events to their own states.

In chapter 9, independent researcher Micki Lavigne's use of Google is an eye-opener, while Roland Halpern's use of federal public records shows how these lesser-known resources can reveal previously unknown information.

I'm also grateful for the assistance and advice of Denver probate attorney Joseph K. Reynolds, as he reviewed chapter 10 on pitfalls and legalities. Detective Stuart Somershoe also offered several helpful topics to include.

Chapter 11 is an in-depth look at one specific case that grew out of my correspondence with many people. Special thanks go to Minnesota resident Deb Anderson, who, for more than a decade, advocated for "Blue Earth Jane Doe," culminating with her identity as Michelle Yvette Busha. Deb and I spent many hours online and on the telephone, and she put me in contact with former Faribault County sheriff Roger Fletcher and former chief investigator Jerry Kabe. Getting their perspectives on this case from 1980 added important historical context. Also enlightening were comments from Phil Lerman, whose half-sister Jackie (once thought to have been the Jane Doe) is still missing.

Others who corresponded with me on the Jane Doe/Busha case included *Faribault County Register* reporter Chuck Hunt, Blue Earth Community library director Eva Gaydon, Ramsey County medical examiner Dr. Michael B. McGee, assistant Ramsey County medical examiner Dr. Butch Huston, Minneapolis Police Department police support technician David Peña, Matagorda County Sheriff's Office sergeant Teresa Jeremiah, Minnesota Missing and Unidentified Persons Clearinghouse manager Kris Rush, Minnesota Department of Safety public information officer Jill Oliveira, and members of the Faribault County Sheriff's Office. Thanks to all of you for your valuable input.

Chapter 12 includes the plight of the unknown, at least at the time of this writing. John Piearson is to be commended for his continued advocacy in the case of "Independence Pass John Doe." Marcia Martinek's story in the *Herald Democrat* hopefully will bring in new leads. Similarly, former Yavapai

County Sheriff's Office cold case investigator Brendan Fillingim's dedication to "Little Miss Nobody" reflects the same community spirit that was evident at the time of the child's burial. Thanks also go to the Yavapai County Sheriff's Office, in Prescott, Arizona, which still is investigating "Little Miss Nobody's" case. I also appreciated hearing from Clay Bonnyman Evans, who shared his story of recovering his grandfather's remains from a tiny island in the central Pacific Ocean.

Each one of these diverse and talented people offered a different perspective, and each is a part of the book as a whole. The following individuals and organizations also contributed photographs:

- Gina Hoogendoorn
- Lyon County Sheriff's Department chief Deputy Jerry Birkey
- Robert Gates
- Richard Drew, *Associated Press*
- Detective Stuart Somershoe
- Sean Stipp, *Greensburg Tribune-Review*
- National Center for Missing & Exploited Children®
- David Egerton
- Janet Franson
- Celeste Shaw
- Sergeant 1st Class Gordon Hyde, Army National Guard
- George Kirchhoff
- J. Todd Matthews, director, Case Management and Communications, NamUs on behalf of the National Institute of Justice
- Jay Raveill, *findagrave.com*
- Faribault County sheriff Michael S. Gormley
- Deb Anderson

I'm grateful, too, to Dina Carson for her technical expertise with several of the photographs. For overall guidance and peer review, I relied on Phoenix Police Department Detective Stuart Somershoe, as well as J. Todd Matthews, director, Case Management and Communications, NamUs. Thank you, both of you, for reviewing the manuscript, and please realize that your ongoing commitment to the missing and the unidentified is greatly appreciated. I also wish to thank my friend and colleague R.H. Walton, whose years of encouragement have helped to keep me focused and motivated.

Lastly, special thanks go to my sister, Marilyn Mildrum, with fond memories of our numerous cemetery visits, and to my husband, Ed Raines, my sounding board and best friend.

Chapter 1

Why Finding the Missing Is Important

In 2003, the author was present at a meeting of various law enforcement officials when the Boulder County sheriff was asked if the remains of a Jane Doe buried in a cemetery in Boulder, Colorado, in 1954, could be exhumed and identified. One of the first questions that came up was, why bother? After nearly fifty years, who would be around to care?[1]

Six years later, with the support of the local community and the help of the sheriff's office and forensic specialists, as well as many dedicated individuals that grew to include the young woman's family, a DNA comparison identified the Jane Doe as Dorothy Gay Howard. In 2010, her surviving sister and more than thirty other family members traveled to Boulder from all over the country to hold a memorial service and place flowers on her grave—with her own name on it, at last.[2]

Some long-term missing persons are found alive, while some are never found at all. Others may exist only as skeletal remains—the result of a natural death, a self-inflicted death, or even murder. When their remains are found, however, their discovery brings resolution. The uninformed will refer to this process as closure, but it is not. For most family members, the pain of the loss never goes away. At the same time, the discovery process often opens old wounds. Individuals react differently, and some family members find that the wounds are so deep that all they can do is to try to move on with their lives. Other family members, however, *need* to know what happened to their loved one, and they need tangible proof of their remains.

It is important to find missing persons (and, in this context, long-term missing persons) for the following reasons:

- Provides resolution for families
- Aids in the arrest and conviction of criminals (possibly preventing other deaths)
- Gives dignity and justice to victims

PROVIDES RESOLUTION FOR FAMILIES

Richard DeWayne "Rick" Herren drowned in a boating accident in Flaming Gorge Reservoir, near Green River, Wyoming, on May 4, 1997. An initial search and rescue effort failed to locate his body, and local officials told his daughter Gina to learn to accept the fact that he would never be found.[3] For them, the case was closed. For Gina, the enormity of her loss had only begun. Fifteen years later, a promise of hope and the results that followed changed Gina's life forever. The following is Gina's story, and her love for her father gives testimony to the human spirit.

Gina and Her Dad: Returned Identities

Gina's parents grew up as childhood sweethearts in Colorado Springs, Colorado. Deeply in love, they married, started a family, then moved to Green River, Wyoming, where Rick had a job. The Herrens, see figure 1.1, both inherited Native American ancestry—Rick was part Cherokee, and his wife Linda was part Navajo/Blackfoot. In email correspondence with the author, Gina Herren, now Gina Hoogendoorn, stated, "My dad always made a point to take time with my brother and me and tell us about nature and how important it is, and that we were just a piece of the puzzle in this world."[4]

Rick was a mechanic by trade, but he loved the outdoors and to hunt and fish. The Herrens were fishing and camping with friends on the fateful day of Rick's drowning, in 1997. Ever since, according to Gina, her mother has been consumed with guilt that she had been unable to save him.

"Losing my dad was so hard," said Gina. "I was 18. I needed him for so many things in my life. I felt so alone. No one I knew had a loved one missing. I was Gina, the girl who lost her dad in a drowning."[5] Indeed, Gina's loss had become a part of her identity. She said that it was glued to her and that was attached to her whenever she was introduced to someone. The conversation would go like this:

"This is Gina. Do you remember that guy who drowned at the lake? That was her dad." "Oh, that guy that fell in a few years ago? Do you think the fish have eaten him or what? Nice to meet you."[6]

Figure 1.1 Linda and Rick Herren. Rick Herren could not take his eyes off his wife, Linda, when this photograph was taken in 1986 or 1987. Fifteen years after his accidental drowning, his family finally was able to recover his remains. *Source:* Photo courtesy of Gina Hoogendoorn

With her mother, Gina attended a grief support group, but the women ended up feeling somewhat resentful of the other survivors whose loved ones were tangible. Said Gina, "I felt like they didn't know how lucky they were that they could have kissed, held, hugged that dead person and cried at his grave or held his ashes."[7]

Two weeks after the accident, Gina's aunt (her father's sister) led the family in a releasing ceremony that involved prayer, music, and symbolic acts that in Native American culture allow the spirit of the deceased to be released from limbo.

To Gina, though, time seemed to stand still. Eventually she married, started a family, and moved to Rock Springs, Wyoming. One night, in the spring of 2012, Gina and her husband were watching a television show about a drowning victim who, at a later date, was found and recovered. The concept of searching for longtime missing drowning victims was new to Gina. The next morning, she googled the topic and located the website of search and recovery specialists Gene and Sandy Ralston. Gina read of their work online, then summoned the courage to call them.

Once on the phone with Gene, she blurted out how she had come to contact him and quickly ran through her story. Then she hesitantly asked if finding her father's remains was something he and his wife could do. According to

Gene's correspondence with the author, his reply was, "I don't know, that has been a long time, but we are more than willing to try." He remembers a brief silence when Gina was overcome with emotion, adding that it was also a very powerful moment for him.[8]

"I immediately felt this HUGE black something pull up from the pit of my stomach and fly up through the top of my head," said Gina. "I KNEW then and there, my life would never be the same." Two weeks later—on April 28, the Herrens' 39th wedding anniversary—the Ralstons, with their side-scan sonar, located Rick's remains.[9]

The Ralstons are an Idaho couple in their sixties who have assisted with underwater searches and recoveries of more than 103 sets of remains. They do not charge families for their services, asking only for reimbursement for the expenses of pulling their boat and equipment behind their motor home. Once they reach a body of water where a search is to be performed, they drag their six-foot sonar device behind their boat, then map the area and record images in real-time on a computer screen.

Assisting in the search and recovery was John Linn, of Tip Top Search and Rescue in Sublette County, Wyoming. He took Gina's mother out in his boat and asked her to show him where Rick had fallen into the water. The GPS coordinates were noted, then given to the Ralstons who searched the area and found what they believed to be a body in only eight minutes. Then, a remote-operated vehicle (called an ROV) was lowered into the water, which allowed them to live video the reservoir's floor.[10]

By this time, Gina and her mother were in a boat with Linn. He had helped with the initial search, and the women were unable to contain their excitement. "Finally," Gina said, "we saw what we had waited to see for fifteen years. There was my dad's jacket sleeve! My dad's pants! My heart leaped out of my chest and flew in the air! My mom and I were holding hands so tightly! We looked at each other, and we both knew it was him!"[11]

Rick's remains were only 75 feet from their estimated location, remarkable in a 91-mile-long body of water. A local dive team brought the remains to the surface a few weeks later, while also unleashing a myriad of emotions for Gina and her family. "I was scared of what I was going to see, what would happen, if the scuba divers would be okay, and what condition my dad would be in," said Gina, adding that "those were some crazy, awful, scary, anxiety-ridden weeks."[12]

Gina thought the actual recovery would be easy, but she was not prepared for the flood of emotions that came back. "I was so excited to hold him again, but I knew it would be fleeting and that I would have to let him go . . . again," she said. "I felt as if his death was fresh and new."[13]

As the sheriff's boat slowly pulled Rick's remains in a large mesh bag (with a protective frame to hold the bag open), Gina waited on shore, shaking nearly out of her skin. With her mother and brother, she watched as the coroner and the local search and rescue team transferred Rick's remains to a black body bag. At the time, Gina's dad was the longest underwater victim the Ralstons had ever found. According to Gene Ralston, Rick's heavy clothing and the cold water temperature had aided in his preservation.[14]

"As they laid him down on the dock," said Gina, "my mom, brother, and I ran to hug him. He felt like him. He still had form to him. Then the coroner put him in the truck. I looked up at the sky and saw a big circle rainbow around the sun. It had been there the whole time since he emerged from the water and stayed until the truck holding him drove out of sight."[15]

Later, at the funeral home, Gina and her mother had some time alone with Rick's remains, still inside the black body bag. Gina poured out her grief, but also her anger, an emotion she did not know she had buried deep inside.

Instead of burying Rick in a cold grave, the family decided to have him cremated. Gina, particularly, wanted him nearby. Now, like the family members in grief support groups, she, too, has a tangible part of him she can hold in her hand, that is, the piece of the puzzle lost so many years ago. Gina keeps her dad's ashes in a china hutch in her kitchen, alongside Rick's wallet and identification that were recovered in his clothing.

Gina also has something else that was returned to her. No longer is she "Gina, the girl who lost her dad in a drowning." Thanks to her determination to reach out to the Ralstons, their skill and response, and the work of the search and rescue team, Gina has reclaimed her own identity, as well.

"In the end, there was an answer and a light at the end of this tunnel," said Gina. "It gave me even more certainty that there are bigger things out there than us and that this truly is a miracle. I do miss him terribly still, but I also know I will see him again."[16]

AIDS IN ARREST AND CONVICTION OF CRIMINALS

When unidentified remains reveal that a John or Jane Doe was a victim of homicide, the identity of his or her remains often leads to the prosecution of the person's killer. The identification of a woman known only as "Jane Doe" (1989–2005) is a good example. Now, her murderer is behind bars, possibly other deaths were prevented, and Lisa Kay Kelly has been given back her name.

Lisa Kay Kelly and Her Killer

Sightseers on Lookout Mountain, in unincorporated Jefferson County, Colorado, stumbled upon a woman's body on March 24, 1989. Seven months later, in the same geographical area, college students panning for gold in Clear Creek Canyon found the body of a second woman. Both had been murdered. The Jefferson County Sheriff's Office identified the first victim as twenty-eight-year-old Lanell Williams and returned her remains to her family.[17]

On a sunny summer day in 1990, the Jefferson County Coroner's Office buried the second victim, still unidentified. The woman's remains, in a blue body bag in a donated casket, were lowered into a donated plot at the Golden Cemetery. A jail chaplain officiated at the graveside service, where a deputy sang the "Lord's Prayer," with members of the sheriff's and coroner's offices in attendance. At the time, only a small bronze-colored marker pointed out her grave. But the county's victims' compensation fund later donated a gravestone with the inscription, "Jane Doe 1989, Known Only to God, May Her Soul Rest in Peace."[18]

No one knew who had killed the women, and there was no indication, at the time, that their murders were related. In 1989, DNA technology was not sufficient to produce the evidence needed to determine a suspect, let alone file charges. The women's cases simply went cold.

In the early days of the investigation, a composite drawing, with some distinctive damage to the woman's front teeth had been circulated, and all responses had been systematically eliminated. A search based on one available partial fingerprint had not produced any results. In 2005, after new advances in technology, it was time to look at the Jane Doe case again. The Sheriff's Office assigned Investigator Cheryl Moore to the job.

Investigator Moore sent the Jane Doe's fingerprint to her agency's lab to be resubmitted to the Automated Fingerprint Identification System (AFIS). At the lab, a diligent technician manipulated the parameters in order to enter the fingerprint into the system in three different ways. In just four hours, the technician had a hit and excitedly called the investigator to tell her that she had a match. The previously unidentified fingerprint had belonged to a woman named Lisa Kay Kelly. The victim, determined to have been thirty-three years old when she was murdered, had been fingerprinted following arrests for shoplifting and prostitution.[19]

"We used good old-fashioned police work to identify Lisa," said Investigator Moore, who demonstrated that she would rather "think outside the box" than prioritize cases based solely on DNA evidence.[20] The victim's identity then opened up new possibilities in investigating her murder. As Investigator Moore worked on Lisa's case, she began to see similarities in the circumstances of Lisa's murder and that of Lanell, the other woman whose body had been found the same year. Like Lisa, Lanell also was black, they were of similar age, and both had been involved with crack cocaine.[21]

Investigator Moore submitted clothing and other items found with Lisa and Lanell to the Colorado Bureau of Investigation (CBI) for DNA analysis. Lisa's had little-to-no physical evidence and did not produce results, but Lanell's came back with matches to Billy Edwin Reid. His criminal record showed that in 1987 he had been paroled to Colorado on a Kansas sex assault case. Subsequently, he was rearrested for various offenses, but his DNA profile did not get into the Combined DNA Index System (CODIS) database until 2002, when he was released from prison in Kansas.[22]

In May 2006, Investigator Moore was ready to arrest the alleged perpetrator for the murder of Lanell when Reid was pulled in on a traffic warrant in Denver. When the investigator questioned him about the victims, he denied even knowing them, but in the Denver County Jail he began talking with a fellow inmate who took detailed notes. Eventually, those notes, along with Reid's own writings, played a key role in getting him off of the streets for good.[23]

Figure 1.2 Lisa Kay Kelly's Gravestone. Lisa Kay Kelly's name, along with the inscription "Never Lost, Always Loved," is now on her gravestone in the Golden Cemetery, in Golden, Colorado. *Source:* Photo by author

Investigator Moore and the prosecution team from the Jefferson County District Attorney's Office then began to build their case. In September 2008, Reid was convicted of "first degree murder after deliberation," "first degree murder—felony murder," and "first degree sexual assault" in the murders of both Lanell and Lisa. Reid also was linked to the murder of a third woman, in Denver, although no additional charges were filed. His sentencing followed, three months later, with grateful members of all three families in attendance.[24]

In 2008, when District Attorney Scott Storey of Colorado's First Judicial District was asked about Reid's prosecution, he told a *Denver Post* reporter, "These are as tough as it gets. The bottom line is that without Jefferson County Sheriff's Cold Case Unit, we would never have brought justice to the families of these two young women."[25] After sixteen years, Lisa's siblings saw her killer convicted. And, as shown in figure 1.2, they were finally able to dignify her grave with her name.

GIVES DIGNITY AND JUSTICE TO THE VICTIMS

Former sheriff Blythe Bloemendaal is the type of law enforcement official who likes to get things done. In a telephone interview with the author he stated, "I was the kind who wanted to kick in the door."[26] It is not surprising that, in 2001, when he first was elected sheriff of Lyon County, Iowa, and inherited a Jane Doe cold case file, he picked it up and ran with it. Identifying a murder victim the agency affectionately called "Our Girl," and then solving her homicide became his passion. Wilma June Nissen now has her own name on her grave, and Bloemendaal is optimistic that, one day, her killer will be behind bars. Although this sheriff is retired, he still has his foot in the door.

Retired Sheriff Is "Our Girl's" Best Advocate

Sheriff Bloemendaal, a native of Michigan, moved with his parents to the Midwestern prairies of Iowa, where his father became a minister. At first, Bloemendaal managed a feed and grain elevator. Then, in 1983, at the age of 23, he decided to do what he had always dreamed about doing and started a career in law enforcement. In looking back, he says he wanted to make a difference, but he admits he had always been a bit of an adrenaline junkie. He thrived as an undercover drug agent for the Lyon County Sheriff's Department, seeking out offenders in the extreme northwest corner of Iowa that borders the states of Minnesota and South Dakota.

Then Bloemendaal moved up the ranks to chief deputy and handled most of his agency's investigations. One of the case files on his desk was the Sheriff's Department's only unidentified murder. On October 4, 1978, a telephone company employee laying cable found the young woman's badly decomposed and half-naked body in a roadside ditch between the towns of Inwood and Larchwood, eighteen miles southwest of Rock Rapids, the county seat. Whether she was killed there or dumped is unknown. At the time, the Sheriff's Department only had six deputies. Investigators did what they could, but no one knew the victim's identity or who was responsible for her murder. No one from the local community had been reported missing.[27]

The victim was fingerprinted, then buried in Rock Rapids's Riverview Cemetery with a small metal marker that read, "Unidentified Woman." After initial, and brief, publicity, most people in the small town forgot about her.

A few years later, when Bloemendaal reviewed the Jane Doe file, he was saddened by how the case had already gone cold. With changes in technology and increased awareness in cases of longtime missing persons and unidentified remains, he knew there was much he could do, including traveling to another state to interview a possible suspect in prison. But, Bloemendaal's requests were always hampered by a lack of funds. That all changed in 2001 when he ran for office and was elected sheriff. For the first time, he was in control of the budget. "Then I had my detective (now chief deputy) Jerry Birkey to work with me, and this is when we made some real strides."[28]

A new resource for law enforcement during this time was the Integrated Automated Fingerprint Identification System (IAFIS), a national automated fingerprint identification and criminal history system maintained by the Federal Bureau of Investigation (FBI). Although the FBI has been the national repository for fingerprints and related criminal history data since 1924, it had only launched IAFIS in 1999. The system houses more than 70 million subjects in its criminal master file, including more than 34 million civil prints of individuals who have served, or are serving, in the US military or have been, or are, employed by the federal government.[29] Well aware of the need to keep up with the latest advances in cold case research, Sheriff Bloemendaal realized that he needed to submit the victim's fingerprints to this new system.[30]

The sheriff's first obstacle, however, was to find Jane Doe's fingerprint card, eventually located in a warehouse at the Iowa Division of Criminal Investigation (DCI) in Des Moines, Iowa. Once submitted to IAFIS, a computerized search produced several possible results, through which DCI agent

Dan Moser searched to make a comparison. The prints were narrowed down to a thumb print from a 1978 arrest made by the Los Angeles Police Department and forwarded to the FBI. The print belonged to a former California resident, Wilma June Nissen. A mug shot became her first-known photo. No one knew how she ended up murdered in Iowa.[31]

"Once in the system, it only took a matter of weeks to get a match," said Sheriff Bloemendaal. "I was out of my head. Finally, in January 2006 [twenty-seven and one half years after she was found], we had something to work with. It was one of the happiest times of my life."[32]

The first item of business was to hold a press conference. The resulting nationwide publicity brought forward a daughter, born approximately one year before Nissen's death. A friend of the daughter had contacted her after reading a newspaper article in her local California paper. Both women had been searching for Nissen for years. Sheriff Bloemendaal then began an investigation to learn as much as he could about the young woman's short, and troubled, life of twenty-three years.

Nissen was born on October 19, 1954. When still a young child, she, along with a sister, had been abandoned by her mother and neglected by her father. Authorities in the state of California moved the sister to an institution, while Nissen, at the age of 10, began passing through the homes of several sets of foster parents. After that, she married one husband and then a second, who is the father of the daughter who came forward. The daughter had been adopted by the last of Nissen's sets of foster parents. At the time of Nissen's identification, both her parents were deceased.[33]

Along the way, Nissen, whose nickname was "Boots," created a handful of aliases and gave birth to another child who has not yet been located. Sheriff Bloemendaal is adamant that law enforcement should never be judgmental about lifestyles and is open about the fact that Nissen had lived on the streets and, several times, had been arrested for prostitution.[34]

In control of his agency's purse strings, Sheriff Bloemendaal and his chief deputy traveled to California where they managed to contact several people who had known the young woman. The investigators learned that in February 1978, the year of Nissen's death, she had traveled to Atlanta, Georgia, with a man who told them that he woke up one morning a few days after they had arrived, and she was gone. Most likely thinking she would return, the man did not file a missing persons report. Back in Rock Rapids, Iowa, Sheriff Bloemendaal and his chief deputy made a ten-foot-paper timeline and hung it on their office wall, keeping the case in front of them at all times.[35]

As Sheriff Bloemendaal was beginning to flesh out his case, a Sioux Falls monument company stepped forward and donated a pink granite headstone. On it was etched a partially open rose along with the words:

Wilma June Nissen
"Our Girl"
Oct. 19, 1954–1978[36]

On June 3, 2006, Sheriff Bloemendaal and more than seventy others gathered for a memorial service at Nissen's quiet and peaceful gravesite in Riverview Cemetery. The young woman's photo, at the age of 18, was placed on a pedestal, along with a dozen white roses. Among those who came to pay their respects were Craig Vinson (the Lyon County Sheriff, in 1978), the couple on whose farm Nissen was found, and others who had stopped, from time to time, to place flowers on her grave. Also present was Nissen's first foster family from California, and the woman who helped Nissen's daughter find her mother. (The daughter was unable to come, but she visited the grave a few months later.)[37]

Also in the crowd was Blue Earth, Minnesota resident Deb Anderson, with her mother and her then two-year-old daughter. At the time, Anderson was searching for the identity of her own community's Jane Doe murder victim. "These women do matter and their families matter," Anderson told a reporter at the time.[38] (In March 2015, the Blue Earth victim was identified as Michelle Yvette Busha.) For Anderson's role in the Blue Earth Jane Doe story, see chapter 11, "Retrospect: Inside a (Previously) Cold Case."

"Somehow, someway, I hope that today we have taken away the words 'unidentified female' and putting Wilma Nissen on this gravesite will now allow her to rest in peace," stated Sheriff Bloemendaal during the service. (See figure 1.3 for a recent photograph of the sheriff at Wilma's grave.) Nissen's foster father added, "For the past 30 years, we have been praying for Wilma and wondering why she didn't contact us. Did something happen to her? Though it is not what we would like to hear, at least we know." A Catholic priest led the assembled group in prayer, followed by a guitarist who played John Michael Talbot's hymn, "Be Not Afraid." The attendees joined in singing: "Be not afraid, I go before you always. Come follow Me, and I shall give you rest."[39]

In August 2007, Sheriff Bloemendaal obtained a court order, as well as Nissen's daughter's permission, to exhume Nissen's remains in the hopes of

Figure 1.3 Sheriff Blythe Bloemendaal. Former Lyon County (Iowa) sheriff Blythe Bloemendaal, shown here in 2015, has reopened the murder case of Wilma June Nissen. She had been buried as a Jane Doe in 1978, and he identified her in 2006. *Source:* Photo courtesy of Lyon County Sheriff's Department Chief Deputy Jerry Birkey

learning more about the manner of her death and who was responsible. The exhumation was held on a rainy September day, with Nissen's daughter watching from under an umbrella. Nissen's coffin had been placed in an inexpensive non-sealing concrete vault. The vault contained a cloth coffin and, inside of that, a metal Ziegler case, which contained a body bag with Nissen's remains. Unfortunately, the metal case also held approximately 40 gallons of water.[40]

Although the water dashed any hopes of obtaining the killer's DNA, Nissen's remains were sent to the Iowa DCI Criminalistics Laboratory in Ankeny, Iowa, where her bones were examined by a forensic anthropologist whom Sheriff Bloemendaal had flown in from New York. Analyzing Nissen's bones turned out to be a long process, but the manner of her death eventually was determined. It has not been released by the Sheriff's Department, however, as the sheriff notes that the specific facts are known only by himself and by the killer.[41]

In February 2009, the Sheriff's Department established a website, a hot-line, and offered a $10,000 reward leading to Nissen's killer's arrest. In addition, deputies revamped their efforts and went door-to-door to talk with people living within a five-mile radius of where her body was found. The Department nearly doubled during Sheriff Bloemendaal's time and now has eleven deputies. Rock Rapids still is a quiet little town, and, as the former sheriff states, "a perfect place to raise a family."[42] Lyon County has no John or Jane Does and no open missing person cases. Nissen's case is the department's only unsolved homicide, and the investigation is ongoing.

In 2013, after three four-year terms as sheriff and thirty years total in the Sheriff's Department, Sheriff Bloemendaal accepted his retirement and started another job in order to care for a disabled family member. He had summed up his commitment at the time of the exhumation when he told a *Sioux City Journal* reporter, "Wilma was a human being and deserves to be handled that way, not just in life but now in death. Wilma deserves an end to this, and I am going to give that to her."[43] On the telephone with the author he added, "It was hard for me to walk out, but we'll make it. And I still believe we'll solve this case."[44]

[Note: Wilma Nissen's identification was made prior to the launching of the NamUs System in 2009. NamUs's dual databases for the Missing and Unidentified now are important resources for both law enforcement and the public in identifying John and Jane Does, discussed in chapter 7, "NamUs: An Investigative Tool." However, the importance of IAFIS should never be underestimated, as is so clearly demonstrated in this case.]

Chapter 2

Categories of Long-Term Missing Adults

The use of the word "long-term" missing has different meanings for different people. In New York City, the Office of Chief Medical Examiner defines long-term as "missing for sixty (60) or more days."[1] The New Jersey State Police, however, in its "Missing Persons Investigative Best Practices Protocol," defines the phrase as "Any person that has remained the subject of a missing person investigation for over thirty (30) days."[2] But, for many families, the definition fits as soon as the initial flurry of police and media reports falls off. Family members find themselves left in an unfathomable void, not knowing if their loved one is dead or alive.

The search for long-term missing persons and/or their remains is a very complex topic. Unless there are suspicious circumstances, or if a person is known to be at risk, there is no easy way even to speculate, let alone to place a long-term missing person into one of several broad categories. And, even within the following categories, many scenarios overlap. The topic of long-term missing children will be addressed in chapter 3, "Children: Helping to Bring Them Home." For the purpose of this discussion, the categories of long-term missing adults include:

- Suspicious Circumstances
- Adults at Risk/ Endangered
- Voluntary Disappearances
- Natural or Accidental Death Most Likely
- Undetermined

SUSPICIOUS CIRCUMSTANCES

In most families, when a loved one goes missing, the initial fear is that "something happened" to him or her. Usually, that is not the case, unless the person went missing under suspicious circumstances. Perhaps the disappearance is completely out of character for the person's lifestyle, or a threat was made and/or a crime may be in progress. *If* a person's life is thought to be in danger, it is essential to immediately file a missing person report with the police and to be as thorough and forthcoming as possible. This information needs to include people the missing person associated with, as well as activities the person was involved in, even if illegal. (Contrary to common myths, there is no twenty-four-hour waiting limit.) The first forty-eight hours are the most crucial, as missing person cases can turn into homicides.

According to the California Commission on Peace Officer Standards and Training, "Officers should assume the missing person is in immediate danger or at risk until the facts contradict that assumption."[3] Unfortunately, "suspicious" is a subjective term. The Commission gives the example of an eight-month-pregnant woman, living with her parents, who fails to return home from a shopping trip after being last seen getting into a vehicle with two men.[4]

Jeanne Overstreet

Missing person cases that *could* be suspicious but are not handled as suspicious can become cold case homicides in the years to come, leaving law enforcement scrambling for documentation. Consider the case of Jeanne Overstreet. In September 1982, the nineteen-year-old from the Tucson, Arizona, area left her home to hitchhike downtown to meet her boyfriend for lunch. She never showed up, and her family knew there was no reason for her to voluntarily disappear. The family filed a missing person report with the Tucson Police Department and shortly afterwards handed over Jeanne's dental records.[5] Did the fact that Jeanne planned to hitchhike raise any red flags? Did the police receive any leads and/or consider her case suspicious, or did they just file the report? The answers are unknown, and the case soon went cold.

Twenty-two years later, in 2004, when DNA technology had advanced to the point that it was used in missing person cases, Jeanne's sister Jackie gave a DNA sample to the same police department. Jackie's DNA was run through a national database, but nothing turned up. Then, in 2011, Jeanne and Jackie's parents each submitted their DNA to supplement the sample given years earlier by Jackie. Finally, in April 2012, nearly thirty years after Jeanne's disappearance, the family was notified of a match. Ever since 1983,

Jeanne's remains had been in storage, in Tucson, in the office of the Pima County Medical Examiner (PCME)![6]

Fourteen months after Jeanne had missed her lunch date, her remains had been found along a highway north of Tucson. Dr. Walter Birkby, the Medical Examiner's former forensic anthropologist, thoroughly analyzed the remains and prepared a detailed dental chart, but his chart did not match the dental records of any persons known to be missing at that time. No one has offered an explanation, but, apparently, neither Jeanne's dental chart (given to the police by the family) nor her missing person report ever made its way to the PCME. In addition, according to the *Arizona Daily Star*, Jeanne's original case file had disappeared completely. Only after a DNA profile finally was obtained from Jeanne's stored remains and matched to the parents' samples taken in 2011 did anyone make the connection.[7]

The event that led up to this discovery was an ambitious project that had been undertaken in August 2010 by Dr. Bruce Anderson, a forensic anthropologist for the PCME. With the use of grant money, Anderson began to submit, for testing, DNA samples from a backlog of approximately 800 sets of unidentified skeletal remains found in Southern Arizona. Most of his samples came from remains discovered during the previous decade, which coincided with a major influx of undocumented border-crossers. Almost one-hundred others were individuals from the 1970s through the 1990s. According to Chief Medical Examiner Dr. Gregory Hess, many of these were unidentified US citizens. Jeanne's remains were among them, but no one knew that at the time.[8]

"My mom never gave up hope that she was alive," Jeanne's sister, Jackie, told a newspaper reporter in 2012. "This hit my mom so hard. She was in complete denial. We all, after some time, said, 'Something happened to her. She's not with us anymore.' But we always had that little bit of hope. We'd see somebody who looked like her, a blonde girl, and just couldn't help but look." In the same interview, Jackie continued, "Right now the emotions are very up and down. We now at least know where she is. That's going to be very helpful, but there's still always going to be the question of what happened."[9]

ADULTS AT RISK/ ENDANGERED

The term "at-risk adults" generally means those who have physical or mental limitations which restrict their abilities to carry out normal activities. This category overlaps "suspicious circumstances," as these missing persons may also be in the company of others who endanger their welfare, or they are drug-dependent or may intend on harming themselves. According to the Connecticut Police Officer Standards and Training, "A missing person is at risk when missing under circumstances in which the individual is in danger of serious physical injury or death. This policy presumes that every missing person or missing adult person will be considered at *high risk* until a reasonable and articulable basis to conclude otherwise exists."[10]

The California Commission on Peace Officer Standards and Training defines an "at risk" person as including, but not limited to, "the person missing being the victim of a crime or foul play, in need of medical attention, has no pattern of running away or disappearing, the victim of parent/family abduction, or mentally impaired."[11] For stories of three different missing adults with mental illnesses, see the following:

- Chapter 5, "Civilian Searchers," David and Rosemary: Face of a Friend
- Chapter 6, "Celeste's Sister Sara: Found Alive in Mexico"
- Chapter 7, "NamUs: An Investigative Tool," Paul Daniel Kirchhoff: The Man on the Train

The elderly fit in the at-risk category as well, and some are prone to wander due to autism, Down syndrome, Alzheimer's disease, dementia, and other cognitive disorders. Some states have what are called "Silver Alerts." In Florida, the statewide initiative evolved in 2008 after an 86-year-old woman who suffered from dementia drove away from her assisted living facility in her white Chrysler convertible and never returned. Her body was found a week later ten miles away in the Intracoastal Waterway, and her submerged car was found nearby.[12]

For a Silver Alert to be issued in Florida, the following criteria must be met:

- Missing individual is driving a car or lost on foot,
- Missing person is 60 years or older, and
- There is a clear indication that the individual has an irreversible deterioration of intellectual faculties (i.e., Alzheimer's disease). This must be verified by law enforcement.

OR:

- Missing individual is driving a car or lost on foot,
- Missing person is 18–59 years of age,
- Missing person has irreversible deterioration of intellectual faculties, and
- Use of dynamic message signs (i.e., large electronic signs that hang over major highways) may be the only way to rescue the missing person.[13]

When worn, personalized wristbands that emit a tracking signal can help to locate elderly or at-risk persons prone to wandering. Project Lifesaver International is a company that produces these wristbands, enabling search teams to more quickly find the wearer. In addition, they give the missing persons' families peace of mind. "[The wristbands] literally can make the difference between life or death," stated Santa Barbara County sheriff Bill Brown, in a KSBY televised news story. "We have instances where people have walked into wilderness areas and to remote areas that are potentially life-threatening if not located quickly."[14]

According to the company's website, its employees develop public outreach programs to educate others about the issue of wandering and constantly work toward developing public policy and effective law enforcement response to help save lives and fulfill its mission in "Bringing Loved Ones Home."[15] Similarly, proponents of the Alzheimer's Aware Initiative attempt to increase awareness of Alzheimer's disease, provide educational opportunities in the community, and encourage the use of locative technologies in saving the lives of patients.[16]

Family members of suicidal missing persons, however, have found that some of those who do commit suicide choose to be away from home in order to spare their families the pain of finding their bodies. It is not unusual, for instance, for a missing person's car to be located at the trailhead of a favorite hiking trail, with the person nowhere to be found. Most families will, and should, file missing person reports. But, if they have found a suicide note or feel certain that the person is taking responsibility for his or her own death, they may accept the fact and respect that the person chose to take his or her life. The police will keep open a missing person report until a body or skeletal remains are found. But, after an initial search, they may not actively investigate the case if the family conveys that it is reluctant to reopen old wounds. Other families may feel completely differently and need the resolution of finding their missing persons' remains. People grieve in various ways, and there is no right or wrong way to handle the situation.

VOLUNTARY DISAPPEARANCES

Most family members, like those of Jeanne Overstreet had done, still hold out hope that their long-term missing person may be alive; and some are. The police are the first to tell families that anyone over the age of 18 is an adult and has the right to leave home without an explanation or forwarding

address. This can be devastating for family members who are left not knowing, but fearing the worst. Missing persons under the age of 18 are discussed
in chapter 3, "Children: Helping to Bring Them Home."

In cases of incest and domestic abuse, however, husbands, wives, sons, and
daughters may flee for their own safety or to start a new life. Others have been
known to skip out on large financial debts, while fugitives disappear in order
to avoid apprehension by law enforcement authorities.

Upcoming court appearances and unplanned pregnancies have also motivated people to disappear, as was the case of Katharine Farrand Dyer, a
likely candidate for the identity of "Boulder Jane Doe." Katharine had been
reported missing by her landlady in Denver, Colorado, a few days before
hikers found a young woman's body, matching Katharine's description,
in 1954. Fifty years later, the Boulder County (Colorado) Sheriff's Office
reopened the Jane Doe case. Then, in 2009, Katharine turned up in Australia,
living under an assumed name. Her sister, who never knew that Katharine
had been reported missing so many years earlier, revealed that Katharine had
voluntarily disappeared to avoid a divorce hearing with her husband because
she was pregnant with another man's child.[17] (In 2009, "Boulder Jane Doe,"
a murder victim, was identified as Dorothy Gay Howard, a runaway from
Phoenix, Arizona.)[18]

Some people, dubbed the "maliciously missing," establish new identities
without telling their families, and their actions can create unforeseen, and
devastating, consequences. This situation is depicted by the fictional Don
Draper in "Mad Men," a period drama television series that aired from 2007
to 2015. Don had come from a poor and troubled background, then switched
identities with a dying soldier burned beyond recognition during the Korean
War. A few years later, in the 1960s, Don emerged in New York City as a
highly successful executive in a Madison Avenue advertising agency. Meanwhile, his own brother had searched for him and finally found him, but Don
refused to have anything to do with the brother or his former life. The (fictional) brother was so distraught that he hanged himself.

There are many cases of real-life missing persons who, also, have walked
away and did not want to be found. The author has been in correspondence
with an Oregon woman who stated that she was one of three children in her
family and that both of her parents had been heavy drinkers. Her father had
been violent when drunk. So, she and her siblings were separated and placed in
foster homes in the Midwest. After a few years, the woman lost contact with her
mother, as well. The woman stated that during the fifty intervening years, she

constantly searched for—and recently found—both her sister and her mother. When she did, she had to deal with her resentment that neither of them had looked for her. The mother is now deceased and, of the sister, the woman wrote, "I have some reason to believe that she may not have wanted to be found."[19]

Ellenor Hacker

Another example of a person who did not want to be found is a late resident from Boulder, Colorado, Ellenor Hacker. More than half a century ago, in December 1959, the then-55-year-old widow went out her back door, early in the morning, to take out the trash. Eleven years later, the Boulder police found her in Victoria, British Columbia. During the intervening years, no one—not even her family—knew where she was.[20]

Initially her sisters and grown children feared that Ellenor had been murdered. The back door to her house was left open, and her purse and glasses were left behind. The family filed a missing person report, and police interviews show that relatives and friends agreed that Ellenor was "a very stable, efficient, and forceful woman." No one could think of a reason why she should drop from sight. He daughter added that she had been baking fruit cakes and cookies, and was planning for the upcoming Christmas holidays.[21]

As it turned out, the Christmas baking was a façade, and Ellenor did leave voluntarily. She assumed a different name and lived for several years in San Francisco, California, where she worked as a housekeeper for an invalid woman and then a nurse before retiring and moving to Canada. The Boulder police were tipped off when she tried to apply for Social Security benefits. When confronted, Ellenor admitted she was the missing woman.[22]

According to a newspaper reporter who interviewed her in 1971, she was "furious" with the Social Security Administration for giving her then-current address to the police. She even admitted that she had tried to make her disappearance as intriguing as possible because she "liked mysteries." A spokesman for the police department said Ellenor had a moral obligation to contact them and admitted that the cops did not even want to think about her case again. When the news broke, she reluctantly was reunited with her children.[23]

In a newspaper interview, at the time, Ellenor finally filled in the gaps on her disappearance. She said she had purchased a new dress and purse the day before she left and took only a toothbrush, hairbrush, and a one-way train ticket to San Francisco. "I've had a happy busy life, and a useful one," she told the newspaper reporter. "There wasn't any quarrel, I just left. I had a little money saved, and I just thought the heck with it."[24]

Brenda Heist

More recently, and also voluntarily missing for eleven years, was Brenda Heist. On February 8, 2002, the attractive 42-year-old brunette left her home in Lititz, Pennsylvania, with her two children (ages 8 and 12) and dropped them off at school. When the children came home, the house was empty. Brenda's car was gone, and there was no sign of a struggle. Her husband reported her missing to police. Four days later, her car was found undamaged in a nearby city. Local, state, and federal authorities spent years investigating her disappearance, interviewing dozens of relatives, friends, neighbors, and coworkers, and entering her into several national missing persons databases.[25]

In 2010, Brenda's husband had her declared legally dead. He collected on her life insurance and remarried. The children grew up and moved on with their education and their lives. For more on presumption of death, see chapter 10, "Pitfalls and Legalities."

Then, suddenly, in 2013, Brenda revealed her identity at the Monroe County Sheriff's Office in Key Largo, Florida, following her arrest for a stolen driver's license. She told authorities that she and her husband had been going through a divorce, and she left after she snapped under financial pressures.[26]

Brenda said she had left her home, family, and identity to hitchhike with homeless people she had met in a park, then panhandled and dumpster-dove for food. When she got to Florida, she worked odd jobs and lived with the homeless population, under bridges or in a tent. Her photo, published by the media in 2013, shows her aged and unkempt, barely resembling her former self. However, conflicting reports by people who knew Brenda (under an assumed name) in Florida, say that, at times, she worked as a housekeeper and did have a roof over her head.[27]

According to news reports, when Brenda's former husband learned that she was alive, he responded with anger, questioning how she could have put her children through so much hurt and pain. Brenda claimed to have thought of them every day, yet—for whatever reason—she never picked up the phone to say she was okay. Former neighbors were in disbelief.[28]

In a WGAL television report on May 2, 2013, Lititz Borough Police detective John Schofield stated, "I was shocked. Our department was shocked. Cause I will tell you, I was convinced something horrible happened to her years ago." In an effort to rebuild her life, Brenda has since moved to Texas to live with her mother.[29]

NATURAL OR ACCIDENTAL DEATH MOST LIKELY

As shown in "Gina and Her Dad—Returned Identities," in chapter 1, "Why Finding the Missing is Important," Rick Herren's family knew exactly where his boat had capsized, but they were unable, for many years, to retrieve his remains. Other families who do not know of specific locations are still waiting and hoping for answers.

Some family members still seeking unrecovered remains are descendants and relatives of more than a dozen men presumed to have drowned in northern Idaho's Priest Lake. Like Flaming Gorge Reservoir, where Gina's dad, Rick, lost his life, Priest Lake also is very large and is more than 300 feet deep. Its earliest-known victims were four men from Spokane, Washington, who, along with their guide, disappeared on a fishing expedition in 1919. Shortly afterwards, searchers found their fishing boat, along with the body of a fifth man. More men were reported to have drowned in 1945, 1948, 1950, 1960, 1987, 1996, and 2004. Newspaper and television publicity surrounding a recent unsuccessful recovery attempt brought forth generations of family members seeking to close the chapters on their missing fathers, uncles, and grandfathers.[30] (Apparently, no women are presumed missing.)

Meanwhile, as searches continue deep under the water, family members and others have spent decades scouring the summits of mountains for missing skiers and hikers. One man still missing is Joseph Laurence Halpern, a graduate student from Chicago who disappeared without a trace, in 1933, in Colorado's Rocky Mountain National Park. When Joseph's parents died, the missing man's brother continued to look for him and now Roland Halpern, Joseph's nephew, has taken up the search. Joseph's case has been entered into the NamUs Missing Person's database in the hopes that, someday, his remains will be found and identified.[31]

For more on NamUs, see "How Families Use NamUs" in chapter 7, "NamUs: An Investigative Tool." More of Roland's search is described in "Public Records" in chapter 9, "Gather Information, Document, and Do the Research."

Floods and hurricanes contribute to what are called the "catastrophic missing." Included in this category are persons who went missing following Hurricane Katrina. The severe storm hit New Orleans, Louisiana, in August 2005, but, nine years later, 705 people still had not been found.[32] Natural and/or accidental deaths often occur in the homeless population, as well. When these people die without identification, finding one or more of their family members can be very difficult. The homeless may be alienated from their families or may not have anyone who knows they are missing, let alone file a report. They, and others, fall into what are called the "missing miss-ing."[33] When their remains are found, they, too, add to the growing lists of the unidentified.

Alaskan Adventurers Find Answers for Families

On the evening of March 12, 1948, Northwest Airlines Charter Flight 4422, en route from Shanghai, China, to La Guardia Airport in New York City, crashed into Mount Sanford, a 16,237-foot peak located 200 miles northeast of Anchorage, Alaska. Along with six crew members, the Douglas DC-4 was carrying twenty-four United States Merchant Marines who were returning home after three months at sea. They had left Philadelphia, Pennsylvania, in an oil tanker, picked up a load of oil in the Middle East, and then delivered it to Chinese government officials in Shanghai.[34] Waiting in New York to meet the plane were wives, children, and other family members. The men never made it home, nor were they forgotten by their families.

The next day, searchers in the air positively identified the wreckage by the Northwest Airlines insignia on the plane's vertical tail fin. But, a rescue oper-ation was ruled impossible because the scene of the accident, at 11,000 feet, was an active glacier and deemed inaccessible. A dog sled team, however, did attempt to reach the site on foot, but gave up when its members realized conditions were unsafe. Five days later, another Northwest DC-4 flew over the crash site, while Protestant, Catholic, and Jewish clergymen conducted airborne funeral services. After prayers, they opened a passenger door and dropped several colorful wreaths in tribute to the thirty victims. By then, all of the wreckage had been swallowed up in the ice and snow.[35] For decades, afterwards, rumors swirled around the downed plane, with speculations of a lost payroll, diamonds, or even gold bullion.[36]

Nearly a half century later, Kevin McGregor and Marc Millican, both former US Air Force pilots, took up the search. Initially, for them, the quest to find the site of the wreckage was part back-country adventure, mixed with the possibility of hidden treasure. Beginning in 1994, the two men made three attempts. (They never did find any treasure, but they did find a rope, ladder, and remnants of an old campsite that suggested explorers had been there before them.) In-between excursions, they read newspaper articles, accident reports, and court records to research the victims. They also compiled lists of family members so that, if they found the plane, they could share with them the news of their discovery.[37]

Finally, in 1997, after landing Marc's Piper Super Cub in the wilderness and then hiking sixteen miles across rough and treacherous terrain, they came across two huge propeller blades and then a radial engine with serial numbers that matched Flight 4422. In Kevin's book *Flight of Gold*, he wrote:

> As we looked around at the jumbled mess of airplane parts, ice, and rock, our mood changed from the excitement of adventure to the sobering realization that we were in the midst of a long-hidden grave. Real people, each with a personal story, had lost their lives here, and these inanimate metal parts strewn over the cold and desolate expanse served as their tombstone.[38]

Within weeks of this discovery, Kevin and Marc talked with the families of almost all the victims. According to Kevin's publisher, Valerie van Heest, the family members found comfort knowing that the accident and their loved ones had not been forgotten.[39]

Kevin and Marc returned to the site two years later, in 1999, and made a startling new discovery. Lying atop the melting ice was a frozen human left forearm and hand, still containing soft tissue after being preserved in ice for half a century. The men marked the location so it would be visible from the air and left the remains in place.[40] The Alaska State Police were able to recover the arm and hand, which they delivered to the Office of the Medical Examiner in Anchorage. Then, images of the fingerprints were compared to the mariners' fingerprints, archived at the National Maritime Center in Arlington, Virginia. But, the remains were too degraded to yield results, at least for the technology in 1999. Initially, DNA extraction was not successful, either.[41]

Fortunately, fingerprint and DNA technologies advanced significantly within a few years. Rehydration techniques brought out ridge detail on the fingertips of the recovered hand. Then, silicone rubber molds of the fingertips yielded casts that then were dusted with fingerprint power, scanned, and compared with the fingerprints on file. Meanwhile, the Armed Forces DNA Identification Laboratory (AFDIL), in Rockville, Maryland, was able to extract DNA, while forensic genealogists painstakingly tracked down relatives and descendants of the victims. (DNA family reference samples were found for twenty of the victims, while fingerprint cards identified the other ten.)[42]

Eventually, the forearm and hand were identified (by both fingerprints and DNA) as belonging to 36-year-old Seaman Francis Joseph van Zandt, a former resident of Roanoke, Virginia. Since then, the man's nephew has donated the remains to the AFDIL to be used for further scientific research.

So far, his is the sole piece of human remains recovered from the crash that killed thirty people.[43]

UNDETERMINED

Gloria Jean Baird

"My name is Stephanie and I want to know what happened to my mother," states a California woman in her Where is Gloria Jean? Facebook group.[44] Stephanie Siegel (LaPoint) was only three months old, in 1967, when Gloria walked out the door of her home in Atlanta, Georgia, where her husband (Stephanie's father) was a chemical engineering student. In email correspondence with the author, Stephanie explained that Gloria had left a note saying that she would be back in ten minutes. She did not come back, and Stephanie never saw her again.[45]

A month later, Gloria wrote to her husband from Louisiana, asking for a divorce. However, around the time of Stephanie's first birthday, Gloria again wrote and stated that she did not want to give up her child. Yet, she never arrived with promised presents, and the couple finalized their divorce a couple of months later. Gloria then married and divorced again, before enlisting in the Army in August 1969. Details are hazy, but Gloria was thought to have been last seen in the company of three men at a New Year's Eve party in Atlanta, Georgia, on December 31, 1969. In January 1970, her parents received notification from the Army that she was "absent without authority."[46]

Mixed in with the basic facts of Gloria's disappearance is an alleged shaking incident by Gloria of her baby, as well as bouts of drinking and association with men with criminal backgrounds.[47] Did the slender 23-year-old walk away from her husband, child, friends, and the Army and start a new life for herself, afraid to come forward for fear of being absent without leave? Or, was her young life ended after the party, and will unidentified remains someday turn out to be hers? Stephanie's DNA is on file, just in case. In NamUs-MP #543, under "circumstances," is stated: "Baird was on an approved leave from the Army at the time of her disappearance [and] had been stationed at Ft. Benjamin Harrison in Indiana (now closed) and Ft. McClellan in Alabama. Her abandoned Volkswagen Beetle [allegedly] was found on the side of a road in Georgia, though no one saw her walking."[48]

Today, Stephanie struggles between the conflicting emotions that either her mother is long-deceased, or that she is alive and has chosen not to contact her. Stephanie's hurt and anger of not knowing, however, is not directed at Gloria, but rather at Gloria's parents (now deceased) whom, she states, never told her anything about her mother until Stephanie started gathering information on her own. Stephanie realizes that if Gloria's remains were to be found, the resolution, albeit bittersweet, would provide some answers. In recent correspondence with the author, she added, "If Gloria is/was anything like me, she would say hello, somehow. The pain can be unbearable. I have only recently learned that holding onto that pain is dangerous, and a waste. I can't help it though sometimes. I am who I am."[49]

John William Gates

Also still looking for answers is Robert Gates, grandson of John William Gates. According to a document titled "Mother's Compensation Act" on file in the Colorado State Archives, in Denver, Colorado, "John W." (as Robert likes to refer to his grandfather) disappeared from his home in Longmont, Colorado, more than a century ago, on April 23, 1916. There have never been any leads, and the remains of the missing man have never been found. Or, if they have, they have never been identified. Like the nephew of Joseph Laurence Halpern (the young man missing on a mountaintop), Robert explained in email correspondence with the author that he wants to solve

Figure 2.1 John William Gates and Family. John William Gates is remembered by his family from this portrait, taken in 1912 with his wife Delphia and their three children. Grandson Robert Gates is the son of Herman Albert Gates, the older boy in the photograph. *Source:* Photo courtesy of Robert Gates

his family's mystery and discover what happened to his long-lost family member.[50]

According to census records, John W. (see figure 2.1) was born in Iowa in 1882 but had moved to Colorado prior to 1900. At the time, his occupation was listed as a farm laborer. He married Delphia Carrie Peterson in 1903, and the couple settled in Longmont, in eastern Boulder County, where their oldest son Herman Albert Gates was enrolled in school. By 1910, John W. was working as a teamster. According to family lore, he delivered mining supplies to miners in the mountains, in western Boulder County.[51]

Rumors passed down through the family suggested that John W. may have been murdered by a brother-in-law who served some time in prison for other crimes. But, the missing husband and father could just as easily have suffered an accidental death away from home. He was thought to have held a lease in a mine and may have fallen (or been pushed) down a shaft or become buried in a rock fall without any word reaching Delphia.[52] In 1916, Boulder County, Colorado, was considered the tungsten capital of the world, due to great demand by the federal government during World War I. One- and two-man tungsten (and, also, gold) mining operations were common, and safety concerns were minimal.

Meanwhile, in 1913 and long before public welfare, the Colorado General Assembly had established the "Mother's Compensation Act." Individual counties were in charge of distributing funds for the assistance and protection of women who were unable to properly care for their children. The "Mother's Compensation Act" application, filed by John W.'s wife Delphia on May 21, 1917, is the only known existing document that sheds any light on the missing man's case. Delphia's application states:

> John W. Gates, husband of applicant and father of children. He left home April 23, 1916 for no reason known to applicant who does not know of his where-a-bouts now and has had no word from him since leaving. Previous to leaving, he was a good provider, a good husband, and a kind father. Applicant fears he met with an accident. Has no income or help from any source other than her labor at day's work and that only when she can have one of the older children at home to take care of the youngest child. Many people object to her having the baby with her at work.[53]

A "Western Newspaper Union News Service" article in a local newspaper, published one month before John W. went missing, gives some interesting insights. From 1915 to 1916, the number of Colorado families receiving the financial assistance numbered 148 [*sic*]. Ninety-eight of the mothers were widows. In the remaining families, thirty-one of the fathers (as would John W.) and three of the mothers were said to have "deserted" (presumably the county gave the assistance to the fathers), and seven of the parents had been divorced. In four of the families, the father was in prison. In four others, the father was sick.[54] There was no category for missing under suspicious circumstances.

Delphia died in 1960. Of John W., her obituary merely stated, "She was married to John W. Gates, and the couple moved to Longmont to make their home."[55] Robert Gates speculates that John W. may have left home to fight in the war, perhaps under an assumed identity.[56] Or, perhaps his remains were one of several unknown skeletons found, years later, tucked away in mountain canyons. Case files, if they even existed, have, unfortunately, disappeared along with the evidence, but newspaper articles still document findings of skeletal remains. One is of a skull found in 1938 at the base of a thirty-five-foot cliff, in Big Thompson Canyon, in neighboring Larimer County.[57]

John W.'s case is one of the oldest that has been entered into the NamUs Missing Persons database. Robert Gates recently gave his DNA in the event that it can be matched to skeletal remains that, if found, could likely belong to his grandfather.[58]

Chapter 3

Children

Helping to Bring Them Home

For those of us who remember the 1980s, the topic of missing children conjures up photographs of kids on milk cartons. Half-gallon cartons featured the smiling faces of two children, while the half-pint cartons handed out to children in school lunches had one image. The faces of today's missing children now are part of direct mail advertising that arrives in mailboxes all over the country, complete with a "Have You Seen Me?" headline, as well as website and hotline contacts to the National Center for Missing & Exploited Children® (NCMEC), 1-800-THE LOST (1-800-843-5678).[1]

The private nonprofit organization was established in 1984 to help prevent child abduction and sexual exploitation, that is, to find missing children and to assist victims of child abduction and sexual exploitation, as well as their families and the professionals who serve them. Who are these kids and how many of them are there? The number of missing children (as with adults) is difficult to determine because only the reported cases can be counted. However, basic categories of missing children can be defined as follows:

- Runaways
- Abductions
- Lost, Injured, or Otherwise Missing Children
- Critically Missing Young Adults

RUNAWAYS

Of the approximately 100,000 people of all ages who are missing at any one time in the United States, many are runaways aged 17 and under. The good news is that the majority of these teens are found alive or return, within a short time, on their own. As to who they are, consider New York State, with the highest runaway statistics in the country. In the year 2014 alone, 96 per cent of the state's 20,000 missing children were runaways, defined by the New York State Division of Criminal Justice Services as "children under 18 who are missing from their homes without their parents' consent."[2] (The NCMEC's statistics for 2015 put the national percentage of missing children as runaways at 86 per cent.[3]) More often, the runaways are girls—62 per cent, according to news reports, as opposed to 38 per cent for boys. New York statistics also are higher for teens of color.[4]

In the 1970s and 1980s, religious cults such as Hare Krishna and the Moonies (followers of Sun Myung Moon) gained a reputation for luring some of the nation's youths. However, most runaway teens today leave home because of domestic conflicts—often after coming out as lesbian, gay, bisexual, or transgender, then facing the disapproval of their parents. According to the National Coalition for the Homeless, 35 per cent of New York City's young homeless people are lesbian, gay, bisexual, or transgender, having fled homes in the South and the Midwest.[5] (Many of those in the western states gravitate toward Los Angeles and San Francisco.)

According to 2015 NCMEC statistics, one in five of reported endangered runaways of all sexual orientations become victims of sex traffickers, one of the most common types of sexual exploitation. And, of these sex-trafficking victims, 74 per cent were in the care of social services or foster care when they ran away.[6] Offenders prey on minors, coercing, enticing, and manipulating them to engage in sexually explicit conduct. Under federal law (18 U.S.C. §2256(2)(A)), "Sexually explicit conduct is defined as actual or simulated sexual intercourse, including genital-genital, oral-genital, anal-genital, or oral-anal, whether between people of the same or opposite sex; bestiality; masturbation; sadistic or masochistic abuse, or lascivious exhibition of the genitals or pubic area of any person."[7]

The sex traffickers then visually and illegally depict the sex acts with photographs, films, videos, and computer-generated images. They also violate federal laws by knowingly possessing, manufacturing, distributing, and accessing with intent to view child pornography (18 U.S.C. §2252(b)).

The offenders who violate the federal laws may face state charges, as well. Victims suffer from depression, withdrawal, anger, and other psychological disorders, while experiencing feelings of betrayal, powerlessness, worthlessness, and low self-esteem. Every time their image is viewed, traded, printed, or downloaded, the child in the image is victimized again.[8]

The outlook for teens caught up in the sex trade industry is bleak. Many males and females alike become addicted to hard drugs such as cocaine and heroin and turn to prostitution to finance their drug habits. Statistics vary, but studies agree that prostitution is not only the oldest "profession," but it is the most dangerous. The use of heroin, in particular, has become an epidemic. According to a recent *New York Times* article, the demographics have changed, as nearly 90 per cent of first-time heroin users in the last decade were white.[9] The drug-users' lifestyles often put them at greater risk of contracting sexually transmitted diseases, as well as dying of overdoses or becoming victims of violent crimes, including assaults and homicides.

Support is available for both families and for youths with the National Runaway Safeline. If a runaway wants to return to his or her family or guardian, for instance, a trained counselor from Safeline will talk with the teen and contact the family, as well as provide a bus ticket and follow-up support once the runaway gets home.[10]

Within the runaway category are what are called "thrown-away" children, (usually) teenagers whose caretakers make no effort to recover them. Thrownaways also include those who have been abandoned or deserted or have been asked to leave their homes and not allowed to return. While not necessarily reported to authorities as missing persons, children in this category frequently come to the attention of law enforcement. For an example, see the case of Shannon Aumock in "Detective Stuart Somershoe—A Voice for the Victims," in chapter 4, "Proactive Police."

As mentioned in chapter 2 in relation to the homeless population, those who are not even reported missing are often referred to as the "missing missing." Unless they are found, statistically, they do not exist.[11]

Missing children who are suicidal may fit into the runaway category, as well. In June 2002, seventeen-year-old Ben Mauer, of Piscataway, New Jersey, disappeared from his family's home in the middle of the night. The very next day, a young man with no identification jumped off of a building in New York City. For nine years (before Ben was identified by DNA comparison) his remains lay in an unmarked grave in the New York Cemetery on Hart Island, part of the Bronx and east of Pelham Bay Park in Long Island

Sound.[12] This cemetery is the largest potters' field in the United States, with one million graves of indigents and unknowns.

Whether Ben's family knew or considered that the teenager was suicidal is unknown. A background investigation, by the police, did not raise any red flags, but some of Ben's friends revealed to police that he had some personal problems.[13] At his family's request, Ben's remains were exhumed from Hart Island, as are approximately 100 sets of remains that are identified and disinterred by family members each year. However, one-tenth of the burials—a tremendous number—remain unidentified.[14] Ben is now buried in his hometown. His was a long journey, but his family finally brought him home.

ABDUCTIONS

According to the NCMEC organization's statistics for 2015, the second highest category of missing children (at 10 per cent) are abductions of minors made by a member of a child's family (or someone acting on behalf of a family member) who takes a child from, or fails to return a child to, his or her custodial parent.[15] These noncustodial family members keep the children in a country or place other than that of their normal residence. Their actions are against the other parent's will and are in violation of court orders, decrees, and/or other legitimate custodial rights. This is also referred to as parental kidnapping and custodial interference.

Citing the same statistics, only 1 per cent of children are taken by strangers, or nonfamily perpetrators. These abductions involve children who have been wrongfully taken through the use of physical force, persuasion, or threat of bodily harm.[16] An example is 17-year-old Marion Joan McDowell, abducted from a suburb of Toronto, Ontario, in 1953. The young woman was parked with her boyfriend in a "lovers' lane" when the boyfriend was hit over the head. When he resumed consciousness, he saw a man stuff Marion into the trunk of another car, then drive away. Despite intensive searches, and even the help of world-renown detectives, no traces of her, or her remains, have ever been found.[17]

Another long-term likely abduction is the case of Frederick "Freddie" Holmes. The almost-two-year-old was last seen in May 1955, walking in the driveway of his family's rural home near Grahamsville, New York. In recent years, Dorothy Holmes Brown (the missing toddler's only surviving sibling) corresponded with the author. Dorothy was 14 years old when Freddie disappeared and she remembers him well. In 2013, in her email correspondence, she wrote:

Freddie was well loved and a special baby to us. We were from a large family, not much money but for sure lots of love. Since we did not have a TV in those years our Freddie was our source of entertainment. We older kids taught him to sing, dance, say clever things. He was precious! . . . My parents grieved as you can imagine. My father died in 1968, a victim of suicide. He simply could not handle the grief and stress. My mother died on her sixty-first birthday of a sudden heart attack. She often told us that she had a hole in her heart related to the loss of her baby son.[18]

Dorothy remembers Sheriff officials ripping up the floorboards of the family's farmhouse, digging up her mother's newly planted garden, and questioning her parents with polygraph machines, while busloads of men from a nearly Air Force base scoured the woods for any shred of clothing or human remains. Yet, when she inquired of the police years later, she was told that, other than newspaper clippings, there was no case file.[19] Was it misfiled, missing, or destroyed? No one knows. But times have changed, and in 2009 Dorothy filed a new missing person report. She educated herself about long-term missing persons, got Freddie entered into the databases of the NCMEC and the National Missing and Unidentified Persons System (NamUs).[20] And she gave police her DNA for comparison.

Dorothy believes that someone abducted Freddie, perhaps to sell him to someone else who wanted a blonde little boy. "I feel certain that he is still alive and does not really know who he is. I always have hoped whoever wanted a beautiful baby boy was sweet and kind to Freddie and that he was not abused." She added, "When Freddie was first taken, can you imagine how sad and frightened and alone he must have felt? Just plain evil and cruel. So, if he were returned to us today, joyful I would be, but, that does not erase the years of grief."[21]

When stranger-abduction cases are solved, they become high profile. Jaycee Dugard was found alive in 2009 after being held captive eighteen years. Amanda Berry and Georgina DeJesus were found alive and living together with Michelle Knight (age 21 at the time of her abduction), in 2013, after more than a decade of captivity in Cleveland, Ohio. In addition, Amanda gave birth to a child in captivity.[22]

Profiled below are two additional well-known victims—Elizabeth Smart and Polly Klass. Elizabeth Smart survived, while Polly Klass was the victim of murder. Elizabeth has set up a foundation, as has the father of Polly. Both have become important resources for parents of missing children:

• Elizabeth Smart Foundation, http://elizabethsmartfoundation.org/
• Polly Klass Foundation, http://www.pollyklaas.org/

Elizabeth Smart

On June 5, 2002, Elizabeth Smart, then a 14-year-old junior-high student, was abducted at knifepoint in the middle of the night from the bedroom of her comfortable Salt Lake City home. The only witness was her younger sister, Mary Katherine, who was able to tell her parents that Elizabeth's abductor might have been a man who once worked at the family's home. Police released a sketch of the man, the case received a lot of publicity, and the search for the missing girl was featured on John Walsh's television show.[23]

Unknown to police and family at the time, the suspect identified by the sister actually was Elizabeth's abductor. He and a female accomplice held and sexually assaulted the girl against her will, only a few miles from her home. The trio then traveled to San Diego, California, where they camped and panhandled. Elizabeth was told that if she tried to flee, she and her family would be killed. Often she was restrained with leg irons. Nine months after her abduction, on March 12, 2003, she was found alive—walking down the street of Sandy, Utah, with her captors.[24] The next day, Elizabeth's father, Ed Smart (see figure 3.1), discussed her safe return with John Walsh.

A few weeks later, Elizabeth and her mother met with US president George W. Bush at the White House, in Washington, D.C., where the president signed the "PROTECT Act of 2003," a child-protection bill that stands for "Prosecutorial Remedies and Other Tools to end the Exploitation of Children Today." One of the PROTECT Act's components was to encourage states to establish the AMBER Alert Program to instantly create public awareness to assist in the search for a missing child.[25]

The Program, named for Amber Hagerman, a 9-year-old girl abducted and murdered in Arlington, Texas, in 1996, is a voluntary partnership among the US Department of Justice, law enforcement agencies, broadcasters, and the wireless industry. AMBER alerts use the eyes and ears of the public with broadcasts on radio, television, road signs, and all available technology outlets.[26]

In 2008, Elizabeth and four other kidnapping survivors authored the US Department of Justice booklet, "You're Not Alone: The Journey From Abduction to Empowerment." In this guide for survivors, Elizabeth told other victims, "We all have different ways of getting through our experiences after we come home. One of the ways I did this was to set goals, to work continually toward those goals, and then to set new ones. Finding healthy emotional outlets helped me a lot as well. One of my outlets was playing my harp. I could put my soul into my playing, which in return, for me, expressed how I felt better than talking to someone might have done."[27]

Figure 3.1 Ed Smart and John Walsh. Ed Smart, father of kidnapped Utah teenager Elizabeth Smart, talks via satellite to host John Walsh during the "The John Walsh Show" in New York, on March 13, 2003. Elizabeth was found alive in a Salt Lake City suburb after being missing more than nine months. *Source:* AP Photo/Richard Drew

Elizabeth was able to move on with her life. She triumphantly testified in the trial of her abductor, who is now in prison for life. Meanwhile, Elizabeth graduated from Brigham Young University and established and is president of the Elizabeth Smart Foundation. She also has married, started a family, and is active in her church, while continuing her work to prevent and stop predatory crimes.[28]

Polly Klass

Like Elizabeth Smart, Polly Klass's case also received national attention, but her outcome was very different. In 1993, the 12-year-old, like Elizabeth, was abducted at knifepoint in the middle of the night from her bedroom, which was in Petaluma, California. Eventually, her killer confessed to strangling her. Nine weeks after her abduction, he led authorities to Polly's buried body.[29]

LOST, INJURED, OR OTHERWISE MISSING CHILDREN

Lost, injured, or otherwise missing children comprise 2 per cent of missing children, again according to the NCMEC's statistics for 2015.[30] The incidents may range from young children wandering away in the woods, or children who are hurt and cannot be found immediately during sports activities or at youth camps. Usually there are happy endings when the children return or are found. But an even smaller percentage of the otherwise missing children involve those who were abducted without witnesses. Their fate can parallel the abduction cases, without anyone aware, at the time, of an abduction. Tragically, some of these cases turn into homicides.

A missing person case that has been solved is that of Surette Clark. The Navajo child was only four years old when she was murdered by her stepfather in 1970, in Phoenix, Arizona. According to court reports, the stepfather punished the child for disobedience (resulting in her death) while her mother was at work. Without revealing where he had dumped the little girl's body, the stepfather then fled to Canada with the child's pregnant and terrified mother.[31]

At the time, no one reported the child missing. Nine years later, in 1979, a young child's skeletal remains were found in the city of Tempe, not far from Phoenix. The remains, however, were misidentified as Caucasian, then put on an evidence shelf and forgotten. Meanwhile, the stepfather confessed to family members, in Canada, that he had killed Surette. But, the family kept quiet, and the case went cold.[32]

Often, in cold cases, the passage of time will bring forward new witnesses. That is what happened in 1993—twenty-three years after the crime was committed—when the killer's sister could no longer keep the family secret and contacted police. Three years later, and without a body, an Arizona court convicted the stepfather of second-degree murder, even though the court was unaware that unidentified remains (that turned out to be Surette's) had been found.[33]

In 1997, while the child's stepfather was serving time in the Arizona State Prison, the Tempe Police Department received a federal grant to reexamine its unsolved cases. The police took the remains of the unidentified child (labeled "Little Jane Doe") off of the evidence room shelf and created a facial reconstruction. No one, at the time, connected the child to Surette, however, as the remains were still thought to have been Caucasian.[34]

Little Jane Doe was still unidentified in 2009, when Surette's stepfather was released from prison on parole. At the same time, detectives from the Phoenix Police Department had requested a list of unidentified child victims from the NCMEC. The organization then encouraged the Tempe Police Department to perform a DNA comparison between its unidentified child and Surette's biological mother and father. Finally, in 2010, forty years after Surette's murder (and after the stepfather's release), police identified "Little

Figure 3.2 Paul and Ramona Blee. Colorado residents Paul and Ramona Blee hold a framed photograph of their daughter Marie Ann Blee, missing since 1979. *Source:* Photo by author

Jane Doe" as Surette Clark. Her remains have since been returned to her mother.[35]

Marie Ann Blee: Someone Knows What Happened

Marie Ann Blee was one of the children whose photograph was featured on a milk carton. Now her photograph (as well as an age-progression digital image) is listed in the NCMEC's database of missing children, searchable by anyone who goes on the agency's website. Not shown behind every one of these faces and brief descriptions, however, are the details of their disappearances and the heartache of their families.

At the time of this writing, the specific facts surrounding 15-year-old Marie Ann Blee's decades-long disappearance are still unknown. Her parents, Paul and Ramona Blee, see figure 3.2, stated in an interview with the author that they agree with current law enforcement officials that their daughter most likely is deceased. They believe that someone knows the location of Marie's remains, and they are dedicating the rest of their lives to finding them and bringing them home. The Blees are still grieving, but they have persevered, and their willingness to help others is an inspiration to all.

The last time Paul and Ramona saw Marie was the night before Thanks-giving, on November 21, 1979. The blonde-haired, blue-eyed high school sophomore was headed off to a dance, seventeen miles away at the Moffat County Fairgrounds Pavilion in the town of Craig. Her date picked her up at the family's home in Hayden, a small town in Routt County, in northwestern Colorado, where her father Paul worked as an electrician. Marie, at the time, was active in 4-H club, had just gotten her ski pass for Steamboat Springs, and was excited about getting her driver's permit. Friends saw her at the dance, as well as at a party afterwards in a private home. Her date for the evening accompanied her to the party, but he did not bring her home. He later told the Blees that she got a ride home with someone else—someone he did not know.[36]

"The next morning," stated Ramona in the couple's interview with the author, "I got up at 6 a.m. to put the turkey in the oven. I looked in Marie's room, and she wasn't there. At first I thought that maybe she had spent the night with one of her friends." Thanksgiving plans were set aside, as Paul and Ramona started calling Marie's friends, as well as local hospitals. They also filed a missing person report with the Hayden Police Department, where an officer tried to brush off the parents' concerns by suggesting their daughter had run away.[37]

A few days later, while neighbors joined Paul in a search party, Ramona stayed home to be near the telephone. And, the telephone rang. An anony-mous caller demanded a $5,000 ransom for Marie's safe return. By then, both the Routt County and Moffat County sheriffs' offices had become involved, and sheriff's deputies tapped the Blees' telephone and stayed at the family's home for several days.[38]

The next week, the police arrested the caller. He was the same teenage boy who had taken Marie to the dance and the party. He denied involvement in her disappearance, but he was given a suspended sentence for extortion.[39] (In June 2015, the same man, now in his fifties, was arrested for kidnap-ping another teenage girl. According to news reports, he allegedly sexually assaulted the girl and then turned her free in the same vicinity and only a few months before Marie went missing.[40])

With no new leads and a turf war among the three involved law enforce-ment agencies, Marie's case went cold. Finally, twenty years later, in 1999, investigators from the Routt and Moffat County sheriffs' offices and the Hayden and Craig police departments, as well as local prosecutors and the FBI formed a task force. They included the Blees in their monthly meetings.[41]

For the first time, law enforcement investigators interviewed many of the teens who were at the party. And, during the next couple of years, the task force tracked down hundreds of leads and explored several theories that included the possibilities that Marie either overdosed on drugs and frightened partygoers disposed of her body, or that she was abducted and killed. Authorities excavated several burial sites and dug up numerous wells. Bone fragments discovered in 2000 were compared to DNA from a lock of Marie's hair and a sample from her orthodontic retainer, but none matched.[42]

The Blees were appreciative of the task force's efforts, but their daughter's case remained unsolved. On many anniversaries of Marie's disappearance, Paul and Ramona wrote letters to the editor of the *Craig Daily Press*. The following was published on November 24, 2003:

> To the Editor:
> Nov. 22 is not only the anniversary of the death of JFK, it is also the 24th anniversary of the day our daughter, Marie Blee, disappeared. Marie had gone to a dance in Craig and never returned to our home in Hayden.
> We thank the task force from the Routt County Sheriff's Department and the Moffat County Sheriff's Department and the Hayden Police Department for the work they have done and continue to do in the investigation of this unfortunate incident.
> They say time heals all, but whoever said it probably never had a missing child and never lived such a nightmare of 24 years.
> What happened that Thanksgiving Eve, Nov. 21, 1979?
> Was Marie's demise preplanned? Was Marie overdosed with drugs and left somewhere to die or freeze to death and later moved to the place where no one would find her?
> Was Marie a victim of date rape and senselessly beaten to keep her from talking?
> Where is her body stashed?
> We have been left with so many questions, but the biggest one is, "Where is my daughter?"
> Someone knows what happened and where she is.
> When the people who know what happened and where she is gather with their families on the holidays, we hope they reflect on the past and what they stole from us on Thanksgiving Eve 1979.[43]

By writing their letters, Paul and Ramona recognized the importance of keeping Marie's story in the public eye. On the twenty-fifth anniversary, the Blees started a scholarship, in Marie's name, that is given each year to a girl from Hayden High School who is going on to college. And, although Paul is now retired, neither of the Blees have taken to their rocking chairs. Now living in Grand Junction, Colorado, they keep busy while directing their energies in helping others. In 2001, Paul had a heart attack. Afterwards, he started volunteering in the Veterans Affairs Medical Center and continues to this day. "It helps them out a little bit," he said.[44]

One of Paul's jobs is to drive disabled veterans to their medical appointments. One day, a decade or more ago, while transporting veterans in a van, he listened to a radio interview with Howard Morton. The father of a long-term missing son had recently founded an organization called Families of Homicide Victims and Missing Persons (FOHVAMP). Before long, Paul and Ramona became active members, meeting with others in similar situations and educating themselves on actions to follow. Ramona is now the organization's president.[45] For more on FOHVAMP, see "Support Groups" in chapter 8, "Become Your Long-Term Missing Person's Advocate."

Meanwhile, Ramona has been, and continues to be, a volunteer victim advocate in the Mesa County Sheriff's Office, in Grand Junction, where she is on call for twelve-hour shifts. Recently, she was called to comfort a mother with a missing 15-year-old daughter. "When the girl was found," said Ramona, "the mother cried and cried and collapsed in my arms."[46] No victim advocate had been with Ramona when Marie disappeared or during or after the telephone harassment, but Ramona was perfectly suited to be at this mother's side. Ramona has also volunteered with the Mesa County Meth Task Force.

Paul and Ramona both have served as family representatives on the Colorado Department of Public Safety's Cold Case Task Force, where they interact with law enforcement officials and members of other families with long-term missing persons and cold case homicides. The day of their interview with the author, the Blees had joined other families at the Colorado State Capitol Building, in Denver, for a state-designated day to remember and honor all missing persons in Colorado. Following a reading of the Resolution, along with each missing person's name in the Senate Chambers, family members gathered on the Capitol Building's steps for a prayer vigil and balloon release.

Paul and Ramona Blee are involved in the lives of their other children and enjoy their grandchildren and even a great-grandchild. But, every day, Marie is on their minds. When asked what advice they would give to other parents, they stated:

- maintain hope—keep going
- keep asking questions
- learn about new techniques
- educate law enforcement and district attorneys
- keep being a "squeaky wheel"[47]

CRITICALLY MISSING YOUNG ADULTS

The fourth basic category of missing children actually is called "critically missing young adults." These are young adults ages 18 through 20, who have an elevated risk of danger and are missing in circumstances outside of their normal patterns of behavior. Included in the NCMEC's statistical breakdown, Critically Missing Young Adults comprise 1 per cent of its cases.[48]

This concern for critically missing young adults is reflected in Suzanne's Law, a provision of the "PROTECT Act of 2003" that extends the same reporting and investigative procedures to individuals under the age of 21 as was already provided to children younger than 18.[49] Suzanne's Law was named for Suzanne Lyall, a 19-year-old student at the State University of New York at Albany, who has been missing ever since she got off of a bus near her dorm, in 1998.[50]

The statute now requires law enforcement to enter the reports of missing young adults ages 18 through 20 into the FBI's National Crime Information Center (NCIC) database without delay and to subsequently conduct an investigation. Additionally, this law lets the NCMEC open cases regarding missing young adults at the request of law enforcement.[51]

NCMEC: BEHIND THE SCENES

The mission of the National Center for Missing & Exploited Children ® (NCMEC) is "to serve as a resource center for law enforcement, families, and the public to help find missing children, reduce child sexual exploitation, and prevent child victimization."[52] When a child or teenager runs away or disappears, the organization advises families to immediately contact them and to contact their local law enforcement agencies. A case management team then will communicate with the family and with law enforcement to generate leads and provide resources and support. Readers in need of *immediate* assistance are urged to go to the NCMEC's website and follow the instructions on the If Your Child is Missing website page.[53]

Remember—There is *no* waiting period to report a missing person.

In addition to addressing time-sensitive concerns, many of the NCMEC's resources are specifically designed for families of *long-term* missing children. No missing child is ever forgotten, even after twenty, thirty, or more years. The organization's forensic artists create age-progression images to show what a missing child would look like many years after his or her disappearance, while staff members specifically assist families of long-term missing children through the following:

- Forensic Imaging Team
- Project ALERT®
- Biometrics Team
- Forensic Services Unit

Forensic Imaging Team

The NCMEC's team of full-time forensic artists use their artistic and computer skills to assist law enforcement agencies with cases of missing children and unidentified child remains. In cases of long-term missing children, the artists produce age-progression images to show what the children might look like as teenagers or adults. In cases of unidentified deceased children, the artists can alter or reconstruct postmortem photos to produce images of what the children may have looked like in life. If the child's remains are skeletal and the law enforcement agency can provide a computed tomography (CT) scan of the skull, the artists use 3-D sculpting software and Adobe Photoshop to create a digitally rendered facial reconstruction. That image is then publicized along with a synopsis of the case. For an excellent example, see "Jane Doe 1967," now identified as Teala Patricia Thompson, in "Trooper Brian Gross and the Westmoreland County Girls," in chapter 4, "Proactive Police."

If law enforcement and/or coroners and medical examiners have photographs of a child's clothing or personal effects, the image can also be cleaned up digitally and provided as part of a case poster. The goal of the Forensic Imaging Team is to produce images suitable to show to the public in order to prompt someone who may recognize a photograph to call authorities. In 2015, an image produced by the Forensic Imaging Team and widely circulated in the national media resulted in the identification of Bella Bond, a two-year-old girl whose body was discovered on the shore of Deer Island near Boston.[54]

Project ALERT®

Project ALERT® works closely with the Forensic Services Unit (see below) to provide on-site support to law enforcement agencies with long-term missing child cases. The project's members assist law enforcement with case reviews, comprehensive analyses, and searches and rescues, as well as biometrics collection and integration of all other available resources to help find the missing children. At law enforcement's request, the NCMEC will send one of approximately five forensic anthropologists to assist in an exhumation. (The anthropologists donate their time, and their number fluctuates.)

During an exhumation, the anthropologists provide guidance to authorities, help identify the grave site, provide full anthropological assessments, and help identify factors that include race, age, skeletal anomalies, and trauma. The NCMEC also utilizes the anthropologists on every skull facial reconstruction that is completed by one of its forensic artists to ensure the artists are creating features representative of the skull.[55]

Biometrics Team

The objective of the Biometrics Team is to aid in the identification of unknown children through the collection and sharing of enhanced data that includes DNA, dental records, and fingerprints. Once collected, this data is uploaded into the NamUs System and the FBI's NCIC database. Team members then search the databases, submit the biometric data, and compare the data to that of unknown victims believed to be children.

The Biometrics Team then assists law enforcement, medical examiners, and coroners by:

- Ensuring DNA has been collected and profiled from both missing children and cases of unknown children. The Team also searches against missing-children-family-DNA-reference samples in the FBI's Combined DNA Index System (CODIS).
- Facilitating collection of dental records for forensic odontology coding on missing unknown children for upload to national databases including NamUs and NCIC.
- Facilitating the collection and coding of fingerprints for entry into national databases.
- Documenting all personal belongings found with a deceased child, such as jewelry and clothing, for dissemination to the public and law enforcement via posters to help identify an unknown child.
- Searching and analyzing data for possible matches in the NCMEC missing child database, as well as in NamUs and the NCIC.[56]

Forensic Services Unit

The NCMEC's Forensic Services Unit is responsible for cases of long-term missing and abducted children, as well as child homicides and cases of unidentified remains. These are the most complex and challenging cases, requiring case workers to become intimately familiar with the children and families involved in order to provide the best resources and guidance. The duties of the Unit's staff include consolidating, analyzing, and evaluating leads from various resources and agencies, as well as preparing progress reports, conducting computer database searches, assisting in a nationwide DNA Project, and communicating with law enforcement, state agencies, and family members.

Specific resources for Unidentified Child Cases, as noted on the NCMEC's website, include:

- Forensic artists and imaging resources for facial reconstructions, image enhancements, and digitization. (See Forensic Imaging Team, above.)
- Poster distribution through specialized geographic and population targeting.
- Media announcements on anniversary dates, featured articles on NCMEC's website and the Help ID Me Facebook page.
- Assistance with other national missing and unidentified person databases such as NamUs, NCIC, and Violent Criminal Apprehension Program (ViCAP).
- Ensuring biometrics (DNA, dental records, fingerprints) are collected, analyzed, and searched proactively for every case.
- Conducting searches and comparisons to missing persons, and ensuring all exclusions are forensically verified.
- Providing case analysis and technical assistance using a variety of public record databases, social networking websites, and internal databases to enhance case information and develop leads.
- Facilitating assistance by forensic professionals such as forensic anthropologists and forensic odontologists (dental specialists).
- Providing evidence review, that is, assessing evidence and making recommendations that could help identify the child and or perpetrator(s).
- Exhumations and search-for-remains assistance by forensic anthropologists and search-and-rescue (SAR) experts.
- Organizing and hosting two-day case reviews, that is, using panels of experts to help evaluate case information and making investigative and forensic recommendations to increase the solvability of cases.
- Utilizing federal liaison resources including: the FBI, United States Secret Service (USSS), US Marshals Service (USMS), United States Coast Guard (USCG), Naval Criminal Investigative Service (NCIS), Interpol, US State Department, and the US Postal Inspection Service (USPI).[57]

Carol Schweitzer: A Privilege to Speak for the Children

Senior Forensic Case Specialist Carol Schweitzer began her work with the National Center for Missing & Exploited Children ® (NCMEC) as an intern in 2005. It happened to be the day that the organization opened a Katrina Hotline to help reunite families that had been separated during Hurricane Katrina. The agency's headquarters, in Alexandria, Virginia, was packed full of staff and volunteers hooked up to phones and computers. "The energy in that building was overwhelming, a feeling I will truly never forget," stated Carol in email correspondence with the author. "People were there helping because there was nowhere else they would rather be."[58]

"My eyes and ears were open, and I absorbed a lot those first few weeks with so much going on around me," she added. "That first day I was asked to help follow up with family members who were trying to locate their displaced child. The first person I spoke with on the phone was distraught and crying, but by the end of our conversation the woman knew where to go to find her child. I had met someone during a crisis and made an impact. I wanted to do more, so I decided to stay. The people and the mission were inspiring."[59]

In 2006, Carol was hired as an assistant case manager, researching active missing child cases including runaways, family abductions, nonfamily abductions, and critical missing child investigations. In addition, she provided technical assistance and resources to law enforcement by searching family members and social service agencies, and she provided technical assistance to federal analysts developing the Innocence Lost Initiative. Then, as a Forensic Case Specialist, she managed a caseload of long-term missing child cases, providing technical assistance and recommendations to investigating law enforcement agencies, while also communicating directly with searching family members.[60]

Now in her current role as Senior Case Specialist in the Forensic Services Unit, Carol is focused specifically on cases of unidentified remains, working with medical examiners, coroners and law enforcement. Her desk is in a cubicle quad near a window, and she has a bulletin board jammed with photos of missing and unidentified children, success cases, Bible scripture, funnies, and team photos that keep her smiling and motivated every day. Carol's responsibilities encompass a large area, as she handles all cases in the eastern half of the United States (east of the Texas eastern border). Her counterpart, Ashley Rodriguez, handles the West. Their combined caseload, at the time of this writing, totals 712 sets of unidentified child remains.[61]

While some of these unidentified remains cases are being matched to long-term missing children, many of the cases that come across Carol's desk are children who, sadly, never were reported missing to police, or are those who were neglected, thrown away, or forgotten. Carol said she is drawn to the complicated stories that surrounded her cases and enjoys putting the pieces together to help discover their names. "Every child deserves a name," she said. "I now have the distinct privilege to be able to speak for these children who no longer have a voice. At NCMEC, we never stop having hope and never stop fighting, nor do we stop searching for answers and justice for these children we serve."[62]

Her position also allows her to unveil the previously unnamed children's life stories—where were they born, where they spent their childhoods, and who are their families. She's interested, too, in other aspects of their lives that include their traditions, how they dressed, how they wore their hair, and habits they might have had. "I get to help create a picture of what these children looked like and acted like, as if they were standing right next to me," she said. "It's a challenge to do that, but it's also an honor. And when we get it right some days, and we help give a child back his or her name, it's a humbling good day."[63]

Carol likes to recall the words of her mentor, former Forensic Services Unit supervisor, Jerry Nance, who once told her that families with long-term missing children wake up every day with one foot in the past on the day their child disappeared and another in the present. And every day they have to make a choice on whether they are going to dwell in the past or take a step forward, just remembering where that other foot is but still moving ahead. "Remembering that helped me through many difficult conversations with family members of missing children," Carol said. "We are meeting these families on the phone when they are going through their worst nightmare, and we have an opportunity to make that day a little bit better for them. My job allows me to be a voice of encouragement, empowerment, remembrance, and hope to those family members still waiting for answers."[64]

The Case of Curtis Huntzinger

One missing child case that has stuck with Carol is that of Curtis Huntzinger. According to news reports, the 14-year-old Native American was last seen at his sister's home in Humboldt County, California, in May 1990. Shortly before he went missing, he had told his parents that he had been sexually molested by a male family friend. When the teen failed to return to his sister's home, his parents filed a missing person report. Instead of investigating, the local police assumed that he had run away. No one had any idea, at the time, that the family friend had killed Curtis by crushing his skull with a barbell, then burying him in a clandestine grave.[65]

In a newspaper interview nineteen years later, after Curtis's body was found, his sister told a reporter that the former family friend not only killed

Curtis, but he had destroyed an entire family. "We were walking in frustration and inside all of us was a permanent ache," she said. "Life as we knew it was over. There were no more big holiday festivities, no more big family picnics. If there was a gathering that was meant to be happy, it was marred by the fact that one of us was missing."[66]

For a short time, the police did take Curtis's case seriously and formed a task force, but it quickly disbanded. Then came a false murder confession by a convicted felon already in prison. Curtis's mother, Nancy, however, correctly believed that her son was dead and the killer was the former family friend. In 1999, she confronted him. He confessed and said he wanted to kill himself. That prompted Nancy to take the man to her church to be baptized, and she begged him to take her to the wooded site where he told her that he had buried her son. The man agreed, but the search proved fruitless and remained so for nine more years.[67]

The Humboldt County District Attorney's Office took over the case in September 2008. By that time, District Attorney Investigator Wayne Cox had requested the organization's help. He was often on the telephone with Carol who provided support and resources every step of the way. She stated, "Investigator Cox and his team spent days in the woods searching for Curtis. Every couple of hours he would call me with updates and would always say, 'We're not leaving this mountain without Curtis. He is here and we're going to find him.'"[68]

A few days later, a volunteer, working with the team, arrived with a metal detector. After several false leads that turned out to be spent bullet casings, the man's metal detector picked up on Curtis's watch. When the dirt was dug away, the investigators found the watch, still on the teen's wrist in his shallow grave. It had been overgrown with poison ivy and blackberry brambles, and Curtis's remains had been entwined in the roots of redwood trees.[69] But even before the teen's remains had been unearthed, Investigator Cox had arrested the former friend who pled guilty to voluntary manslaughter.[70]

Carol spoke highly of the investigator and his team, but she also heaped praise on Curtis's mother, Nancy, admitting that she was the first mother who made her cry. "She described the day she went into the woods with her son's killer searching for her son's grave and, at one point, got on her knees and just started digging with her bare hands," said Carol. "She [Nancy] dug and dug looking for her own son's remains. She brought hope, courage, love, and peace into that case that will always stay with me."[71]

For more on Nancy and her son's case, see "Civil Lawsuits" in chapter 10, "Pitfalls and Legalities."

Chapter 4

Proactive Police

Modern technology and the Internet have revolutionized the way that police approach cold cases, including those of the long-term missing. Today, there is new hope for family members that their loved ones will be found. And, helping to find them are many motivated and dedicated people. The following pages give a behind-the-scenes look at three law enforcement professionals.

CSO BETH BUCHHOLTZ: MAKING A DIFFERENCE IN HER COMMUNITY

Community Service Officer (CSO) Beth Buchholtz is a noncommissioned civilian in the Detective Division of the Longmont Police Department. The detectives in this city of 89,000 residents in Northern Colorado are fortunate to have her, as she brings to the job a unique set of skills that qualifies her to focus on a topic of special interest—missing persons and unidentified remains.

Names for the Unknown

In an interview with the author, CSO Buchholtz said that she always liked to solve puzzles. She holds a master's degree in anthropology and previously worked as a medical investigator with the Boulder County Coroner's Office. While there, in 2004, she took vacation time to assist the Boulder County Sheriff's Office and members of the Vidocq Society in the exhumation of a Jane Doe murder victim from 1954, briefly mentioned in chapter 1, "Why Finding the Missing is Important." The coffin had disintegrated underground, but CSO Buchholtz and forensic anthropologist Dr. Walter Birkby spent two long days removing the remains. DNA from the victim's tooth, when compared with DNA from a surviving sister, revealed her identity as an 18-year-old teen missing a half century earlier from Phoenix, Arizona. CSO Buchholtz compared the exhumation to an archeological dig and called the experience both "grueling" and "satisfying."[1]

In her role as a medical investigator, CSO Buchholtz also spent six years searching for the family of a John Doe, whose skeletal remains had been found on a mountainside near Boulder, Colorado. His cause of death was undetermined. From his bones, teeth, and hair, however, CSO Buchholtz was able to give his physical description, including approximate age and height. The coroner's office then submitted a bone sample to a lab in Baltimore, Maryland, resulting in a full DNA profile. In those pre-NamUs days, CSO Buchholtz undertook the daunting task of manually comparing her John Doe with a list of more than 700 missing young men, using dental charts and DNA, when available.[2] For more on NamUs, see chapter 7, "NamUs: An Investigative Tool."

Eventually, the John Doe's remains were interred in a peaceful rural cemetery, but his case was not forgotten. Prior to his burial, the young man's DNA had been submitted to the FBI laboratory for entry into the Combined DNA Index System (CODIS) to enable automatic searching for potential matches. In 2007, CSO Buchholtz entered his case information and description into the then-new NamUs—Unidentified Persons database.[3]

In 2009, the same year that the Unidentified Persons database was merged with the Missing Persons database to create the NamUs System, two members of the family of missing 16-year-old Cristobal James Flores contacted their local law enforcement agency, as well as the National Center for Missing & Exploited Children® (NCMEC), to request that his missing person case be reopened. (Cristobal had originally been reported missing in 2001.)

In 2012, family members provided DNA samples to their local police who then had the familial profiles entered into CODIS via its DNA laboratory. Cristobal's case information was also entered into the databases of both NamUs—Missing Persons and the NCMEC.[4] For more on the organization, see chapter 3, "Children: Helping to Bring Them Home."

After the family members had submitted their DNA, CODIS produced two "cold hits," identifying John Doe as Cristobal James Flores. By then, however, CSO Buchholtz had taken on her current position at the Longmont Police Department. When speaking of her role with a newspaper reporter at the time of Cristobal's identification, she stated, "It's important in any death investigation to have a balance between the science and the emotional part of it. But it's always a person to me. I don't think anyone should die without having a name."[5] Now, Cristobal has his name, and his remains have been returned to his family.

Prevention and Best Practices

CSO Buchholtz carries this same commitment and passion into her current work at the Longmont Police Department. Initially, she was put in charge of the pawn unit and also assisted with search warrants—tasks which she still performs along with other duties involving property crimes. Before long, however, she realized that her department had a handful of new missing person cases each week, but, because of limited resources, the only ones the detectives followed up on were those determined to be endangered or missing under suspicious circumstances. CSO Buchholtz then began attending missing person conferences and training sessions to learn about long-term missing persons, as well as to keep the ones that were missing and then found from going missing again.[6]

At the Longmont Police Department, the responding officers and initial report-takers question the reporting parties and make the first call in determining if a missing person is endangered. Risk factors include, but are not limited to, age (under 13 or elderly), mental or behavioral disability, drug dependency, inconsistent or suspicious circumstances under which the disappearance has taken place, and/or the company of others who could endanger the person's welfare.

Once a week, CSO Buchholtz updates a spreadsheet on her department's missing persons. Most are runaway teenagers, and 95 per cent of them come back on their own. Some, commonly referred to as "frequent flyers," run away and come back multiple times. In those cases, CSO Buchholtz looks for reports of previous police contact with the family or the child to see if there are any indications of child abuse, domestic violence, or substance abuse that would suggest returning home might not be in the best interest of a minor child (17 years old or younger). Said CSO Buchholtz, "It's important to find the underlying issues instead of just entering, and then removing, the missing person [from the database]. If we can determine the underlying cause of the runaway episodes, we can refer the family or the child to the proper resources."[7]

In Longmont, responding officers can refer parents of out-of-control kids to "Children, Youth, and Families," a division of the City's Community Services Department, where short-term counseling services are provided to help youth and/or their families assess issues, set goals, improve communication, mediate conflicts, and provide a direction for the future. When there are mental health concerns, professionals from "Mental Health Partners," part of a statewide mental health crisis response system, will accompany an officer and visit with families directly.

For those who do not have at-risk factors or unusual circumstances, CSO Buchholtz also speaks with family members/reporting parties in order to follow up on runaway and missing adult cases. When there are pieces of information that were not collected in the initial report, she follows up to get more information and requests photographs if none were provided. She then creates bulletins for officers to be on the lookout for the missing persons. When her department believes that a missing person has traveled to another jurisdiction, she shares the bulletin with other agencies.[8]

CSO Buchholtz also provides training to her department about missing persons; this includes local and national statistics about missing persons and unidentified remains cases, best practices for response and documentation of missing person cases, and potential dangers to frequent runaways, as well as discussions about local and national resources for families and children who have frequent runaway episodes. She added, "We are just beginning to form a 'missing person task force,' which will consist of officers and staff members who would like to spend additional time addressing this issue and following up with families and children who return."[9]

Matching the Missing and the Unidentified

With the identification of John Doe as Cristobal James Flores, CSO Buchholtz is passionate in emphasizing the importance for family members of the long-term missing to give their DNA to their local police agencies who then enter the profiles into the national databases. Family members should know their DNA is only compared to the DNA profiles of unidentified deceased individuals. She also believes that it is essential to every investigation to have a complete description of the missing person's tattoos, scars, and history of previously broken bones. According to CSO Buchholtz, it is also necessary for families to find and retain their missing person's medical and dental records, including X-rays. When families retain copies of these records, they eliminate the danger of them being purged by a medical or dental office.

"Families also need to be completely honest and tell police who the person was hanging out with and what they were doing," added CSO Buchholz. "That's where the leads come from. Sometimes family members are not eager to share the details of their loved one's lifestyle out of embarrassment or a belief that the investigator may think less of them. It's essential the investigator have all available information surrounding the missing person's activities and state of mind at the time of the disappearance."[10]

Familial DNA is needed to compare with the DNA of unidentified remains, but not all long-term missing persons are deceased. CSO Buchholtz has also had success in finding those who are still alive. In doing so, she has uncovered spelling errors in previous records and stresses the importance of checking with families and/or online databases to make sure the missing persons' names and Social Security numbers have been correctly entered into reports. Then, with a Social Security number, she can look for employment activity, and she also searches by name on social media, through public records, and even Google. In addition, she accesses genealogical information via RootsWeb.com and other databases that do not charge fees.[11] For additional resources, see chapter 9, "Gather Information, Document, and Do the Research."

For those who are missing for a long term, though, CSO Buchholtz periodically checks the NamUs databases for possible matches and new activity. At the time of this writing, the Longmont Police Department has three listed missing person cases, including 33-year-old John William Gates, missing for a century—since 1916. For more on this case, see "John William Gates" in chapter 2, "Categories of Long-Term Missing Adults."

The department's only case with unidentified remains is also an unusual one. A man's remains were found in 2013 in the basement of a Veterans of Foreign Wars Hall, but were thought to have been recovered elsewhere, and long ago, as an archeological specimen.[12]

In CSO Buchholtz's spare time, she volunteers with the NCMEC's Project ALERT®, a team of approximately 170 law enforcement professionals who gather biometric data of missing and unidentified cases from all over the country for entry into the NamUs System.

There are approximately 700 unidentified remains cases across the United States with an estimated skeletal age less than 25 years old. The biometric team members of Project ALERT® provide technical assistance and consultation to law enforcement agencies and coroner and medical examiner offices to help facilitate identification of these unidentified individuals. The NCMEC organization can also provide agencies some assistance if exhumation is determined to be the best avenue for identifying these individuals.[13]

To keep up with advances in her field, CSO Buchholtz recently took a week-long forensic workshop in 3-D facial reconstruction, taught by NCMEC forensic artist Joe Mullins and cosponsored/hosted by the Florida

Institute for Forensic Anthropology and Applied Science at the University of South Florida (USF) in Tampa, Florida. Additional classes are taught in computer imaging (to complete a digitally rendered facial reconstruction), but this class was based on clay sculpture and consisted of twelve students selected from various law enforcement agencies across the United States. The students worked on nine actual-cold-unidentified cases comprising two juveniles and seven adults. The oldest case dated back to 1967. All had been submitted by detectives from local Florida law enforcement agencies.[14]

When creating any kind of facial reconstruction, protecting the integrity of the actual skull is of utmost importance. Traditionally, when using clay, a forensic sculptor would make a plaster cast of a skull and then apply the clay to the cast. Now the method is to make digital scans (CT or laser scans) of the skulls and use the resulting 3-D imagery to print "skull copy" replicas in white plastic. CSO Buchholtz and the others were taught the Manchester Method of Facial Reconstruction, in which they learned about bone structure, the various muscle attachments of the face and skull, and the use of tissue-depth markers as a guide.[15]

"Some of the process is intuitive," stated CSO Buchholtz. "The goal is not to produce an exact likeness of the person, but to produce a face that provides a spark of recognition for someone who knew the person in life."[16] For the story of a successful outcome, see "David and Rosemary: Face of a Friend" in chapter 5, "Civilian Searchers."

Sculpting was not new to CSO Buchholtz, as she had taken several art classes, including sculpture, while pursuing her undergraduate degree, and she later attended a facial reconstruction (sculpture) class at Colorado State University. She stated that even though the use of clay in facial reconstructions is not new, recent advancements in tissue depth estimates have made the process more accurate. Previous scientific studies of facial tissue depths had been conducted on deceased individuals, but more recent studies use live individuals. The more recent studies have also had larger sample sizes drawn from various ancestry groups. The use of 3-D printed skulls (instead of creating a plaster cast from a mold of the actual skull, which can damage the delicate bones of the face) is a brand new technique, one that CSO Buchholtz considers "an awesome demonstration of how this technology can be used."[17]

CSO Buchholtz's assignment in the class was to complete a reconstruction on an estimated 28- to 34-year-old John Doe homicide victim, whose skeletal remains were found in 1988 in Hillsborough County, Florida. The man's remains originally were thought to be Asian, but a more recent anthropological study assessed him as black. All of the students were provided with anthropological reports of their assigned remains, including descriptions of the person's hair (if it was recovered at the scene) and any information about clothing sizes in order to determine the wearer's body size and build. The facial reconstruction CSO Buchholtz sculpted in the NCMEC/USF class was her second, but it was the first one she did for an active case.[18]

The final busts were revealed at a press conference at the end of the week of the class. CSO Buchholtz and the other students were on hand, along with representatives of the law enforcement agencies in charge of the cases, to answer reporters' questions about the reconstruction process and the cases themselves. CSO Buchholtz's reconstruction has since been posted on the NamUs Unidentified Persons database as UP-201.[19]

"I learned a lot in the class," she stated in email correspondence with the author. "I felt a great responsibility to get the reconstruction right and knew if the face I completed was similar to the way he looked in life, there was a possibility his family might see the reconstruction and call the detective. All of the artists in the class hoped that the faces they were sculpting would lead to identifications and provide answers for searching families"[20] For more information on the NCMEC's Forensic Imaging Unit, see "NCMEC Behind the Scenes" in chapter 3, "Children: Helping to Bring Them Home."

In addition to her full-time job, CSO Buchholtz recently organized Colorado's first-annual "Missing in Colorado Day," based on similar successful events, also held annually, in Michigan and Arizona. Family members at these events are encouraged to give their DNA for entry into CODIS and their case information into NamUs and other databases. For more on these events, see "Missing Person Day Events" in chapter 8, "Become Your Long-Term Missing Person's Advocate."

When asked about resources needed for the future, CSO Buchholtz said she would like to see a statewide grant for exhumations. Even though the investigation of missing persons (and unidentified remains) is not the main part of her job, that is where her heart is. And, one case at a time, she is making a difference in her community.

DETECTIVE STUART SOMERSHOE:
A VOICE FOR THE VICTIMS

Detective Stuart Somershoe is one of those fortunate people who has found his niche in life. In email correspondence with the author, the twenty-year veteran of the Phoenix Police Department quips that he is "a sucker for unidentified person cases."[21] Focusing on the nameless and voiceless, however, has become his life work.

After majoring in English at La Salle University, in Philadelphia, the future detective managed a bookstore, but, as he states, he was "dulled by the stultifying routines of retail." Then, his brother, an officer in the Los Angeles Police Department, took him on a couple of ride-alongs, and Somershoe was drawn to the variety, excitement, and challenges of law enforcement. In 1996, he entered the Arizona Law Enforcement Academy, then continued with specialized training in a variety of fields. For eleven years, he patrolled the streets of Phoenix, claiming it to be one of the best schools of learning about human psychology and behavior.[22]

Now a detective in the Phoenix Police Department's Missing and Unidentified Persons Unit, Detective Somershoe firmly believes that all people deserve to have their names when they die, and that one's name is the one thing we are given in life that we take into our death. "The most satisfying part of my job is solving the puzzle—finally getting an answer to a mystery," he said. "And putting bad guys away is also a bonus!"[23]

Missing and Unidentified Persons Unit

Phoenix is a city of nearly 1.5 million people. To serve them, the Phoenix Police Department employs approximately 2,900 officers. Even so, the agency is understaffed. One segment of the Detectives Section is the Family Investigations Bureau, a work group that includes the following investigative units: Sex Crimes, Cold Case Sex Crimes, Sex Offender Notification, Domestic Violence, Internet Crimes Against Children, Child Crimes, and Missing and Unidentified Persons.

The Missing and Unidentified Persons Unit is staffed by eight detectives and one supervisor. Detective Somershoe is one of two detectives (within the eight) who deals solely with cold case missing and unidentified persons. However, he will fill in and cover new missing person cases if one of the other detectives is out of the office, or if a new case requires extra work. (See figure 4.1 for a photograph of Detective Somershoe and some of the other investigators.)

Spread among the other six detectives are all of the city's recently missing persons (both adult and juvenile), a staggering caseload of approximately 7,000 per year. An overwhelming number (roughly 80 per cent) are runaways. A large portion of those cases are repeat offenders—what the Unit calls "chronic runaways" (and what CSO Buchholtz calls "frequent flyers"). One troubled child or teen may generate a couple of dozen reports in a year's time.[24]

A smaller percentage of the new cases are adults that include the mentally ill, the suicidal, the elderly, and drug users. An even smaller percentage of the new reports are cases with "suspicious circumstances," which sometimes turn out to be homicides. Although these are exceedingly rare, the challenge of recent missing person cases is that all of them have the potential of being a crime. "The cases don't come to us with helpful labels so we can know which ones represent actual crimes and not just irresponsible behavior," said Detective Somershoe. "We can spend a lot of time and resources looking for someone who just doesn't want to talk to his or her family."[25]

Because the number of new cases is so high, the detectives have to prioritize them through a constant triage process. For instance, the very young (under 11 years) and the elderly go to the top of the pile. Cases involving victims with health issues or disabilities such as Alzheimer's disease and autism receive special attention, as do people who are suicidal and have the means and ability to hurt themselves or others.[26]

"Then," said Detective Somershoe, "there are those cases that are somewhat indefinable. *These are the cases that 'just don't feel right' and raise red flags for investigators.* This could be the man who has never missed a day of work who suddenly fails to show up for his scheduled shift, or the woman who is in a domestic violence relationship who has disappeared without taking any of her belongings. The circumstances vary, but there is usually a distinct break in the life pattern of the missing person that indicates something has happened."[27]

Based on high-profile cases that families see in the media, Somershoe has found that family members tend to indulge in "worst-case scenario" thinking when someone disappears. "The reality," he said, "is that almost 90 per cent of missing person cases resolve within a few days or weeks, with the person being found alive and well."[28]

Long-Term Missing Persons

There are, however, a troubling minority that end in tragedies that include suicide, a fatal accident, or homicide. An even smaller percentage linger on, unresolved. Those cold cases are the ones that Detective Somershoe and his fellow cold case investigator are trying to solve. Between the two detectives they have, at any given time, approximately 200 open cold cases. Of those, about 130 are long-term missing person cases and approximately seventy are cases of unidentified persons.[29]

Sadly, of these long-term missing person cases, many are homicides in which the suspect has "successfully" erased the victim, disposed the body, and cleaned up the scene. Some of these are domestic violence situations. Others are high-risk victims (such as prostitutes or drug addicts) of serial killers. The scenarios are endless, but the common denominator is a smart suspect who attempted to circumvent a criminal investigation by destroying or hiding the basic element of the crime, that is, the body.

In Phoenix, the Maricopa County Attorney's Office prosecutes cases in its jurisdiction but teams up with the Phoenix Police Department as the agency prepares and submits its cases for prosecution. Specifically, law enforcement's role is twofold—to find the missing body or remains, as well as to gather the forensic evidence in order to bring the killer to trial. Without a body, and usually without a crime scene, investigators not only lack this evidence, but they also lack witnesses. "In investigating these cases," said Detective Somershoe, "we face the extra burden of not only proving someone killed a victim, but that the victim was killed in the first place."[30]

According to Detective Somershoe and under the direction of Sergeant Bryan Chapman, the Unit works hard to pursue "no body" homicides. "Many of our long-term missing person cases are obvious homicides, in which a body was destroyed or successfully hidden," said Detective Somershoe. "These cases were often crippled with the outdated notion of 'no body, no crime.' Sergeant Chapman emphasized that the body is just one piece of evidence. We now have chalked up half a dozen 'no body' homicide prosecutions and have more on the horizon."[31]

Cold case investigations are driven by either a change in technology, or a change in relationships. And, as noted above, missing person cases typically lack evidence, so tapping into a change in relationships becomes essential. That can mean lots of interviews of former boyfriends and girlfriends, ex-spouses, former friends, and family members in order to build a circumstantial case.

Detective Somershoe is quick to point out, however, that his work is vastly different from all the drama and excitement that viewers see on television. He might engage in a dramatic interview, but then he will spend hours and hours behind the scenes to document the interview. On a typical day, he can be found at his desk trying to locate witnesses and leads, looking for new investigative strategies, and reviewing reports.

The reports, particularly old ones, can be a real challenge. Some are not as thorough as currently written reports. Said Detective Somershoe, "I wish

I had a time machine to go back and tell past detectives to do things differently."[32] But, he has found that many former detectives, like today's, had to deal with tremendous caseloads. Sometimes the detectives just did not recognize that the case of the particular missing person they were investigating might actually turn into a homicide.

Jane Doe 92-1169

Detective Somershoe has had many accomplishments in his career. But one that he is most proud of is the identification of Shannon Aumock. She was born in Flagstaff, Arizona, in 1976, to a teenage mother who gave her away at the age of three to Arizona Child Protective Services (now Arizona Child Safety and Family Services). Then a Flagstaff family adopted her and subsequently moved to Phoenix. By the age of 12, Shannon had become a challenge for her adoptive parents who handed her back to the state agency. After that, the troubled young teen was placed in a series of foster homes and group homes from which she ran away forty times![33]

On May 28, 1992, an all-terrain-vehicle driver in north Phoenix came across a young woman's clothed, but mostly skeletal, remains in a trash-dumping site in the desert. The body had no identification, although prescription eyeglasses with pink frames were found nearby. The unknown and unclaimed victim (later identified as Shannon) became "Jane Doe 92-1169." Her autopsy revealed that she had been brutally strangled. Investigators reviewed all of the Phoenix Police Department's open missing person reports (as well as many from other jurisdictions), but no matches could be found. As it turned out, the last time Shannon had run away no one had reported her missing. The 16-year-old fit the textbook example of what is now referred to as a "thrown-away" teen.[34]

While investigators entered the Jane Doe's basic information into the NCIC, the county buried her remains in the Twin Buttes Cemetery. Unlike a traditional cemetery with manicured lawns and perpetual care, this cemetery is for the indigent and is covered with gravel. A few weeds manage to poke through its surface. There are very few headstones and most graves are marked with small, flat metal disks that contain the barest of information. Those for Jane and John Does have only the Medical Examiner's Case number and date of death. Said Somershoe, "It is not a place I would want a loved one to end up."[35]

In 2004, after the use of DNA had become widely acceptable as an investigative tool, forensic scientists profiled the victim's DNA from tissue that had been preserved during her autopsy. That profile then was entered into the CODIS. Also, at that time, forensic odontologist, Dr. John Piakis, charted Jane Doe's dental records and entered them into the NCIC database. He also sent bulletins to a dental association newsletter in hopes that a dentist who had treated the young woman would recognize her unusual dentition, as she still had some of her baby teeth.[36]

Throughout the intervening years, all of the usual procedures were followed in an attempt to identify Jane Doe. Several different composite sketches were created and released to the media, along with photos of her clothing. The television show "America's Most Wanted" profiled the case on its website, and the unidentified young woman was entered into databases that included the Doe Network, as well as NamUs, as soon as it became available. The NCMEC distributed fliers and placed the case on its website. The years passed and detectives retired. Jane Doe was still without her name.

Shannon: Once Lost and Now Found

In 2010, in Detective Somershoe's role as a detective with the Phoenix Police Department, he began a systematic review of all of the department's unidentified person cases. He located approximately 100 reports from as early as the 1970s that involved unidentified victims ranging from infants to the elderly. Their cases included natural deaths, suicides, traffic fatalities, and homicides. The reports were scattered across various work units within the department, and there was no standardization on how they had been investigated.[37]

Detective Somershoe approached Sergeant Chapman, his supervisor in what then was called the Missing Persons Unit, and showed him what he had learned. The men agreed that all of the missing and unidentified cases needed to be placed within one work unit. In 2011, they renamed themselves the Missing and Unidentified Persons Unit and began working on John and Jane Doe cases. "Sergeant Chapman looked through the cases I had brought to him," said Detective Somershoe. "He plucked Jane Doe #92-1169 from the pile and said, 'If we do nothing else in 2011, we will identify this girl.' "[38] And, they did.

When a full review of the case revealed that it had received extensive media coverage, and that all of the traditional means of identifying a body had been attempted, it was time to try a new approach. Recognizing that Jane Doe might have fallen through the cracks, Detective Somershoe realized that, sadly, thrown-away kids often are abused or molested. He then combed through 1,600

Figure 4.1 Phoenix Investigative Team. Detective Stuart Somershoe, Sergeant Bryan Chapman, Detective William Andersen, and DNA Analyst Kelley Merwin are shown, in 2011, leaving Shannon Michelle Aumock's exhumation at the Twin Buttes Cemetery, in Tempe, Arizona, where she had been interred as a Jane Doe. *Source:* Photo courtesy of Detective Stuart Somershoe

closed missing juvenile reports (from the time period and within Phoenix's jurisdiction) of females with a similar physical description as Jane Doe.[39]

Detective Somershoe and two other detectives then conducted background investigations on each reported missing person, looking for proof of life after May 28, 1992, when the body of Jane Doe was discovered. When the detectives found a subsequent police report, an arrest record, or a state identification issued after that date, they crossed that person off their potential list. After months of work, they whittled down the list to 100 cases that required deeper investigation. Detective Somershoe began back at the beginning. Fortunately for him, the names were listed alphabetically, and Shannon Aumock was near the top of his list.[40]

Investigating some more, Detective Somershoe tracked down Shannon's biological mother and obtained her DNA. When it was profiled, the Phoenix Police Department's lab confirmed that the mother's DNA matched Jane Doe #92-1169. With the positive identification of Jane Doe as Shannon Aumock, homicide detectives were able to further investigate her murder.[41]

"This investigation has taught many lessons," stated Detective Somershoe, who admits to getting wrapped up in his work and sending emails to colleagues at 2 a.m. In email correspondence with the author, he stated:

There is an underlying assumption that with all the databases we use to compare unidentified and missing persons that for every John or Jane Doe found there is a corresponding missing person report. Sadly, this is not true, for many of our unidentified are the dispossessed of our society, with no loved one to file a report on them. Further, we all know some jurisdictions fail to take missing person reports or close reports that should have remained open. As investigators, we need to sometimes think outside the box and use techniques beyond media releases and entry into CODIS, NamUs and NCIC. These databases, while essential, are only tools and cannot be expected to solve a case by themselves.[42]

Since Shannon's identification, her remains have been exhumed from the indigent cemetery. She then was reburied, with a real burial ceremony, thanks to charitable contributions by the Christ Church of the Valley and the Sunwest Mortuary, in the Heritage Sunwest Cemetery, in El Mirage, Arizona. Paty Rodriguez (the cemetery's Family Care and Cemetery Specialist) chose the location near, but not in, a children's section of the cemetery called the "Cherub Garden" (See figure 4.2).[43] Added Detective Somershoe, "We all felt strongly that Shannon, who spent most of her life not having a home, at least deserved a home in death."[44]

Sergeant Chapman chose the words for the plaque on Shannon's gravestone—a line from the hymn "Amazing Grace"—which Detective Somershoe agrees is very appropriate. It reads:

SHANNON MICHELLE AUMOCK
I ONCE WAS LOST,
BUT NOW AM FOUND.
MAR 2 1976   MAY 27 1992[45]

For more on the Amazing Grace epitaph, as well as a close-up photograph of the inscription on Shannon's grave, see chapter 12, "Final Words."

TROOPER BRIAN F. GROSS AND THE
WESTMORELAND COUNTY GIRLS

Trooper Brian F. Gross, a recently retired Criminal Investigation Assessment Officer with the Pennsylvania State Police, proactively sought the identities of two Jane Does in his jurisdiction. In 2015, he took the lead in reopening the cases of the unidentified females—a young black teen and a newborn Caucasian baby—in Westmoreland County, east of Pittsburgh. The cases are

Figure 4.2   Cherub Garden, Heritage Sun West Cemetery. Shannon Michelle Aumock's new grave is on the left and in back of a section of children's graves called the Cherub Garden, in Heritage Sunwest Cemetery, El Mirage, Arizona. *Source:* Photo by author

unrelated, but the two were found in 1967 within weeks of each other and were buried in the same grave.[46] Now, one of them has regained her name.

"I've always felt that children are the truest of victims and have always gone out of my way to help them," stated Trooper Gross, in email correspondence with the author, of the Westmoreland County girls. Their remains had been found one and a half years before the trooper was born.[47]

A native of Pittsburgh growing up in Plum Borough, Allegheny County, Trooper Gross graduated with a degree in administration of justice from the University of Pittsburgh. Then, in 1991, he entered the Pennsylvania State Police Academy and began his career in law enforcement the following year, at the age of 22. Stationed in Troop A, Greensburg, he initially worked as a patrol trooper. Then, in October of 1996, he obtained a specialized position in the Records and Identification Section (now called the Forensic Services Unit) processing crime scenes. In 1998, he became a criminal investigator in the Crime Unit.[48]

Back in Time

Initially, Trooper Gross learned about the case of the unidentified teen from his Crime Unit Supervisor, then read newspaper reports of the infant. Next, Gross read through his agency's original case files, the coroner's autopsy reports, and the few newspaper articles he could find. In forty-eight years, there had been no credible leads as to the victims' identities. A newspaper article of September 26, 1967, from the *Greensburg Tribune* stated the following:

Deaths Mystery: Court Orders Burial of Infant, Teenager

Common Pleas Court Judge L. Alexander Sculco Monday signed separate orders permitting the "potter's field" burial of an infant and a teenager whose unidentified bodies were found weeks ago in different areas of Westmoreland County.

Both are believed to have died as a result of foul play, although police and county detectives have been unable thus far to produce any leads on the identification of the bodies or precisely how they met their deaths.

The orders by Judge Sculco, with District Attorney Joseph M. Loughran consenting, refer only to "the burial of an unknown white female infant" and unknown minor Negro female."

Several Calls

Edwin Gordon, chief of the county detective bureau, said his office has received several telephone calls in regard to the two mystery deaths. However, he said, none of the informants have been able to provide any worthwhile information.

The body of the infant female was discovered Aug. 27 lying against a grate inside the Jeannette Sewage plant in Penn Township. Police theorize that the infant's body was thrown into a storm sewer in Jeannette and was carried several miles through a sewer line to the treatment plant.

A medical examiner's report showed that the infant died of suffocation by drowning and, presumably, was alive when thrown into the sewer.

The second body, that of a teenage girl ranging in age from 14 to 16 years, was found September 18 at the Colvar Sanitary Landfill in Salem Township.

Her body was decomposed to the extent that usual identification could not be made. By the same token, the decomposition was such that an autopsy did not show the cause of death.

Near Landfill

A spokesman for the county coroner's office said the girl's body was found a few yards off a road which leads to the landfill. It was partially buried when discovered.

The "potter's field" burials, as approved by the court, means that the bodies will be placed in cemetery plots located on the county's institution district property south of Greensburg.[49]

Additional media coverage indicated that the teen had been found near the Colvan Sanitary Landfill, "on County Road about 1/8 mile off of Route 66, roughly 2 1/2 miles west of Slickville" by a passerby who saw a foot sticking up out of the ground and called authorities. The teen was unclothed, except for a white "footie" on her left foot, and she was clutching a piece of white cloth in her right hand. A green, zippered clothing bag was found with her body.[50]

According to the *local* newspaper articles, there were no reports of missing persons who fit the description of a five-foot-tall female weighing approximately 100 pounds.[51] Meanwhile, a search was on for the mother of the newborn. The infant had, apparently, been tossed into the sewer no more than an hour after birth.[52] The remains of the teen and the infant were buried. And, before long, they were forgotten.

Fast-Forward to the Present

The combined grave of the unknown victims was one of 610 separate graves located on county-owned grounds of the former Westmoreland County Home/Poor Farm. For more than a century, the large imposing brick building on South Grande Boulevard south of Greensburg, Pennsylvania, had sheltered the homeless and indigent. As was the custom in the late 1800s (and long before federal welfare), these public-run institutions also housed the disabled and elderly. Residents were expected to work, as they could, on the premises. The since-demolished county home was built after fire destroyed an even earlier building in December 1878. A hospital annex was added in 1955 to provide for nursing care. In 1975, the older building was torn down, and Westmoreland Manor, a modern nursing care facility, took its place.[53]

According to cemetery records maintained by the Manor, the combined grave originally was marked with one small square marble stone, engraved with the number A-608. But, there is no existing map of the stones, and many of them are now so worn that they are unreadable. In September 2015, when police and county officials made a preliminary search for the stone, there were none with the A-608 inscription. County Coroner Ken Bacha told a reporter, at the time, "We have no idea what we're getting into."[54]

What was known, however, was that the Westmoreland girls needed to be exhumed in order to obtain bones or teeth for a DNA analysis. Lined up to assist the state police were members of the NCMEC which agreed to provide financial assistance, a forensic anthropologist to examine the remains, and a 3-D cranial facial reconstruction.[55] (As it turned out, a NCMEC anthropologist was not needed, after all, as the coroner brought in a forensic team from Mercyhurst College. A NCMEC consultant, however, was present at the exhumation.[56])

In October 2015, before any digging could begin, Trooper Gross contacted his District Attorney's Office to obtain court orders for both the teen and the infant in order to show reasonable cause for their exhumations. Each of the legal documents was titled "Motion for Exhumation and Examination of Unidentified Human Remains" and spelled out the few known facts about each case, most of which had already been stated in the original newspaper reports. For the teen, the order also noted that (at the time) "hair samples and dental records were obtained in an effort to make an identification of the body."[57]

The court's intent was not only to identify the victims, but also to identify their killers. For each of the victims, the court order stated,

> Trooper Gross of the Pennsylvania State Police is presently investigating this case and has consulted with the Westmoreland County Coroner's Office, the Westmoreland County District Attorney's Office, and other agencies including the National Center for Missing & Exploited Children®. It is their belief that exhumation and examination of the remains will assist in obtaining the identification of the victim and will provide information as to the identification of possible suspects.[58]

Also quoted in the court orders were parts of the Pennsylvania Coroner's Act which further specified,

> If this petition is granted, upmost respect for the deceased would be maintained at all times. If any surviving next of kin are located, inquiries will be made to determine if the family wishes to take control of the remains and reinter them in another location. If so, the remains will be provided to the family in the manner prescribed by law."[59]

As District Attorney John Peck stated when he filed the papers, "If they have an identity, at least they'll have a starting point."[60]

In addition to DNA technology and bringing in the NCMEC's support, Trooper Gross realized the potential of the NamUs System. As a result, the Westmoreland County Coroner's Office entered the teen into NamUs as UP-13512.[61] For more on NamUs, see chapter 7, "NamUs: An Investigative Tool." The trooper also brought in the press.

Exhumation

The exhumation was scheduled for three days later, on October 30, 2015. The long lines of marble stones (see figure 4.3), some in disarray, filled a grassy area between woods and a tree-lined lane. The last burial in the cemetery

Figure 4.3 Westmoreland County Gravestones. Small square marble stones mark the county-owned cemetery, in Westmoreland County, Pennsylvania, where two Jane Does were buried for nearly forty-eight years. Their remains were exhumed in 2015. *Source:* Photo courtesy of the *Greensburg Tribune-Review*, Sean Stipp, photographer

had taken place in 1972. Prior to 2015, no remains had ever been removed. The late fall weather was clear and cool as Trooper Gross, along with other investigators, the coroner, and the media huddled around a backhoe. Also with the small group was Dr. Dennis Dirkmaat, chair of the Department of Applied Forensic Sciences at Mercyhurst College, in Erie, Pennsylvania, and a handful of his students.[62]

Finding the grave, however, proved to be a challenge. The members of the forensic team began their search at the end of the row of the old stones, thinking that the cemetery had run out of stones and later burials had been unmarked, but that area of the cemetery turned up empty. Then they shifted to another location where there was only one unmarked stone. After several hours, they finally unearthed a pine box that contained the remains they were seeking.[63] "We knew how many graves were recorded in the records, so we knew how many were missing or unmarked," stated Trooper Gross. "Once we found a grave we continued to dig until there were no more graves. Then we counted backward to find the grave we were looking for. The remains of the unidentified female matched the autopsy records, so we knew we had found the correct remains."[64]

In continued email correspondence with the author, Trooper Gross added, "The wood from the box was in good shape but the lid had split down the middle which allowed water to infiltrate the wooden box. The unidentified female was in a body bag, but the infant was not. We were able to remove the body bag, and then the remaining contents were removed archeologically."[65] A television reporter (with cameraman) was on the scene, adding that the investigators had found a dozen or so small bones of the infant as they sifted through the bones belonging to the teen.[66] Anxiously following the news was Pittsburgh resident Mary Thompson, who had learned of the exhumation from a television report on the day the court order had been granted. Thompson believed that the teen was her sister Teala, who was thirteen when she went missing from the Homewood neighborhood of Pittsburgh in September 1967.[67]

Identification

After the exhumation, the skull of the teen was taken to the Children's Hospital of Pittsburgh for a CT scan, which used X-rays to create pictures of cross-sections of the skull. The skull was then turned over to Dr. Dirkmaat, while the images were forwarded to the NCMEC in Alexandria, Virginia. There, forensic artist Paloma Galzi used 3-D sculpting software and then Adobe Photoshop to create a digitally rendered facial reconstruction, as shown in figure 4.4. Meanwhile, DNA from the bones was analyzed at the University of North Texas Center for Human Identification to compare with databases of missing children and their families.[68]

Five and a half weeks after the exhumation, police released the reconstruction showing the facial features of the unidentified teen. Before making the image public, Trooper Gross showed it to Mary Thompson who agreed that there was a family resemblance. Mary was four years old when her sister Teala Patricia Thompson went to school one day and never came home. The teen found in the landfill had been too decomposed to recognize, but Mary added that her mother knew about the body, at the time, and always believed it was Teala's.[69]

Back then, without fingerprints on file and in the pre-DNA days, there was no way to make an identification. And, as so often happens in cold cases, there was a breakdown in communication. According to the family, Teala's parents had reported her missing to the Pittsburgh Police Department. (And, recent research uncovered an October 3, 1967 article on the girl's disappearance, published in a newspaper in Pittsburgh, less than an hour's drive away from where she was found.[70]) At the time of the exhumation, however, the police no longer had record of the report. At the recent urging of the NCMEC, the Pittsburgh Police filed a new missing person report for Teala and began

Figure 4.4 "Jane Doe 1967." Forensic artist Paloma Galzi of the National Center for Missing & Exploited Children® (NCMEC) created this digitally rendered facial reconstruction of "Jane Doe 1967." The process is a mixture of science and art. *Source:* Photo courtesy of the National Center for Missing & Exploited Children®

the process of entering her into several national databases, including the NCMEC, the National Crime Information Center (NCIC), and the National Missing and Unidentified Persons Data System (NamUs).[71]

In December 2015, Mary told a television reporter that she only had one wish if the DNA results proved that the teen was Teala. "I want to bring my sister home to her family, her loved ones," she said, through tears. "She's been missing all this time, lying there by herself. I want to put Teala with her mother, brothers, and sisters. I want her to have a proper burial, and make her safe."[72]

"This has haunted all of us," Mary said. "There has been a hole in our hearts."[73]

In August 2016, completed DNA tests confirmed that "Jane Doe 1967" *was* Teala Patricia Thompson. When interviewed by a newspaper reporter, Mary said, "We're grateful, but we're still hurting. We're happy, but we're hurting."[74]

The search for the killer continues.

Chapter 5

Civilian Searchers

Finding long-term missing persons is never easy, but it is safe to say that when the family is involved—as in the remarkable story of "Celeste's Sister Sara: Found Alive in Mexico" in chapter 6—the odds are in their favor. As is further explained in chapter 8, "Become Your Long-Term Missing Person's Advocate," the most important action that family members can take, after filing a missing person report, is to give their DNA to police, so the police can enter the familial DNA profile into national databases. Family members can, and should, do this *even though* they still hold out hope that their loved one is alive. It is merely a matter of covering all bases.

Friends are important, too, as shown in the following story. In an unusual twist, New York State resident David Egerton did not initially know that his friend Rosemary Ulrich was missing. But, because of his quest, along with the actions of her siblings, a twenty-year mystery has been solved.

DAVID AND ROSEMARY: FACE OF A FRIEND

In the late 1970s, Rosemary "Ro" Ulrich was a student at Parson's School of Design, in New York City, where she shared an interest in sculpture with classmate and friend, David Egerton. Evidence suggests that, in 1995, Rosemary may have jumped to her death from the George Washington Bridge, adding another Jane Doe to the City's large backlog of unsolved cases. At the time, all that was known about the drowning victim was that she had been found in the Hudson River and was Caucasian, in her thirties, and measured five feet and five inches tall.[1] Meanwhile—for twenty years—her family and friends waited and wondered, as the woman's body remained unidentified.

A few years later, David was flipping through television channels while watching his infant son, and a show on the use of forensic art as a tool to identify the unknown dead caught his eye. "The sculptor demonstrated on a person's skull, shaping and adding clay until a face appeared," stated David in email correspondence with the author. "Instantly I was shocked. The face in front of me was my friend Rosemary."[2] For David, the realization simmered on the back burner for several years, before leading him on a quest to dignify his friend's life by restoring her name.

College Days

At Parson's, David and Rosemary had many of the same classes together, both graduating, in 1980, with a bachelor of fine arts degree. (See figure 5.1 for their 1977–1978 Parson's class photograph.) They were also part of a

Figure 5.1   David Egerton and Rosemary Ulrich. David Egerton is the man in the back, in this Parson's School of Design group photograph from 1977. In front of him is Rosemary Ulrich, who later went missing. *Source:* Photo courtesy of David Egerton

social/philosophical group that met, at first, in vacant classrooms at Parson's. "Our drawing teacher, Roger, had a real impact on us," David explained. "He inspired about ten of us, including 'Ro,' and got us interested in philosophy. We started to meet on a weekly basis to read and discuss the works of [Greek philosopher] Plato. He kept the group going from our sophomore year until graduation and after."[3]

Before long, the Plato reading group began gathering at Roger's house on the west side of the Hudson River, in Weehawken, New Jersey. The meetings evolved into Sunday potlucks that David described as "fun."[4] By this time, he and Lynn, his wife-to-be, had moved across the street from Roger. Eventually, Rosemary and six of the others also moved to Weehawken, creating a mini-artist community. The members formed a nonprofit artists' group and put on art shows. Eventually, they stopped discussing Plato, but that was only after they had read all of his major works and some of his minor works, as well.

David and Rosemary's lives remained intertwined. As part of a core group of eight people, they took day trips together to visit museums and art galleries in New York City. In 1981, David married his fiancée, with both Rosemary and Roger in attendance at their wedding. Along with Rosemary and two other women, David's wife worked in the City at Paul's Patisserie Shop, a concession in the Marriot's Essex House on 59th Street. David worked at the hotel's front desk, convenient for him as he could stop in at the shop anytime he liked for free pastries. As he likes to say, "It was a sweet deal."[5]

Beginning in 1986, however, David's contact with Rosemary became limited. David and Lynn divorced, and, a few years later, David moved up the Hudson River to Dobbs Ferry, New York. It was while living there, in 1998, that he tuned in to the television program on forensic art. The body of the woman whose face strongly resembled Rosemary had been found on March 14, 1995. After seeing the show, David tried to reach Roger, but he, too, had moved away. "Since I didn't really know if 'Ro' was missing or not, I soon put it out of my mind," stated David. "Life got in the way."[6]

In 2005, David's second wife, Judy, threw him a surprise fiftieth-birthday party. And, she was able to contact three people from the "Weehawken group," one of them being Roger. "The subject of 'Ro' came up, and I told the story of watching the forensic program," said David. "Everyone was shocked, except for Roger. He glumly stated that he had seen that same program also and thought the same thing that I did." David and Roger then joined Nina and Charlotte (the others from their group) in raising their glasses of wine to their college friend. Stated David, "We drank a toast to 'Ro'—to wherever she may be. Someone said, 'She would have liked that.' It was a bitter-sweet moment."[7]

Roger also related how, when Rosemary was still living a few blocks away from him, she would come and visit him in his studio. He had tried to talk to her, and help her put things in perspective, eventually telling her that he believed she needed professional help." If Rosemary was depressed, or if a mental illness was creeping up on her, David, at least, never suspected it. "When I knew her," he stated, "she was mostly a quiet person and didn't really engage people she didn't know well in conversation. When she spoke you knew she had something to say."[8]

Pursuing the Search

Now retired and in his early sixties, David enjoyed a successful career in the field of information technology. He also dug into his own family history and researched the histories of his local community's veterans. In 2015, for personal enrichment, he enrolled in an online college-level genealogy class through Boston University. One of his assignments was to write a paper on forensic genealogy, so he pursued the question that had lingered so long in his mind—What had happened to Rosemary Ulrich?

David began by compiling everything he knew about Rosemary, including her birthdate, last-known addresses, and names of her friends. He then hypothesized on her death, reflecting on Roger's comments on her mental health and agreeing with the narrator of the television program that the cause of her death likely was suicide. (The narrator had discussed the evidence that supported the theory that she had jumped from the George Washington Bridge. Specifically, these included injuries on her body, combined with known currents in the river and the exact location where her body had been recovered.)[9]

On the Internet, David googled "Rosemary Ulrich missing" and found a query, on a genealogical message board, from 2001. It was unsigned, but it was from a woman who identified herself as Rosemary's sister, adding that Rosemary was missing and that she had attended Parson's School of Design. There was no doubt that David and the query writer were searching for the same person. However, by the time David read the posting many years later, the sister's two listed email addresses were defunct. The information she provided, however, did confirm that Rosemary had been missing, that she had family, and that, at least, one family member had been looking for her. Online "people searches" brought up names that could have been the sister and other siblings. David wrote to similarly named people on Facebook who he believed could have been related, but got no positive responses.[10]

Jumping into the search, David accessed missing person databases, looking for all white females missing in New York City prior to the sister's query. His search included the Doe Network and NamUs, but he did not find any listings for Rosemary as a missing person. Nor could he find any mention of her as a missing person on any law enforcement websites. Then he began to think that maybe she was not really missing after all. Maybe she was alive, but he was unable to find a current address for her.

On both the Doe Network and NamUs databases for Unidentified Persons, however, David found a Jane Doe that caught his attention. The unidentified female's body had been recovered from the Hudson River, in New York, on March 14, 1995—the same date as the discovery of the unknown woman (also found in the Hudson River, in New York). David's gut feeling that the sculpture that came to life for him *was* the face of his friend. And, the databases showed that, even in 2015, the Jane Doe was still unidentified. David's next mission was to find her family. He wondered if they were searching for her as well.[11]

David also contacted the caseworker from the New York City Medical Examiner's Office, as listed on the NamUs Unidentified Persons website, and described why he believed the missing person was Rosemary. The caseworker stated that Rosemary's name had already been supplied to him more than a year earlier, adding that detectives in a Long Island, New York, county had been notified. David recognized the county as Rosemary's childhood home. But, months after David's telephone call, the NamUs and Doe Network databases continued to show that the body found in the Hudson River was still unidentified. David began to wonder if Rosemary's case had slipped between the cracks.[12]

Finally, the Family

New York City has thousands of cases per year, and progress can often be agonizingly slow. But, sometimes a nudge is needed to give a case higher priority. There's no doubt in the author's mind that David's call to the caseworker moved forward Rosemary's identification.

Meanwhile, David had brainstormed with some colleagues who suggested additional online resources. A public records search led to the names of two siblings—including middle initials—and one lived near Rosemary's childhood home. The brother's middle initial enabled the researchers to zero in on his specific name and address. A little online detective work quickly matched up all the siblings (including the sister) on Facebook.[13]

Within hours, David called and introduced himself to Rosemary's brother. David explained what he knew about Rosemary's disappearance and the facial sculpture that had unfolded, years ago, in front of his eyes. The brother said he was glad to hear from him and explained that, in November 2014, he had joined a program run by the New York City Office of Chief Medical Examiner and had submitted his DNA sample to help with the search for his sister.[14] For more on this medical examiner's office, see "Missing Person Day Events" in chapter 8, "Become Your Long-Term Missing Person's Advocate."

"Her brother also told me that on August 19, 2015, he had received a phone call from the New York City Medical Examiner's Office stating that it had a match with his DNA and the unidentified female found in the Hudson River," added David. "Once I finally knew for certain that Rosemary had died in 1995, I was struck with a sudden sadness. However, sometime after, knowing that I had contributed to putting the final pieces of the puzzle together, I felt gratified. Speaking to her brother was a poignant experience, but I was also happy to know that it would give his family resolution."[15]

David's telephone conversation with Rosemary's brother occurred a few weeks after David's call to the caseworker, who has since archived the case. Thanks to an old friend of a troubled former classmate, one of New York City's unknown now has her name. She, her family, and her friends, can now be at peace.

VICTIM ADVOCATES AND DEDICATED INDIVIDUALS

In addition to the involvement of family and friends, the odds jump dramatically for the unknown dead when interested victim advocates and civilian search teams also get on the trail of missing persons and unidentified remains. As shown in chapter 11, "Retrospect: Inside a (Previously) Cold Case," Deb Anderson is one of a few really dedicated individuals who, for no pay, turned the identification of one specific unidentified person into a priority while, at the same time, juggling her family, home, and career.

Deb and a handful of others have found that when they stayed in the search for the long haul, they eventually earned the trust and respect of law enforcement. Retired investigators, such as sheriff Blythe Bloemendaal in "Retired Sheriff is 'Our Girl's' Best Advocate," in chapter 1, "Why Finding the Missing is Important," also make significant contributions, as they bring in their expertise and liaison with their hometown agencies that often lack the time and money to tackle the cases already on their desks. Consider, too, the valuable contributions made by victim advocates and dedicated individuals who volunteer on behalf of many of the missing, the unidentified, and the families.

Janet Franson: Doing God's Work

Ask Janet Franson what kind of work she does, and she is eager to explain that instead of a job she has a "mission." In email correspondence with the author, she also said she is retired, but her desk is piled with cases of the missing and unidentified. "I work to represent the voices that cannot speak—the lost, missing and unidentified," she said. "I work for God."[16]

Janet, originally from Wyoming, is in her early sixties. After twenty-one years of service as an honorably retired homicide investigator for the Lakeland (Florida) Police Department, she volunteered with the Doe Network, a privately funded database of the missing and unidentified. Then she volunteered for five and a half years for the Project ALERT® program of the National Center for Missing & Exploited Children® (NCMEC) where she was part of a team of approximately 170 retired local, state, and federal law enforcement professionals who donate their time and experience to the law enforcement community. For three and a half years after that, she worked as a regional system administrator for NamUs.

Janet also managed to fit in pro bono case reviews for her friends in law enforcement who realize that sometimes all that is needed is a fresh pair of eyes. Most recently, she has tapped a niche that is really demanding her attention. She and two other women—sisters Ashley Kroner and Megan McWilliams—started the Lost and Missing in Indian Country Facebook page. Within a few months, their "likes" soared to more than 23,000.[17]

Ashley and Megan are both stay-at-home moms with great searching and computer skills. As Megan states on the organization's website, "During my time at home I needed some time for myself to keep myself busy on a project and I knew looking at missing and unidentified cases piqued my interest. I would look at cases in NamUs and compare missing with unidentified persons."[18] Prior to the launching of the Indian Country Facebook page, Megan started, and continues to operate, a Facebook page titled "Wyoming LostNMissing."[19]

The mission and goal of Lost and Missing in Indian Country (both its website and Facebook page) is "to give a place to get/give/ask for information referencing missing persons and unidentified remains in Indian Country" and "to get the word out to the public—to put FACES to these numbers." As stated on the website, "These missing are PEOPLE and they belong to

Figure 5.2   Lost and Missing in Indian Country. The Lost and Missing in Indian Country logo contains an eagle and its feathers, symbols recognized by all Native American tribes. The four sections (each a different color) represent the four directions and four seasons, while the circle is the circle of life. *Source:* Photo courtesy of Janet Franson

somebody. We strive to assist law enforcement, medical examiners, coroners, and families of these missing. We want to bring these lost people HOME."[20]

According to Janet, there is a void of Native American cases that are not getting entered into the system, or not being followed up on if they do get put in the system. The main reason is because the jurisdictional boundaries are blurred in Native American cases due to the unique involvement of several different law enforcement agencies. They include individual tribal police and the Bureau of Indian Affairs (BIA), as well as the Federal Bureau of Investigation (FBI). Stated Janet, "Just trying to figure out who has jurisdiction and who (if anyone) will actively work the case is a nightmare."[21]

The many cases that Janet, Ashley, and Megan handle each day are not numbers. Instead, they represent real people, and Janet and her coworkers deeply care about each and every one. Many of the unidentified cases are the result of homicide. As a retired homicide investigator, Janet knows, first-hand, that her initial job is to identify the victims so that law enforcement can continue its investigations. She added, "Many people talk about the wrongs in the world. I try to right some of those wrongs. I strive to find the lost and give back the names of the unidentified."[22]

One young woman who was given back her name after the launch of the Lost and Missing in Indian Country Facebook page is Regina Marie Curtis, a member of both the Cheyenne and Arapaho tribes. In May 2000, the petite 16-year-old left her home in Oklahoma City to make a telephone call and never returned. In January 2016, Regina's family contacted Janet to update the young woman's photograph, along with the message to Regina, "Words alone cannot even begin to express just how much you are loved and missed!"[23]

Within days, 203 other Facebook readers shared the family's post, along with prayers for Regina's return. On February 4, 2016, her brother, Virgil Curtis, contacted Janet saying that he had received a call from the Oklahoma City Police Department and the state medical examiner confirming that a DNA match to remains they had found in June 2000, in a wooded area in southeast Oklahoma City, were those of Regina Marie Curtis. Her remains had been located one month after her family reported her missing, but the match was not made for nearly 16 years![24]

Virgil then posted on the Lost and Missing in Indian Country Facebook page, "I believe all the prayers from this website brought our sister home. Thank you and Ma'heo, bless you all and your families."[25] [Ma'heo is the Cheyenne name for "Great Spirit, Great One or God."[26]] In a personal email to Janet, which she shared with the author, Virgil wrote, in part, "All the prayers that were spread throughout the land through your website were heard and helped bring her home."[27]

It is fortunate that Janet is not locked into the structure of a nine-to-five job, as she continues to come up with innovative ideas to find missing persons and give names to unidentified remains. In addition to the Lost and Missing in Indian Country Facebook page, she also started the Unidentified Persons Jewelry Facebook page, where she posts photos of rings, watches, necklaces, and other items found on the remains of unidentified persons.[28] Seeing an image of a distinctive ring associated with unidentified remains, for instance, may jog the memory of a loved one.

Janet has no need to travel, nor does she even have to commute to work. Instead, she lives with her husband and three heeler dogs in rural Texas and works out of her home, where her only tools are a computer and a telephone. That is, unless, she temporarily loses her Internet connection and has to take her laptop to the closest coffee shop in a nearby town. In her spare time, she likes to visit historical sites, horseback ride, and hike.

Working from home has other challenges, as well. She has no typical workday, as each day is different from the previous one. Her phone has rung at 4:30 a.m., and chasing leads or following up on new cases often extends into evenings and weekends. She starts her day by trying to update any changes in her cases, then she answers her email and returns phone calls. She also corresponds with multiple agencies and family members, often in different time zones.

Janet said her greatest support is her husband John. Married nearly twenty years, there were times as a homicide investigator that she would be gone for days at a time. "While I took care of other people," she said, "he took care of me when I came home."[29]

Jody Ewing: All Iowa All the Time

To say that Jody Ewing has made the solving of cold cases in Iowa a priority in her life is an understatement. Based in west-central Iowa, the mid-fifties researcher, writer, author, wife, mother, and grandmother was asked by a newspaper editor, in early 2004, to write a series of articles on cold cases in the vicinity of Sioux City, Iowa. In email correspondence with the author, she stated that other writing assignments came and went, but the cold cases—and a desire to see them solved—stuck with her.[30]

So, in 2005, she created a website where she could post summaries for a wider audience. In 2010, after continued research, she incorporated her work on Iowa Cold Cases by founding Iowa Cold Cases, Inc., a nonprofit organization. Jody was, and is, dedicated to getting the word out about these Iowa cases, stating on her website that "hope is never laid to rest."[31]

Her nonprofit has evolved into Iowa's first and foremost repository of case summaries of the state's unsolved homicides, along with persons missing under suspicious, or mysterious, circumstances. She does most of the research and writing herself, personally contacting victims' families. In the process, she has developed many close relationships with family members, and she spends a great deal of time working with them in efforts to resolve the cases of their loved ones.[32]

In recent years, Jody's cold case summaries have grown to include more than 500, from all parts of the state. One of the cases is that of her stepfather, Earl Thelander, who died in 2007 from burns sustained in a house explosion after copper thieves cut and stole propane gas lines at a rural home he was preparing for a renter. At the time, the family expected a speedy arrest. But, as in so many other cases, Thelander's case has gone cold. Jody knows firsthand how important it is to keep all of the cases in the public eye.[33]

As stated on her website, the mission of Iowa Cold Cases, Inc. is "to educate the public about these open cases, share and exchange resources in efforts to publicize these unsolved crimes, and ensure every victim's story is told and kept alive until those responsible are held accountable." Jody has no illusions about solving the cases herself. Instead she (with a team of dedicated volunteers) states, "We work with law enforcement officials at the county, state, and federal level, often serving as a liaison between investigators and those providing information via our website. Our goal is to provide case summaries for each victim while encouraging those with information to contact appropriate law enforcement officials with any known details about the crime."[34]

Acting as a liaison between families and law enforcement, however, is important, and Jody listens carefully to what family members have to say. For instance, there are times when family members disagree with law enforcement as to cause of death. Families may believe their loved one was murdered, but the death was ruled an accident. Jody can relay that information to the proper authorities. Some family members confide in her that no one else will listen to them. In praise of Jody's role, one family member told a reporter, "Jody gives people a voice who know something about the crime—a way to make contact that is not so public. She is not only helping families deal with it, but hopefully one day bring justice. She's at least giving us hope."[35]

With cases well-organized and cross-referenced by name, year, decade, county, and city, Jody has made her website easy to navigate and the case summaries easy to find. Consider, for instance, Wilma June Nissen in Lyon County, as related in "Retired Sheriff is 'Our Girl's' Best Advocate," in chapter 1, "Why Finding the Missing is Important." Although sheriff Blythe Bloemendaal eventually identified the former Jane Doe murder victim, her killer has not (at the time of this writing) been convicted of the crime. Along with a summary on Nissen's case, Jody provides photos, state and county maps, and contact information to the Lyon County Sheriff's Office. Nissen's summary also includes transcribed newspaper articles, a television clip, and extensive links to additional media coverage that spans the years 2006 through 2014.[36]

Quick to acknowledge the work of others, Jody—a member of The American Investigative Society of Cold Cases—states that case summaries for decade-old cases would not exist if not for the countless journalists who doggedly pursued investigators for details, tracked down public records by shoe-leather reporting, and published their findings in newspapers long preceding today's Internet search engines.[37]

As discussed in chapter 2, "Categories of Long-Term Missing Adults," not all long-term missing persons cases are homicides, but there is some overlap when people are missing under suspicious circumstances. Jody has developed an extensive database of unsolved homicide cases in Iowa, dating from the nineteenth century, through every decade of the twentieth century, to those following the year 2000. Some of the cold cases also are included in a second database specifically for missing persons.[38]

As of this writing, the missing persons database includes 136 names and case summaries. They range from Lillian Demaris, a thirty-one-year-old woman missing since 1952 from Mason City to others who disappeared within the past year. Demaris left behind three young daughters who continue to search for her.[39] A case that continues to receive a lot of publicity is that of Jodi Sue Huisentruit, also reported missing from Mason City. In 1995, the petite and pretty twenty-seven-year-old anchorwoman for a local television station was abducted from the parking lot of her apartment building on her way to report the morning news. She has since been declared dead. But her remains, like others in the database who likely are deceased, have never been found.[40]

Another section of the Iowa Cold Case website contains information and links to cases that *have* been solved since the database went online in 2005. One is that of Mark Edgar Koster, a fifty-eight-year-old man from Sac City, Iowa, who went missing in 2009 and whose remains were found in 2012. Jody summarized Koster's case as follows:

> Mark Koster disappeared from Sac City, Iowa, sometime during the summer of 2009, and was reported missing to the Sac City Police Department July 4, 2009. He'd been "last seen with a friend from Florida," and a search warrant served on Koster's house revealed all his clothes and possessions still in the home. His vehicle remained parked in the garage.[41]
>
> On November 5, 2012, a new homeowner renovating Koster's former Sac City home discovered human skeletal remains concealed in the basement and immediately notified Sac City police. Officials later identified the remains as Koster's. On March 25, 2014, officials with the Sac City Police Department and Iowa Division of Criminal Investigation arrested 54-year-old John David Green in Orange Park, Florida, and charged him with first-degree murder in Koster's death. On April 3, 2015, a jury from Boone County, Iowa, found Green guilty of second-degree murder in Koster's death.[42]

Also on the Iowa Cold Cases website, Jody includes a link to the Iowa Department of Public Safety's Missing Person Information Clearinghouse, established in 1985. According to its website, the clearinghouse is "a program for compiling, coordinating and disseminating information in relation to missing persons and unidentified body/persons." Housed within Iowa's DCI, the clearinghouse "assists in helping to locate missing persons through public awareness and cooperation and in educating law enforcement officers and the general public about missing person issues."[43] The state-run list of missing persons is more inclusive than Jody's database, as the state's list is released weekly and includes persons recently missing and under all circumstances. The majority of missing persons on the state-released list are juveniles, that is, under the age of 18. Many of the juveniles are runaways, and many of them return on their own.

It is obvious that in Iowa, missing persons are well-documented. As noted above, all are briefly listed on the state's clearinghouse website, and those missing under suspicious circumstances are included in Jody's Iowa Cold Cases missing persons database. Iowa had a Cold Case Unit (part of the Iowa DCI) that began in 2009 with a $500,000 grant from the US Department of Justice, but the grant ran out in 2011. The Unit had identified 150 cases in a public database that it hoped to revisit and clear using DNA, and it solved two cases during its three-year operation.[44] The DCI, however, continues to assign agents to investigate cold cases as new leads develop or as technological advances allow for additional forensic testing of original evidence.

Without any outside funding other than a few private donations, Jody and her volunteers work long hours for no pay and fill a much-needed gap to help the families they interact with every day. In 2015, the Iowa Newspaper Association (INA) asked Jody if Iowa Cold Cases would consider a partnership with them to profile a different unsolved murder each week that would run statewide in participating newspapers. "Gone Cold: Exploring Iowa's Unsolved Murders" launched in July 2015 and has brought new awareness to the state's unsolved crimes.

At the top of her website's homepage, Jody has links to rotating cases, as well as a link to the *Des Moines Register's* "Gone Cold" article series and an interactive state map. In addition, she is constantly updating her anniversary lists, with links to the summaries of those with known death dates.[45] For readers who are more interested in social media, Jody also administers an Iowa Cold Cases Facebook page with more than 13,000 "likes."[46]

In September 2015, the INA named Jody a "Friend of Iowa Newspapers," an honor the INA management team confers to those who have made significant contributions to the newspaper industry in Iowa. In a newspaper interview, Jody stated that the cases have become important to her because she can relate to what the families are going through. It is the family members, she said, that keep her going.[47]

Jody's commitment to families of the victims is full-time, and others would do well to emulate her empathy and passion. If you want to follow in her footsteps in your state, please do. If you have a long-term missing person in Iowa, rest assured that she is looking out for you.

CIVILIAN SEARCH TEAMS

The civilians in the above stories primarily do their searching and researching at their desks, while others work, in a variety of ways, outdoors. As shown in "Gina and Her Dad—Returned Identities," in chapter 1, "Why Finding the Missing Is Important," Ralston & Associates fulfilled the request of a family member in recovering the remains of Gina's father, a drowning victim. The environmental consulting firm founded and owned by Gene and Sandy Ralston is based in Boise, Idaho, and specializes in water-related services that include underwater search and recovery missions. Ralston & Associates, as well as other volunteer civilian search teams, also work at the request of law enforcement.[48]

Members of Texas EquuSearch, for instance, search on horseback for the lost and missing. The nonprofit organization initially formed in the North Galveston County area of Texas and is dedicated to the memory of Laura Miller, the daughter of its founding director, Tim Miller. Now, with more than 600 members, the organization has been involved in more than 1,350 searches in approximately forty-two states in the United States, as well as other countries including Aruba, Sri Lanka, Mexico, Jamaica, Dominican Republic, and Nicaragua. More than 300 missing people have been safely returned home to their families and, at the time of this writing, the team has returned the remains of 159 missing persons.[49]

Colorado Forensic Canines: Human Remains Detection

Other volunteer search teams use dogs. In May 2015, two members of the Colorado Forensic Canines human remains detection team were called to Dickinson, North Dakota, to search for Eric Haider, a man who had been reported missing three years earlier from a construction site. The local police had been unable to find him, so the man's parents hired private investigators. A team from Discovery Investigations made the decision to call in the dogs. With their handlers, Bonnie Guzman and Kim Sadar, the dogs narrowed down the search area and had two or three unconfirmed hits in the area that Eric was believed to be in. Three weeks later, the investigators found the man's remains, in the same location, buried six feet underground.[50]

Colorado Forensic Canines is based in Colorado, but the organization goes wherever its services are needed. The nonprofit corporation founded in 2011 is run by civilians and does not charge fees, although it accepts tax-deductible donations. Its members specialize in human remains detection, as well as urban, suburban, and wilderness trailing. The trailing teams track down recently missing persons, while human remains detection teams are designed to search for the skeletal remains of those missing for a longer time.[51]

Search dogs have been locating missing persons, both dead and alive, for centuries. Among the best-known historic examples are Saint Bernards, large working dogs that were bred for centuries in order to retrieve lost travelers high in the Swiss Alps. In recent years, Saint Bernards, as a breed, have been replaced by various other breeds that continue to play vital roles in search and rescue teams. Search dogs and their handlers can be found in locations as diverse as wilderness trails to the middle of high-profile disasters, including the World Trade Center in New York City after the September 11, 2001, terrorist attacks. Many police agencies have K-9 (Canine) units, with specially trained "police" dogs (usually German Shepherds, Dutch Shepherds, and Belgian Malinois) used to uncover drugs, explosives, and crime-scene evidence, in addition to tracking criminals and missing persons.

But not every law enforcement agency has its own K-9 unit. And, even when they do, not all are trained to seek out human remains if the person has been missing for any length of time. Civilian handlers and their dogs often work with law enforcement agencies, at their request. They also can be called in by private individuals, as were the Colorado Forensic Canines in the case of Eric Haider. The request was similar to that of Gina Hoogendoorn when she contacted Gene Ralston, of Ralston & Associates, to recover the remains of her father.

A typical search for human remains was one that was done in 2012 at the request of the Jackson County (Colorado) Sheriff's Office. The small agency is located in the large and sparsely populated open mountain valley of North Park, in north central Colorado. Walden, with a population of 590, is the county seat and is the county's only incorporated municipality. More than a decade ago, one of the town's residents was thought to have disappeared (and presumably died) along a drainage south of town. His body was not found at the time, and the intervening years had not brought forth any leads. The area had become overgrown with willow bushes. If any trace of the man were to be found, it would be skeletal remains.[52]

On a late June afternoon, smoke still hung in the air from recent and massive Colorado forest fires as Bonnie Guzman, Kim Sadar, and Morgan Wolf, each in their own vehicles and with their own dogs, made the several-hours drive from their respective homes in the metro-Denver area. Sometimes, when out in the field, they bring camping gear, but this time the women and the dogs stayed in a modest motel on Main Street. They were up before dawn (with the author along to observe and photograph), then were briefed at the scene by Undersheriff Stephen Holland.[53] (See figure 5.3.)

The early start gave the dogs the advantage of optimal temperature conditions in order to make best use of their sense of smell. On this particular summer day, it meant that the ground temperature was warmer than the air temperature and also allowed the search to be completed before the heat of the day. Other criteria helpful in a search include recent moisture to help saturate the ground, as well as some cloud cover.[54]

Any dog in good physical health, with above average intelligence and good listening skills can make a good search dog. The team that searched in Walden

Figure 5.3 Colorado Forensic Canines. During a 2012 search for the remains of a missing man, former Colorado Forensic Canines member and dog handler Morgan Wolf (with her German Shepherd, Lena) is briefed by Undersheriff Stephen Holland prior to entering the search area. *Source:* Photo by author

consisted of Lena (a German Shepherd), Porter (a Doberman Pinscher), and Stoner (a Golden Retriever). Each of the handlers, with her dog, started in different parts of the search area. The dogs knew they were there to work (i.e., not play with each other), and they knew what was expected of them.[55]

Bonnie, acting as spokesperson for the group, added in email correspondence with the author, "When my dogs get in my truck and then see certain gear taken out (including a backpack, water bottle, possibly a dog toy, and a GPS collar), they *know* we are searching. I usually don't have to say anything but oftentimes I will just ask 'are you ready,' and they know what's up. I sometimes will say 'search,' but it really isn't necessary."[56]

All of the dogs have been trained to "alert" (by sitting or lying down) to the scent of human bones, even when buried underground. Often, however, the search for human remains can be complicated by a scattering of animal bones. Both handlers and dogs have to learn, through experience, how to tell them apart. If the handlers have any doubts, they photograph the bones and send the images for review to one or more anthropologists associated with their organization. (Other support members include those in the fields of historical research and ground-penetrating radar.) By midday, the three dogs had worked their way through the entire search area without alerting to any human remains.[57]

Before leaving the scene of the Walden search (and routinely in other searches as well), the handlers conducted training exercises with their dogs so that each dog would be positively reinforced to alert. Then the dogs were rewarded by playing with their handlers who had been training them since they were very young.

As puppies, the dogs had learned to find special toys with a desired scent, then they got to play with their handlers as their reward. The same concept was, and is, continued throughout the dogs' careers.[58] The average person, however, is unaware that play-as-reward training is ingrained in dogs who search for human remains, and onlookers are apt to disapprove. For instance, dog handlers televised at the site of the World Trade Center after the September 11, 2001, attacks were said to have been criticized for playing Frisbee and other games with their dogs at Ground Zero. The handlers were not being disrespectful—they simply were rewarding their dogs for performing their duties.

Members of Colorado Forensic Canines also spend a lot of time in ongoing training, which pays off when their dogs receive annual certification from national law enforcement K-9 testing agencies that include the North American Police Work Dog Association and the Law Enforcement Training Specialists. Meanwhile, in addition to training, their handlers donate their time to a myriad of duties that include making arrangements for searches and corresponding with investigators. Travel costs, including gas for their vehicles, usually comes out of their own pockets.[59]

As of this writing, the search for the Walden man continues. Eric Haider's case, however, is still under investigation. The discovery of his remains was a massive break and allowed his family to confirm his death and give him a funeral. But, they still are seeking resolution. "We don't know who, we don't know why," Haider's mother tearfully stated in a May 2015 television interview. "Normal families, when they lose someone, they know when it happened, why it happened, where it happened—the time, the date. I've waited three years, and I kept saying he was there and people kept saying I was nuts."[60]

For the dogs, human remains detection is all in a day's work, but it is obvious that they enjoy it. When asked what is in it for the handlers, Bonnie replied, "We feel a great obligation to assist in bringing answers to grieving families. We also are strongly allied with law enforcement to bring perpetrators to justice."[61]

Chapter 6

Celeste's Sister Sara

Found Alive in Mexico

Sara, whose full name is being withheld in order to respect her privacy, disappeared for eight years on the streets of Tijuana, Mexico. But, this story is not only about her. The events, as they unfolded, are told through the eyes of Celeste Shaw, her sister, a resident of Colorado Springs, Colorado. Year after year, Celeste pursued Sara's missing person case, and then, suddenly, was swept into complicated international legal maneuverings and flung onto a roller coaster of emotions after a detective from the Colorado Springs Police Department notified her that Sara had been found, and that she was alive.

In a subsequent letter to the Colorado Springs Police Department, Celeste wrote:

> Before Sara was found, one of Detective [Ron] Lopez's volunteers was researching dental records and located two possible matches for my sister. Detective Lopez told me the records were being checked against Sara's for a match. Then, on July 15, 2013, he called me and told me she had been found, and he briefly paused. I realized whatever he said next would forever change my life. When I heard she was alive and had survived over eight years—a single white female, on the streets of Tijuana—it was so hard to believe.[1]

GROWING UP IN COLORADO

Sara, born in 1965, is now in an assisted living facility in Colorado Springs. Although she has contact with other family members, Celeste is her court-appointed legal guardian. The relationship makes sense, as Celeste was the oldest of three children in their family, as shown in figure 6.1. In an interview with the author, she recalls times as a little child when Sara, a year younger, often asked, "Where Sissy go?" When Sara found her, she would cling to her big sister's hand.[2]

The sisters and a younger brother grew up in Teller County, Colorado, where their father worked for the Hewlett-Packard Company, and their mother was a stay-at-home mom. In high school, Sara was pretty and popular, was good at sports, and liked country and light rock music. Even then, however, Celeste was aware that something was wrong, explaining that Sara began to lie and deceive and was extra-rebellious. Sara attended a year of college, but disregarded rules and boundaries.[3]

Figure 6.1 "Sara" and Celeste with Their Brother. Always the big sister, Celeste Shaw, right, posed in this childhood photograph with "Sara" and their baby brother. *Source:* Photo courtesy of Celeste Shaw

THE DOWNWARD SPIRAL

At the age of 19, Sara was diagnosed with one of many future mental illnesses. But, like so many others who are mentally ill, she refused to stay on her medications. For the next two decades, she sometimes lived on the streets, had run-ins with the law, and tried, unsuccessfully, to hold down a series of part-time jobs while, at the same time, giving in to alcohol addiction. When Sara went off her medications, however, as she did many times, she fell into cycles in which she became violent and abusive. And, at the bottom of each cycle, she would flee to California. Celeste then managed to find her, each time, re-medicated in some faraway psychiatric ward. According to Celeste, when Sara disappeared, she disconnected with the family, even telling doctors that all of her family members were deceased.[4]

Functioning Amid Dysfunction

Sara's mental illness was also taking a toll on her family. Because of Sara's sometimes disruptive behavior, her parents started living behind locked doors. Celeste's employers received phone calls from Sara stating that Celeste was embezzling money. And holiday dinners became difficult when some family members preferred to keep their immediate families away from Sara rather than interact. So, when she disappeared, for the sixth time, there was, initially, an understandable sense of relief.[5]

During the end of April 2005, Sara telephoned from Tijuana and asked the family for money so she could come home. That was the first time that Celeste or her family knew that Sara had crossed the Mexican border. It was also the first time—ever—that she had asked them to send money. The family wired her a Money Gram, but it never was picked up.[6]

After three months went by with no word from Sara, Celeste and her mother filed a missing person report with the Colorado Springs Police Department and also with the US Consulate in Tijuana. Along with her mother, Celeste still was determined to bring Sara back. What Celeste did not expect, however, was the fracturing of her extended family that followed. "Their criticism was wearing," she said. "No one thought we were doing too much, but no one would help."[7]

Even when Celeste and her mother filed that last missing person report, Celeste downplayed Sara's mental illness and did not mention, at first, that

Sara had previously been missing. And, as Celeste had been told before—and was told again—a person over the age of 21 is an adult and has the right to be missing. Celeste points out that what was even harder to accept was that in order for the police to do their job, they have to consider family members as suspects in the person's disappearance. She added, "We had to learn to function in all the dysfunction."[8]

An Unlikely Club

Families of missing persons need to hope for the best and prepare for the worst. But, most family members, particularly at first, find themselves completely overwhelmed. As one woman, in another case, stated after the disappearance of her adult daughter, "It's like being spun into a world all by yourself without a single person to tell you what to do."[9] Statistics point out that the majority of missing persons come back on their own or are found. But, statistics are not necessarily comforting. Celeste compares having a family member go missing to belonging to a club that no one would choose to join.[10]

Since Sara had previously gone missing, and had been found, Celeste and her mother knew many of the first steps in a missing person search. Their hope was for Sara's safe return—as proved true—but they knew they also had to prepare for the possibility that Sara might be found deceased.

To cover both scenarios, Celeste stresses the importance of the following:

- Preserve the missing person's laundry. Use gloves and put the soiled clothing in a bag. Also preserve items such as a hairbrush, toothbrush, and cup that the person had used, that is, anything that might yield DNA.
- Obtain (or ask police to obtain) the person's dental records.
- Arrange for two family members to give their DNA to the police.
- If the missing person had been collecting Social Security Disability Insurance, stop the funds and return any that arrived since the person went missing. This is important because if the person is found alive, all documentation regarding the disability insurance (including the dates that the checks were received and returned) has to match.
- If the person had been treated in a local/county psychiatric facility, notify them that the person went missing. That may allow the local facility to keep client records in an "open" status.
- Keep all documents and correspondence, including envelopes (that prove dates), especially those with the missing person's handwriting.[11]

THINKING LIKE AN INVESTIGATOR

Six months to a year went by before reality set in that Sara might actually be dead. "My mind was there," said Celeste, "but I didn't fully accept it."[12] Celeste looked for Sara, alive, with Google searches. But, by the end of 2005, Celeste's searching had turned to websites with unidentified remains, and she began to think like an investigator. She started her online searches with coroners' offices in individual counties within the border states of California, Arizona, New Mexico, and Texas. Then she looked at websites in counties with Interstate highways that led north from the border crossings.[13]

Her search took her to coroner/medical examiner websites such as that of the Office of the Medical Examiner in Maricopa County, Arizona. In addition to basic information on the decedents, many of the sites provide sketches and photographs, when available. Some also include photos of tattoos, piercings, and/or belongings. In addition, Celeste found similar listings in the Unidentified Index of the Doe Network.[14]

Then, when the NamUs System was launched in 2009, Detective Lopez entered Sara's photos and fingerprints, as well as the availability of DNA profiles from the family. By then, both he and Celeste were searching the NamUs database for unidentified remains. Celeste urges family members to familiarize themselves with NamUs and to add information in order to boost their loved one's listing to the five-star category.[15] (Many of the county databases, and also the Doe Network indices, are currently being incorporated into NamUs databases. For more on NamUs, see chapter 7, "NamUs: An Investigative Tool.")

Celeste's Google searches also led her to the CBI Cold Case Files.[16] "No one tells the families that after three years, their missing person has become a 'cold case,'" she said. The classification is not meant to be impersonal but, from the families' perspective, Celeste says it is like a slap in the face—like someone is working against them behind the scenes.[17]

After reading hundreds of listings of unidentified remains on various databases and websites, Celeste began to question some of the data, wondering whether descriptions (such as specifications of race of skeletal remains) may have contained human error. She broadened her parameters on the descriptive data but narrowed them in other ways. For instance, since Sara did not have piercings or tattoos (at least when she disappeared), Celeste looked more closely at bodies and remains that did not have these distinctions, regardless of the stated race, height, or weight. As the years went by, Celeste said she

Figure 6.2   Tijuana, Mexico Border. From 2005 to 2013, "Sara" lived on the streets of Tijuana, Mexico. The United States/Mexican border, shown here, separates the densely populated city from California. *Source:* Photo courtesy of Sergeant 1st Class Gordon Hyde, Army National Guard

was constantly looking at corpses. "It became emotionally difficult, knowing that so many people and their families had suffered," she added. "I felt like I was going to 200 funerals a day."[18]

According to the Social Security Administration, a missing person is presumed dead if he or she has been missing from home and has not been heard from for seven years or more.[19] Said Celeste, "At some point I had to stop and just admit that maybe Sara was in Mexico and fell off a cliff." By then, the seven years had gone by. Celeste was in the process of obtaining the final document needed for Sara's Legal Presumption of Death, when, suddenly, she received word that Sara had been found alive.[20]

MEANWHILE, SOUTH OF THE BORDER

All during the time spent searching, Celeste and her family were unaware that from May 2005 (shortly after Sara's phone call) until December 2012, Sara had been living on the streets of Tijuana. (See figure 6.2.) Little is known of that time of her life, as she has not revealed many details. She was, however, known to have eaten from dumpsters, and she filled her coat with leaves for added insulation on cold nights. Her only possessions were the clothes on her back. She had been hit by a car, but had not received any medical care, leaving her with a shattered ankle, broken teeth, and a large scar on her face.[21]

Then, on Christmas Eve 2012, a Catholic priest found Sara on the street and took her to a locked facility for women. At that time, Sara was mute. She had her own sign language but was unable to explain who she was or where she was from. Celeste says that the people at the center saved Sara's life, but the conditions were primitive. Instead of a bathroom, for instance, the residents used a bucket. Their families were supposed to pay for food and clothing. But since Sara had no financial support, she was only given one minimal meal, such as a bowl of soup or beans, per day. During her stay, she was malnourished and inflicted with severe lice and scabies.[22]

Then came a turning point in Sara's story. In July 2013, a volunteer at the shelter thought that Sara might be an American and called the US Consulate. Kevin Brosnahan, a foreign service officer based in Tijuana, visited Sara and asked her who she was and where she was from. She was unable to even tell him her name, but when he pulled out a map, she pointed to Colorado Springs![23]

Back in his office, Officer Brosnahan began searching the Missing Persons database of the NamUs System, spending three hours looking through entries of women missing from Colorado. Finally he came across the profile of Sara that Colorado Springs Detective Lopez had entered. The officer called Detective Lopez, then forwarded Sara's photo and fingerprints. "It was her," the detective later told a reporter. "It looked like she was aged from living on the street." Brosnahan added, "Not all cases come out with a happy ending. This is beyond a happy ending."[24]

BRINGING SARA HOME

On the day that Celeste received the telephone call from Detective Lopez, her immediate family were all together on vacation, celebrating her parents' 50th wedding anniversary. After the dust settled with the surprising news, hundreds of people—including federal, state, and county officials—became involved in the logistics of bringing Sara home.

Years earlier, Celeste and her mother had learned that the money they had tried to send to Sara in 2005 never was cashed, so they deposited the funds in a Colorado Springs bank account. That, along with other possessions still being kept by the family was enough for the El Paso County, Colorado, Court to prove that Sara's affairs were in its jurisdiction. A wide-ranging court order then granted Celeste the flexibility to take any actions, make any decisions, and speak with any immigration officials and physicians to get Sara across the border. With the help of US Congressman Doug Lamborn, Celeste (as Sara's guardian) reinstated Sara's Medicaid and other benefits, and tried to answer the big question—Where should Sara go?[25]

To ensure Sara's secure transport out of Mexico, she had to willingly—as proof that she was not being abducted—get into one ambulance (paid for by the American Red Cross), then at the border, willingly get into another ambulance (paid for by Medicaid). Luckily, someone at the shelter had explained to Sara what was about to take place, and she agreed to go. The family was given photographs taken at the time that show Sara voluntarily getting into the vehicles. Once across the border, a physician who accompanied Sara repatriated her by explaining that she was an American citizen and was safely back on American soil. Stated Celeste, "God got Sara out of Tijuana on a shoestring."[26]

Road Trip

All of Celeste's strengths, and all of her emotions, culminated in Sara's final journey home. Celeste and her family knew (from the previous times that Sara had gone missing) that when Sara was rescued, in order to assure that she stayed in the mental health system, that she had to be admitted to a psychiatric ward, this time in a San Diego hospital. The family was not allowed to be present. But, getting her back to Colorado Springs became Celeste's responsibility, requiring Celeste to obtain another court order.[27]

Then Celeste (with her then-81-year-old mother) drove more than 1,100 miles from Colorado Springs to San Diego to bring Sara home. Sara recognized Celeste and their mother as soon as she saw them and agreed to accompany them. At the San Diego psychiatric ward, Celeste was handed a bag of medications, but she was not given any instructions as to what they were. Many simply were marked "give as needed."[28]

Now, Celeste can joke about the two-day road trip, but traveling with a mentally ill patient in the back seat was not easy. In addition to making all of the arrangements and doing all of the driving, Celeste had to research and dole out Sara's medications. She also bought her new clothes which Sara insisted on wearing in multiple layers. After years with practically nothing, her manner of dressing had become a survival technique. So, too, after receiving only one meal a day at the Mexican facility, was her insatiable interest in food. According to Celeste, every time they stopped for gasoline, Sara would be the first to get out of the car and would grab armfuls of sodas and snacks at convenience stores.[29]

Mission Accomplished

After a stressful four days of driving from Colorado to California and back, Celeste and Sara finally arrived at a hospital in Colorado Springs, where Sara needed to be medically cleared. Celeste, however, was exhausted, so she lay down on a bed, while Sara paced the hall. When the doctor arrived, he initially thought Celeste was the patient. Hospital employees realized that Celeste was totally spent, and they refused to allow her to transport Sara to the psychiatric ward. Faced with saying goodbye to Sara, though, even temporarily, was overwhelming. "I felt lost and, for the first time, I didn't know what to do," said Celeste. "I broke down and sobbed. But my mission was accomplished, and it was time to go."[30]

Today, Sara's needs are met in a group home for the mentally ill, and she receives her regular medications by injection. Now in her early fifties and living as normal a life as possible, she has taken an interest in dishwashing and helps out in the kitchen. Celeste visits her weekly and takes her to all of her doctor and therapy appointments. Sara leaves the facility on Sundays to attend the Lutheran Church (in which both sisters attended as toddlers), sometimes with Celeste and sometimes with their mother.[31]

Celeste currently divides her time between selling real estate and managing Sara's affairs. When asked why she never gave up, she stated, "When I'm on my deathbed, I don't want any regrets. She's family, she's my only sister."[32]

Chapter 7

NamUs

An Investigative Tool

NamUs is an investigative tool, and its key to success is that it facilitates communication. J. Todd Matthews, director of Case Management and Communications for the NamUs System, has called it a "needed bridge" between law enforcement agencies, medical examiners, coroners, and the public. "This is the first time we have had a central system that everyone can use and access," he stated in a National Institute of Justice (NIJ) publication in 2009, when two of the three interlocking databases were launched. "We are all on the same page, looking at the same info, and that is truly important."[1]

Now, family members, too, can play an active role in the investigations and become part of the solution. Instead of being told to sit and wait, NamUs allows families to participate and be proactive, all at no charge and without leaving their homes or offices. This chapter will give readers some insight into:

- How Law Enforcement Uses NamUs
- Melissa Gregory: Representing a Region
- How Families Use NamUs
- Paula E. Beverly: Found by Her Sisters

HOW LAW ENFORCEMENT USES NAMUS

When searching for long-term missing persons, as well as unidentified (and unclaimed) remains, a very productive investigative tool used by both investigators and families is the NamUs System. The account of "Celeste and Her Sister: Found Alive in Mexico," in chapter 6, illustrates how NamUs connected officials in Mexico with a detective in Colorado that led to the identification of "Sara," the woman who lived on the streets of Tijuana from 2005 to 2013.

The following story shows how the same detective—and during the same eight-year period—worked with other investigators to locate, in Texas, the remains of a missing Colorado man, Paul Daniel Kirchhoff. NamUs has jump-started many cold cases by facilitating communication between agencies. Thanks to NamUs, the families of both Sara and Paul, and many others, no longer have to wait and wonder as to what happened to their loved ones.

Paul Daniel Kirchhoff: The Man on the Train

On Friday August 12, 2005, twenty-one-year-old Paul Kirchhoff was in his bedroom, upstairs in the house where he grew up, in an older residential area in Colorado Springs, Colorado. The neighborhood was quiet and so was the house, except for the sound of Paul tearing paper into strips, an activity brought on by his gradually worsening schizophrenia. Paul's father George stopped by his room and noticed that he seemed unusually agitated.[2]

"I said goodnight, and Paul reached up and put his hand on my face," stated George in an interview with the author when asked about his youngest son. The following morning—August 13, 2005—Paul was gone.[3]

In Paul's place were broken car windows, a branch ripped from a tree, and blood in front of the family's home. Paul's parents did everything they could when faced with a family member who suddenly was missing. They called the police and hospitals. Then they called Paul's friends, made and passed out fliers, and even called the jail. "We had hope that he was alive and being cared for by someone," said George.[4] The following Monday, he filed a missing person report and made sure that the police understood that Paul was an at-risk adult.

Meanwhile, a long freight train was making its way from Wyoming to Texas, with car after car filled with coal. Lying in one of the cars on top of a load of coal was the body of a young man. A coroner would later determine that the man had jumped off a bridge onto the moving train, instantly dying from a severed spinal cord. The man on the train had no identification, and, for nearly eight years, no one knew that he was Paul Daniel Kirchhoff.[5]

"We spent every day watching for him. Not knowing was the worst," said George, as he flipped through scrapbooks of Paul's childhood days.[6] The son George remembers smiles back at him in photos of birthday parties, on family vacations, and just being a kid with his two older brothers. His parents never had to worry about him.[7]

Paul had gone to Columbia Elementary School and wrestled at North Junior High School. He enjoyed baseball and skateboarding. Then, at age 16, he began exhibiting disordered thinking and behavior and was diagnosed with schizophrenia. Still, in 2003, he was determined to graduate from Palmer High School. Then his illness worsened. Paul continued to live at home, he jogged long distances, and he enjoyed hiking in the mountains. The last photo his family has of him he took of himself, by holding his camera in front of him on one of his solo hikes.[8]

The first day Paul was missing, his uncle hiked Paul's favorite mountain trail, showing his photo to joggers and posting fliers. Paul's face stood out above the caption, "Have you seen me? Loving family is worried," along with contact information.[9] Every day after work, his mother rode her bicycle to a nearby park, carrying Paul's photo and talking with homeless people, asking if they had seen him. The days turned into weeks and the weeks into months, but for Paul's parents, finding their son was always uppermost in their minds.[10]

The police also made an effort to find Paul, at least initially. George, a longtime city employee, was told that the police were doing everything they could do. By law, they contacted the Kirchhoffs once a year. "The first time the police called, they left a message," said George. "It really got our hopes up, but we learned it was just routine, as they only asked if we had seen Paul. And, we hadn't."[11]

Meanwhile, on August 17, 2005, five days after Paul went missing, an employee at a cement plant in New Braunfels, Texas (in the Hill Country northeast of San Antonio), sat down to eat his lunch before unloading a newly arrived shipment of coal. The rail-yard worker was in a place where he could look down onto the rail cars, and he happened to see, in one of the cars, a young man's body lying on top of a load of coal. He called in the medical examiner who determined the manner of death. The man had no identification, and when members of the Comal County (Texas) Sheriff's Office arrived, they were faced with the challenge of identifying a John Doe.[12]

At the time, there was no mechanism in place for the Colorado Springs Police Department to effectively communicate about missing persons and unidentified remains with law enforcement agencies in other parts of the country. And, even if investigators had considered that Paul's body had been on a freight train to Texas, they would have been overwhelmed in contacting each of the jurisdictions in all of the cities and counties the train passed through in Colorado, New Mexico, and Texas. Without any way to identify the man, the Comal County Sheriff's Office buried him in Bracken Cemetery.[13] The small rural graveyard is covered in native vegetation that includes yucca, prickly pear cactus, and a variety of wild flowers, all under the year-round shade of live oak trees.

The Kirchhoffs, however, continued to wait and wonder, while the case of the man on the train went cold.

In 2009, the NIJ launched NamUs—a dual database for the missing and unidentified. Detective Ron Lopez of the Colorado Springs Police Department was on top of this latest investigative tool and entered Paul's description into the database of missing persons. Similarly, the Comal County Medical Examiner had put his John Doe's description and related information into the database of unidentified remains.[14]

The conversation between the Colorado Springs Police Department and the Kirchhoffs took a different turn when Detective Lopez called the family in 2012. Thinking it was another routine annual call, Paul's parents were surprised when the detective asked if he could visit them in their home. In email correspondence with the author, Detective Lopez explained that he had told the Kirchhoffs about NamUs and the success he was having finding other missing persons. In addition, he swabbed the insides of their cheeks to collect saliva for DNA. When he returned to his office, Detective Lopez entered images of Paul's dental records and sent Paul's parents' DNA samples to the University of North Texas Center for Human Identification so NamUs could enter a familial DNA profile.[15]

In beginning his search, Detective Lopez had to rule out the likelihood of Paul being alive. He looked for, but did not find, any activity in Social Security records or in law enforcement databases. Paul's parents had stated, however, that Paul was an excellent long-distance runner and could have run all the way to Pueblo, forty-five miles south of Colorado Springs. Detective Lopez began—as he had for Sara—to search through the NamUs listings of unidentified remains, this time looking for those of young men who fit Paul's age and physical description. With the possibility of Pueblo as a destination, the detective initiated his search there. On a hunch, he continued to look at locations farther to the south.[16]

One listing in the Austin, Texas, area looked promising, so Detective Lopez contacted the Travis County Medical Examiner. From dental and DNA comparisons, though, that unidentified man was not a match. Then, the medical examiner, who also covered Comal County, put Detective Lopez in contact with the Comal County Sheriff's Office, as that jurisdiction had a John Doe, as well. An initial comparison of the Comal County John Doe's NCIC dental charting to Paul's dental records was not a match either. Fortunately, before burial, the medical examiner had preserved a DNA sample and also had withheld the man's jawbone for possible future comparison.[17]

Meanwhile, Detective Lopez was in contact with former NamUs regional system administrators (RSAs) Jerry Brown and Mike Nance, as well as an odontologist (forensic dentist). "We all educated each other," said the detective. "The odontologist pointed out that dental records can sometimes be entered incorrectly or even backwards. Since the jawbone was available, it was sent to the University of North Texas Center for Human Identification's Forensic Services Unit where it was compared with Paul's dental X-rays. We compared the DNA at the same time."[18]

The DNA from Paul's parents matched the DNA of the unidentified man found in Comal County. The newly recorded dental records matched, too. Once everything was in order, Detective Lopez, via NamUs, sent all related records to the Travis County Medical Examiner for his confirmation.[19]

"This case showed me a lot of things, but the main thing it showed me was that the information is there," added Detective Lopez. "It may not always be correctly or fully entered, but you just have to find it. The most incredible thing I learned, by just talking with the other agency involved, is that its investigators had actually traced the train back to Colorado Springs, put two and two together, and figured out that its unidentified person could possibly be Paul. The agency contacted the El Paso County Sheriff's Office and was told that it had no such case, which was true, as it was a Colorado Springs Police Department case."[20] (Colorado Springs is located in El Paso County, Colorado.)

In addition, Detective Lopez later discovered that a National Crime Information Center (NCIC) printout had also showed the Comal County John Doe as a possible match, but that information, too, had fallen through the cracks.[21] (The NCIC is a federal database that includes listings of missing and unidentified persons.)

When asked about the outcome, Detective Lopez stated, "Oh gosh, it was great to make the match. It wasn't like we just threw in the DNA. The Comal County officials did a hell of a job. The problem was that we just did not communicate. That's what NamUs does. It helps us communicate better with outside agencies."[22]

Less than a year later, in April 2013, Detective Lopez asked, again, to visit the Kirchhoffs in their home. This time he brought along a victim advocate. And, this time he had something to tell them.[23] The outcome is best expressed in the concluding paragraphs of a letter George Kirchhoff wrote on April 25, 2013, to the chief of police of the Colorado Springs Police Department:

> On April 1, 2013, Detective Lopez made contact to request a meeting with me and my wife. He informed us that Paul was deceased and was buried in New Braunfels, Texas. Detective Lopez had made contact with Detective Doug Phillips of the Comal County Sheriff's Office. They had recovered Paul's body on August 17, 2005 but were unable to identify him at that time. With Detective Lopez's help [and] DNA and dental records, Detective Phillips was able to make positive identification of the body as being Paul. While I and my family will always be grief-stricken over the outcome of the case, we will always be grateful for having closure regarding the loss of our beloved son.
>
> I sincerely hope that you will personally pass along our everlasting thanks and gratitude to Detective Ron Lopez and any others that may have helped in bringing a close to this case. Words can never express how much this means to us. It is also our sincere hope that other families with missing loved ones can be helped as well.[24]

Shortly after Paul's identification, his parents visited his grave. "When Detective Lopez first gave us the news, we didn't believe it, as we wanted to believe he was alive," stated George. "But going there helped, and a big weight has been lifted. We'll continue to visit his grave every year."[25] (See figure 7.1.)

Figure 7.1 Paul Daniel Kirchhoff's Grave Marker. Paul Daniel Kirchhoff, formerly a John Doe, now has his name on his grave, in a peaceful rural cemetery in Comal County, Texas. *Source:* Photo courtesy of George Kirchhoff

MELISSA GREGORY: REPRESENTING A REGION

Melissa Gregory is one of eight NamUs Regional System Administrators (RSAs) and is responsible for Region 3—Nebraska, Missouri, Kansas, Iowa, Colorado, New Mexico, and Utah. It is a big area and a big responsibility, but Melissa is upbeat about her work and says that her successes come daily. "Of course the biggest success is to locate a missing person alive or to identify an unidentified deceased," she stated in email correspondence with the author. "But other successes can be locating biometric data that law enforcement has been trying to find for many years, or making contact with a searching family member who is extremely appreciative."[26] She often hears from family members who tell her that before getting her on the telephone, they thought that "everyone" had forgotten about their case. Melissa enjoys explaining the nuts and bolts of the NamUs System to families and also considers it an achievement when law enforcement gets "on board," becoming encouraged with the resources that the system can provide.[27]

After growing up in Nebraska and graduating with a Criminal Justice degree from the University of Nebraska-Lincoln in 2001, Melissa moved to Colorado and earned a graduate degree in Criminal Investigative Psychology. While in Denver, she interned with the Denver Police Department and became knowledgeable in crime analysis and crime-scene investigation and even attended autopsies. Also, she briefly volunteered with a missing child organization where she learned of the resources of the National Center for Missing & Exploited Children® (NCMEC).[28] For more on this organization, see chapter 3, "Children: Helping to Bring Them Home."

In 2006, Melissa accepted a position at the NCMEC, in Alexandria, Virginia. She started as an assistant in the Case Analysis Unit (CAU) and worked her way up to analyst and then senior analyst. In 2011, she took on the role of supervisor with the CAU. While working there, she also learned about NamUs. "Though I thoroughly enjoyed working at NCMEC," Melissa stated, "I was interested in moving back to the Midwest so I kept an eye on the available positions with NamUs."[29] In February 2015, she moved back to Nebraska and began her work as a regional system administrator (RSA).[30]

Although RSAs are employed by the University of North Texas Health Science Center, Melissa and the others work remotely. Being physically located within the region in which she is assigned gives her the opportunity to economically travel throughout her region and to instruct and meet with investigators. Unlike her positions at the NCMEC, where she worked behind the scenes, Melissa has become the "forward face" of NamUs when she meets with law enforcement and coroners/medical examiners. She conducts presentations and trainings for investigators to educate them on the resources NamUs provides, and she continually offers assistance on cases of missing and unidentified persons. She also is working with state agencies to develop Missing Person Day events. Although her official work hours are 8 a.m. to 5 p.m. Monday through Friday, the demands of her job require flexibility. Often she finds herself corresponding with family members and/or law enforcement during evenings and weekends.[31]

The goal of all of the RSAs is to assist the investigators in their regions in resolving their missing and unidentified cases. But, it is a big job, and Melissa wears many hats. Often, she is managing communications between family members, law enforcement, medical examiners, coroners, coworkers, lab personnel, and the general public. In addition, she reviews all of the cases within her region to enhance biometrics (including DNA, dental records, and fingerprints). Her work also includes providing potential matches to investigators and evaluating potential matches provided by the general public.[32]

Figure 7.2   NamUs Logo. The NamUs System of interrelated databases facilitates communication among law enforcement agencies, medical examiners/coroners, and the public. Funded by the National Institute of Justice, it also provides DNA testing and related forensic services. *Source:* Photo courtesy of J. Todd Matthews, director, Case Management and Communications, National Missing & Unidentified Persons System (NamUs) on behalf of the National Institute of Justice

Melissa knows, firsthand, that waiting and wondering is the hardest part of what families endure. When asked how NamUs helps families, she stated, "I want families to know that the NamUs staff will do all we can to assist in locating their missing loved ones whether that be an ear to listen to or someone to bounce ideas off of. We are also here to explain what our resources are pertaining to missing person cases and offer guidance in how to closely work with their law enforcement agency in an attempt to locate their missing family member."[33]

She added, "We also are a liaison between families and law enforcement, and someone to share joy or grief with when their loved one is located."[34] For more on the NamUs System, go online and access NamUs.gov.[35] (See figure 7.2.)

HOW FAMILIES USE NAMUS

The Kirchhoffs were fortunate that Detective Ron Lopez (now retired) was experienced in the use of NamUs. As noted in chapter 8, "Become Your Long-Term Missing Person's Advocate," it is essential for family members of the long-term missing to give their DNA to their investigators *and* to make sure their loved one has been entered as a missing person in the NamUs Missing Person database. At the time of this writing, however, there is no law *requiring* law enforcement agencies to enter their cases. Some investigators simply are not knowledgeable about NamUs. Family members who have filed missing person reports with uninformed agencies (or even a member of the public) can enter the missing person's case themselves. (See "Enter a Missing Person's Case," below.) First, however, the family will need to know if its loved one's case is listed.

The NamUs System consists of three databases—for Missing Persons, Unidentified Persons, and Unclaimed Persons—and is free and accessible to the public.[36] The unclaimed database is searchable by the public using a missing person's name and year of birth. The database lists deceased persons who have been identified by name, but for whom no next of kin or family member has been identified or located to claim the body for burial or other disposition. The missing and unidentified databases are discussed below. The best way to learn about these resources are to use them. Start with the missing persons database to do the following:

- LOOK UP a missing person's case
- ENTER a missing person's case (if a law enforcement agency has not already done so)

- GIVE more information
- TRACK a missing person's case
- PRINT a poster of the missing person
- LEARN about additional resources
- SEARCH the Unidentified Persons database for unidentified remains

It is a good idea, too, to become familiar with all three databases and get involved with one's community. The joint efforts of caring individuals can help to solve others' missing persons' cases.

Look Up a Missing Person's Case

Anyone researching a missing person can go to the Welcome to NamUs Missing Persons page and do a "Quick Search."[37] Any or all of the following fields can be entered:

- First name
- Last name
- Sex
- State

For instance, to see if your family member is listed, simply enter his or her name. If you are interested, however, to learn more about missing persons in your state, enter the state. That will open the "Search Results" page where you can sort by number, name, date last seen, location, sex and race. Clicking on a case will open the Case Navigation page to the following:

- Case Information
- Circumstances
- Physical / Medical
- Clothing and Accessories
- Transportation Methods
- Dental
- DNA
- Fingerprints
- Images
- Documents
- Investigating Agency
- Reports
- Contacts

Each of those pages will then provide more information.

Enter a Missing Person's Case

As noted above, anyone can explore and become familiar with the NamUs databases without registering. But, registration is required in order for public users to enter a missing person into the missing persons database. The required fields need to be filled in, but not all have to be known. For instance, if the person's eye color is not known, then enter "unknown."

- First Name
- Last Name
- Age
- Sex
- Race
- Height
- Weight
- City
- State
- Date LKA (Last Known Alive)
- Circumstances
- Hair Color
- Eye Color

After the basic information is entered, a case manager verifies it with the appropriate law enforcement agency and obtains additional information, including a federal NCIC number, before the case can go "live." Registered users can track cases they initiate, and they can follow their cases and those of others. When law enforcement, however, enters (or adds to) a case, sensitive case material, such as specific biometric information, can be blocked from public view.

No matter who enters a case, it is important to upload one or more photos, as well as descriptions of scars, tattoos, and jewelry the missing person often wore. After verification, law enforcement will obtain (if available) fingerprints and dental records. This is the time, too, for law enforcement to take DNA samples from (usually) two family members. If family members live in different jurisdictions from where the person went missing (or where the report is filed), any local law enforcement agency can obtain the DNA swabs on behalf of the investigating agency. As long as the case has been entered into NamUs, there is no cost to the family or to law enforcement for DNA comparisons, or for the assistance of forensic anthropologists and odontologists (dentists). NamUs is funded (with our tax dollars) through the NIJ.[38]

Give More Information

The more description posted about a missing person, the better. If the law enforcement agency initially entered the missing person's case, then the agency needs to be informed of missing details. If, for instance, your family member had a distinctive ring or always wore a gold chain, let your investigator know so he or she can note those items on the "Clothing and Accessories" page. If dental records have not already been provided, give the investigator the name of the missing person's dentist. Better yet, contact the dentist directly to obtain copies of the missing person's medical and dental records, including X-rays. That way, there will not be any danger of the records getting purged, or of the originals becoming lost. Also, do not forget to give the police a copy of a good clear photograph, as well as descriptions of scars and tattoos.

Celeste Shaw, in "Thinking Like an Investigator," in chapter 6, "Celeste's Sister Sara: Found Alive in Mexico," urges families to boost their NamUs listings to the five-star category. Under Frequently Asked Questions, in the Resource section of the NamUs website, the star-designation scale is defined as follows:

> The 5-star scale ranks each case in terms of the amount of information it contains that is potentially useful for finding a missing person. The system automatically assigns a number of stars based on the amount and quality of data that is entered by the case owner. Essentially, the more useful identification information contained in a profile, the more likely it is that these specifics can be used to help solve a case. For example, a case that includes identification information like specific clothing and accessories, dental records, DNA reporting and fingerprints will have more stars than a record containing only basic features like eye and hair color. The 5-star rating system does not denote any priority level in solving a case, but is used here to encourage users to add as much information as possible.[39]

Track a Missing Person's Case

Registered users of NamUs can "track" their cases and automatically receive emails notifying them when case information has been updated. This constant feedback is just as important to the mother whose child is missing as it is to the investigator handling the case.

Print a Poster

One of the features of the missing persons database is that data can be rearranged into various forms. Anyone can click on "Reports" and then on "Print a Poster" and have the missing person's photograph, description, date last seen, and law enforcement contact information immediately available in a poster format.

Learn About Additional Resources

The Welcome page of the missing persons database includes a drop-down menu called "Resources." Listed there are links to (and a list of) State Clearinghouses, often confusing as these agencies have varying names. For instance, in Iowa the state-run agency is the Missing Person Information Clearinghouse, Division of Criminal Investigation (DCI). Pennsylvania's state agency is the Pennsylvania State Police, Bureau of Criminal Investigation. In Arizona, the clearinghouse is the Arizona Department of Public Safety, Criminal Investigations Research Unit. In Colorado, it is the Colorado Bureau of Investigation (CBI), Missing Person/Children Unit; while in Georgia the name of the agency is the Georgia Bureau of Investigation, Intelligence Unit. Regardless of what the agencies are called, they function to assist other law enforcement agencies within their states.

Some of the states have their own publicly searchable databases. Colorado's is the CBI's Cold Case Files, subdivided into "missing," "homicide," "unidentified," and "other crimes." Stated within this agency's Mission Statement is, "Their voices may now be silent;. . . those who may know the truth are not."[40]

Search the Unidentified Persons Database

As Celeste Shaw stated when searching for her sister, six months to a year went by before she was ready to admit that Sara might actually be deceased. Even thinking about the possibility can be a difficult line to cross, but if there is any likelihood of the missing person being deceased, families should actively search the Unidentified Persons database for remains. Only coroners, medical examiners, and designated law enforcement professionals can enter these cases. (Some states have coroners, while others have medical examiners. Both are elected officials, but medical examiners are required to also be physicians.)

On the Welcome to NamUs Unidentified Persons page, anyone, including the general public, can enter any or all of the following search fields:

- Sex
- Race
- Ethnicity (Hispanic/Latino)

- Date last known alive
- Age last known alive
- State last known alive[41]

There is also an option to perform an "Advanced Search" in which any combination of information may be searched including clothing, dental characteristics, tattoos, scars, and many other possible identifying features. In the event of a likely match, members of the public can go to "Contacts" and find the name of the case manager, then contact him or her to suggest a possible match. Based on FBI policies, only law enforcement, medical examiners, and coroners can officially request a manual comparison of DNA. Once a suggested match is received, it is up to these investigators whether or not to pursue a manual comparison.

PAULA E. BEVERLY: FOUND BY HER SISTERS

One of the best success stories of a public search for a missing person in the Unidentified Persons database was done by the sisters of Paula E. Beverly (aka Paula Beverly Davis) in 2009. The NamUs System, which initially linked only the missing and unidentified persons' databases, had recently been launched and was being introduced to the public. The sisters viewed a Public Service Announcement about NamUs on a television show, then they connected to the Internet. Paula had been missing for twenty-two years, and they found her in the database in only thirty minutes![42]

Paula was twenty-one-years old when she was last seen in Kansas City, Missouri, at a truck stop on Interstate 70. The date was August 9, 1987. The very next day, an unidentified young woman's body was found on an exit ramp, off of Interstate 70 in Montgomery County, Ohio, nearly 600 miles away. At the time, no one made the connection. Paula's mother filed an extensive missing person report with her local law enforcement agency. The case went cold. Meanwhile, the Montgomery County medical examiner was faced with a Jane Doe he could not identify. The body of the young woman found in Ohio was buried in a pauper's grave in a county-owned cemetery, similar to the fate of the Jane Doe victims in Westmoreland County, Pennsylvania. In the spring of 2009, shortly after the launching of the NamUs System, members of the Medical Examiner's Office entered their Jane Doe into the NamUs Unidentified Persons database.[43] For more on the Pennsylvania cases, see "Trooper Brian F. Gross and the Westmoreland County Girls" in chapter 4, "Proactive Police."

When Paula's sisters got online, they, too, entered Paula's description into the Unidentified Persons database. The first parameters they typed were Paula's sex: female, age: 21, race: white, and Missouri, the state where she was last seen alive. But no cases came up as a result of their first search. They knew to manipulate the parameters, so they removed Missouri from the criteria and tried again.[44]

The second attempt produced ten search results. The sisters quickly read through the first nine and ruled them all out. Then they got to the very last profile, which was a description of an unidentified female found in Montgomery County, Ohio, complete with a tattoo of a unicorn on her right breast and a red rose with green leaves on her left breast. They knew from reading the missing person report filed by their mother that Paula had identical tattoos. The sisters immediately knew they had found her, but were in shock and were not sure what to do.[45]

Before long, however, they were on the telephone with authorities in Ohio, explaining that the Jane Doe they were investigating was Paula E. Beverly. Police then swabbed saliva from inside the cheek of Paula's father and compared his DNA with DNA from the exhumed remains of Jane Doe. They were a match. The family then raised the money necessary to bring Paula home. At her memorial service in the Floral Hills East Memorial Gardens Cemetery, in

Figure 7.3   Paula E. Beverly's Niche Cover. On the niche cover of Paula E. Beverly's cremated remains are images of a unicorn and roses with leaves, symbolic of the tattoos that led to the young woman's identification. *Source:* Photo courtesy of Jay Raveill, *findagrave.com*

Lee's Summit, Missouri, was the mother of another missing young woman who stated, "I was in awe of Paula's family. I stood there with kindred spirits, people who fully understood the roller coaster I was on and am still on."[46]

Paula's cremated remains were placed near those of her mother, who died without knowing what had happened to her oldest daughter. On Paula's niche cover, see figure 7.3, is an engraving of a unicorn and roses with leaves. The only words, using the young woman's maiden name, are:

Paula E. Beverly
December 13, 1965
August 9, 1987[47]

Chapter 8

Become Your Long-Term Missing Person's Advocate

Families can rest assured that the search for their loved ones is ongoing. As is obvious from previous chapters, there are many dedicated people working to match the missing and the unidentified, from individual civilians to police investigators to employees of federal agencies. But, action by family members is vitally important, as well. The days of filing a police report and settling in to wait are over. In increasing numbers, family members today realize that they need to be educated, informed, and involved. They need to become their long-term missing person's advocate.

And, because we all like happy endings, consider this rare twist of fate in which the missing person and his advocate were one and the same. In 1986, 21-year-old Edgar Latulip was living in a group home in Ontario, Canada. According to an article in *The Washington Post*, Edgar had mental health challenges and functioned on the level of a 12-year-old. He attempted suicide, then wandered off from the home.[1]

Edgar's mother feared the worst and reported him missing. No one was aware, however, that the boy had suffered a head injury and lost his memory. Somehow, he ended up eighty miles away in another city and started a new life with a new identity. *Thirty* years later, in 2016, he remembered his name, contacted authorities, and gave his DNA which matched that of his overjoyed mother.[2]

For the rest of us, this chapter addresses the following topics:

- Communicate with Law Enforcement
- Get the Case into NamUs and Give DNA
- Missing Persons Day Events

- Support Groups
- When Is It Time to Go to the Media?
- Do I Need a Private Investigator?

COMMUNICATE WITH LAW ENFORCEMENT

As fellow author and criminal justice professor R.H. Walton stated in email correspondence with the author, "If you don't ask questions, you won't get answers."[3] This includes communicating with law enforcement. For the purpose of this discussion, it is assumed that a family has filed a missing person report with the local law enforcement agency in the jurisdiction where the person was last seen and that the immediate steps in the days after the person went missing have been taken. If the person was at risk or went missing under suspicious circumstances, an investigator should have been assigned to the case. Weeks, months, and perhaps years have passed.

Some families are fortunate to have investigators who stay in their same positions for years on end. They may have developed a rapport with a family member and periodically call with updates or to acknowledge an anniversary. More likely, though, there are no updates, and a new investigator has taken the former one's place. It is never excusable for law enforcement to lose or misplace a case file, but instances are known to exist where it has happened. Retired investigators have, on occasion, taken home the files they were working on, while others may even have been purged.

As the years go by, family members often have changes in their lives, as well. They may have moved, married, or the contact person may have died. A newly assigned investigator may try to call, but the telephone number of the family member who filed the report may have been disconnected, or that person's previous email address is no longer valid. Law enforcement databases have powerful people-search functions, but the investigator in charge of a loved one's case may or may not reach the reporting party, that is, the person who originally filed the missing person report. When family members move, it is their obligation to give their investigators their latest contact information.

Whether or not the family needs to provide an update, this would be a good time to order the missing person's case file. As noted under "Police and Sheriff Records," in "Public Records" in chapter 9, "Gather Information, Document, and Do the Research," any member of the public can file an Open Records Request with a law enforcement agency. It is a good way for families to find out what has, and what has not, been done.

Of most importance, family members need assurance that their missing persons have not been forgotten. Keeping the communication open between families and law enforcement will help. Investigators prefer that the family designate *one* trusted member to be its liaison with law enforcement. Getting calls from multiple family members only creates confusion and can take the investigator's time away from the case, where it should be focused. Families also need to be cognizant that some elements of a case will not be discussed in order to protect the integrity of the case. Some information simply cannot be released.

How often should a family seek an update? There is no definite answer. But, on long-term cases, the recommended time is every six months and is most easily accomplished by email. In turn, investigators should assure the families that, in the interim, they will be informed of any major developments. According to a Colorado study that asked "cold case families" what they most wanted from law enforcement, their answer was the need for better, honest, and direct communication. And, it works both ways.[4]

In talking with their investigators, and in addition to providing current contact information, family members need to remember to:

- share information, if applicable, on drug use or other illegal activity. The details may provide necessary clues for the investigation.
- present theories. For instance, if the family believes that the missing person was murdered, and police do not, the family needs to bring its theory to the table.
- understand that investigators may have to keep some information private in a criminal investigation so as to protect the integrity of the case.
- treat members of law enforcement the way we all want to be treated—with respect.

But what if a missing person report was never filed in the first place? No matter how many years have passed, it is not too late. A report would certainly have aided in a quicker identification of "Grateful Doe." In 2015, this victim of a fatal car accident was identified as 19-year-old Jason Callahan from Myrtle Beach, South Carolina. The revelation came after his mother heard a local news broadcast and his brother saw the young man's digitally rendered facial reconstruction (prepared by the NCMEC) on a Facebook page.[5]

The page was created by two individuals, Lesha Johanneck and Alyssa Hillman. All they had to start with was a report that the young man and the car's driver (also killed, but identified) were heading south after attending a Grateful Dead concert at the Robert F. Kennedy Memorial Stadium in Washington, D.C., in 1995.[6]

According to a newspaper report, in 2015, Jason's mother told the police that her son had been a frequent runaway, and that she had not known where to report him missing. The man's half sister stated, "No one ever thought to report him missing because they thought he wanted to be missing." Jason's identification was solved solely because social media forums kept the story alive, posted photographs submitted by Jason's former roommate (who did not know his last name), and kept the then-unidentified man's image in the public eye. Only after the young man's mother contacted the administrators of the Facebook page, did the mother, after twenty years, file a missing person report on her son. Involving law enforcement, even at that late date, facilitated a positive DNA comparison.[7]

In the *New York Times* newspaper article "Grateful Doe is Identified 20 Years After Road Trip Death," Lesha stated, "I'm really stressing to news stations to please mention to people to check in on a loved one if you haven't heard from them in years or even a friend that just up and vanished. A lot of families are split apart and some don't even know if their family member is missing if they didn't have contact."[8]

GET THE CASE INTO NAMUS AND GIVE DNA

The "Grateful Doe" case shows that some missing persons' cases can be solved, even if done in unconventional ways. When families file missing person cases with law enforcement agencies, however, they initiate communication with investigators who are trained to search for missing persons. Similarly, when law enforcement agencies enter their cases into the NamUs System, they finally have effective ways to communicate with each other. In both instances, these open the avenues of communication which are more likely to bring the loved ones home.

The steps for families to take with NamUs are outlined in "How Families Use NamUs," in chapter 7, "NamUs: An Investigative Tool." Families also need to make sure that their investigators are familiar with the NamUs System. Occasionally a small agency, or one that is particularly short-staffed, may not know of this resource for long-term missing persons. If the investigator is receptive, explain the advantages of the missing and unidentified databases. Sometimes, as Paul and Ramona Blee indicated in "Marie Ann Blee—Someone Knows What Happened," in chapter 3, "Children: Helping to Bring Them Home," family members may have to educate law enforcement. In the unlikely case that the investigator is not interested, any member of the public can go to the NamUs website (under "Contact Us") and ask that the Regional Administrator for the state where the law enforcement agency is located contact the investigator directly.

Once a missing person's case has been entered into NamUs, preferably two or more familial DNA samples need to be sent for profiling to the University of North Texas Center for Human Identification. In order to submit the samples under a proper chain of custody, they cannot be sent by members of the public. Instead, collections are performed by law enforcement officers, medical examiner/coroners, or other medicolegal investigators, often in family members' homes. The process is simple, involving a quick swab of saliva from inside the person's cheek.

First-degree relatives, that is, parents, full siblings, or children, are best for Short Tandem Repeat (STR) comparisons. But, a half-sibling, aunt, uncle, niece, nephew, cousin, or grandparent may also be useful in limited STR comparisons, as well as in comparing Y-STR DNA (inherited through the paternal line) or mitochondrial DNA (inherited through the maternal line).[9] If no first-degree relatives are available, additional familial samples may be required, sometimes involving genealogical research to find them. For instance, since mitochondrial DNA is passed down through a common female ancestor, a family sample could come from the daughter or granddaughter of a half sister, providing the missing person and half sister shared the same mother. Family trees on genealogical websites can be very helpful in locating these extended families.

Familial DNA samples (as well as DNA taken from the remains of John and Jane Does), however, are *not* the same as those sent to databases such as Ancestry.com, which claims to provide information on a submitter's ethnicity.

As noted above, there are some cases in which no one ever filed a missing person report. Perhaps the family, like that of Jason Callahan ("Grateful Doe"), thought its long-term missing person would come home on his or her own. Or, perhaps the families were afraid to go to the police. Maybe the families did go, but the police, for whatever reason, did not file the reports. And then there are the cases of Jeanne Overstreet (as discussed in chapter 2, "Categories of Long-Term Missing Adults") and Teala Patricia Thompson (in chapter 4, "Proactive Police") in which, unknown to their families, the missing persons' entire files disappeared.

It is true, however, that some long-term missing persons do not want to be found. And, in some instances, investigators have been told by people they have found that they do not want the reporting family members to know where they are. As long as the persons are adults, law enforcement officials will respect their privacy. Usually, however, those who do not want to be found will agree to the investigators' requests to tell the reporting parties that they are alive and, presumably, well. That information, alone, can be comforting to family members.

Regardless of the circumstances, family members would do well to widen their networks by attending the Missing Persons Day events that are becoming increasingly popular in several states. Families also find it helpful to join support groups, where they can interact with others in similar circumstances. Where these events and groups do not exist, family members may consider starting their own.

MISSING PERSONS DAY EVENTS

Michigan and Arizona have led the way with Missing Persons Days. Other states and localities that jumped on the bandwagon include New York City, New York; Orange County, California; Harris County, Texas; and Cuyahoga County, Ohio as well as Colorado and Florida.

To get one started in your area, one or more law enforcement agencies need to take the initiative to get the ball rolling. Organizers then have to find space in a neutral venue (i.e., nonthreatening so families will feel comfortable), line up missing-person-related displays and people to man the tables, and coordinate workers to divide up the work of advance publicity, scheduling volunteer help, registration, and a myriad of other details. It is a big job, but police, civilians, and family members working together can, and do, make it happen.

All of the Missing Persons Day events are free and open to the public and offer opportunities for families of long-term missing persons to meet with investigators, ask questions, file or update their missing persons reports and give DNA to be profiled and entered into the NamUs System and additional national databases. The daylong events also include private roundtable discussions/support groups open only to family members (no law enforcement or media allowed), as well as dozens of display tables staffed by missing person resource groups to get the word out to the public about missing persons and unknown remains. Most of the events also end with a candlelight vigil.

For many family members, one-on-one meetings with investigators give them a private and secure place to have their questions answered.

Afterwards, many families have said that their missing persons' cases were taken seriously, often for the first time. For some, there were questions as to which agency has jurisdiction, as questions may linger as to where a missing person was last seen. At the statewide events, the hosting agency takes a new report from family members and then contacts appropriate local, state, or federal law enforcement agencies to work the case. If the assigned jurisdiction fails to follow up, the investigation of the case falls back on the hosting agency.

The following pages contain more information about the events in these localities:

• Michigan
• New York City, New York
• Orange County, California
• Arizona
• Colorado

Michigan

Michigan is credited with being the first state in the country to hold annual statewide Missing Person Day events, and they have become models for the rest of the country. Each May, since 2011, "Missing in Michigan Day" has been hosted by the Missing Persons Coordination Unit of the Michigan State Police, and there are no plans to stop in the future. At any one time, 4,000 to 5,000 people are missing in Michigan. Many of them are in the Detroit area, so Ford Field (an indoor stadium in Detroit) was chosen as the venue for Michigan's first event. Approximately 500 people attended, including the families of forty missing persons. During the following years, the Missing in Michigan event has grown and moved around the state—to Grand Rapids, East Lansing, Flint, and then back again to Detroit.[10]

Michigan State Police Sergeant Sarah Krebs, the event's founder and organizer, is proud to see the event flourish year after year. In email correspondence with the author, she stated that she hopes that long after she is gone, that the event, as well as support for missing persons, goes on. In her work with the State Police's Missing Persons Coordination Unit, Sergeant Krebs has interacted with hundreds of families of long-term missing persons and brought resolution to many of them.[11]

Prior to a recent Missing in Michigan Day event, the Michigan State Police announced the following on its website:

- Who Should Attend: Families and Friends affected by the mysterious disappearance of a loved one and the communities and organizations that assist to bring them home.
- What the Day Will Include: This event is a campaign to raise awareness of the issues and impacts surrounding missing persons in the state of Michigan. Families and friends affected by the unexplained and unresolved disappearance of a loved one will be recognized on this day. Officers will take tips on old cases and information on any new cases reported at the event. Local law enforcement will be on hand to answer the community's questions and concerns. Child ID kits will also be given out.
- A private roundtable discussion will be held from 9 a.m. to 11:30 a.m. for family members with a missing loved one. Carol Ryan from the National Center for Missing & Exploited Children®'s "Team Hope" will lead the discussion. Space is limited, please RSVP to reserve your seat.
- What to Bring: Families of missing persons are encouraged to bring at least two biological relatives (for family reference samples) of the missing loved one and any police reports, X-rays, or other identifying documents to update law enforcement digital databases. Families and friends should feel free to wear memorial T-shirts, bring posters and any literature to display and commemorate their missing loved one.
- Registration: Family members of missing people should preregister to ensure their loved one is commemorated.[12]

As can often be the case, many of the families come to Missing Person Day events with negative views of law enforcement. In Michigan, some family members spoke of reporting their missing person as long as twenty or thirty years ago, stating that no one ever called them back. Sergeant Krebs admits that, in those cases, an investigator or an agency along the way dropped the ball. She adds that for the Missing Persons Coordination Unit of the Michigan State Police, Missing in Michigan Day is a chance to make amends.[13]

Michigan has taken its annual Missing in Michigan event a step farther by supplementing it with a second event called Identify the Missing, held at the Wayne County Morgue. According to Sergeant Krebs, the Identify the Missing event is even more successful than the Missing in Michigan event since it targets the families who believe that their missing loved one is probably there. It also is easier to run and costs very little, but it still makes a huge impact on the missing persons' families.[14] Missing in Michigan also maintains a Missing in Michigan Facebook group where families are encouraged to use the site "to exchange information, post about your loved ones, and hopefully find some support from people that understand what you're going through or have been through."[15]

New York City, New York

The New York City Office of Chief Medical Examiner hosted its first ever New York City Missing Persons Day event on Saturday, November 8, 2014. According to the website of the medical examiner, more than 13,000 persons had been reported missing in New York City during the previous year. While most were promptly found, hundreds of people remained missing for sixty or more days. Meanwhile, the medical examiner's office was, and is, conducting a comprehensive review of its backlogged cases of unidentified remains.[16]

In an attempt to match some of the missing with the unidentified, nearly 100 family members of the long-term missing attended the city's first Missing Persons Day event where they were given the opportunity to discuss their cases with professionals and give information, including DNA. Volunteers were also on hand to provide emotional and spiritual support. Less than a year later, DNA provided by family members solved five of the cases of unidentified remains.[17] For one example, see "David and Rosemary: Face of a Friend," in chapter 5, "Civilian Searchers."

The event was held in partnership with the New York Police Department (NYPD) Missing Persons Unit, New York City Department of Health and Mental Hygiene, American Red Cross, and spiritual care volunteers from Disaster Chaplaincy Services, with support from the New York City Office of Emergency Management, New York City Human Resources Administration/ Department of Social Services, New York City Administration for Children's Services, National Center for Missing & Exploited Children® (NCMEC), the Center for HOPE, the National Missing and Unidentified Persons System (NamUs), and the Doe Network, as well as assistance from the Mayor's Community Affairs Unit and the Mayor's Office for International Affairs.[18]

Orange County, California

Orange County, California, based its event on the successes of Michigan and New York City. On October 3, 2015, the Orange County Sheriff's Department (OCSD) Coroner Division hosted its own Identify the Missing Day. Family members of persons missing in southern California were asked to give DNA and to bring in photographs, as well as medical and dental records, if available, of their missing persons.[19]

As posted on the OCSD website, the daylong event included one-on-one meetings with forensic professionals who collected the documentation on the missing persons and performed DNA cheek swabs on (preferably two) family members. Law enforcement officials were also on hand to file missing person reports and to gather and update information on older reports.[20]

Statistics supplied by the California Department of Justice and stated by the OCSD at the time included the following. It is important to keep in mind, however, that they only include the *reported* missing person cases and the unidentified remains that have been *found*.

Missing Persons Cases

• Total in Southern California, 9,974
• Total cases in California, 19, 897
• Total cases in the United States, 84, 274

Unidentified Persons (John/Jane Doe)

• Total in Southern California, 2,179
• Total cases in California, 3,121
• Total cases in the United States, 8,431[21]

Arizona

Arizona's first annual Missing in Arizona Day was based primarily on the success of Missing in Michigan Day. Arizona's event was held on the campus of Arizona State University, in Phoenix, on October 24, 2015, see figure 8.1. Statewide in scope, it was promoted in newspaper articles and on television, as well as on Twitter and through a Missing in Arizona Facebook page. Well-attended and well-received, it was sponsored jointly by the Phoenix Police Department, the Maricopa County Sheriff's Office, and the Maricopa County Office of the Medical Examiner.[22]

Family members who wanted to meet with law enforcement were encouraged to register in advance, although walk-ins were welcomed, as well. Reporting a missing person or adding to an existing missing person's report began at the check-in table. From there, volunteers escorted family members to a secured "counseling" area in the far end of a large open ballroom. In the counseling area, families sat down with law enforcement investigators from the Phoenix Police Department and discussed the circumstances of their missing person cases. Technicians were also on hand to perform the DNA swabs, and family photos were scanned, on the spot, for inclusion in missing person reports.[23]

Figure 8.1 Registration, Missing in Arizona Day Event. Arizona held its first Missing in Arizona Day event in October 2015. Signs on the registration table welcomed both English-speaking and Spanish-speaking participants. *Source:* Photo by author

Meanwhile, NamUs representatives entered the newly reported cases into national databases. According to the investigators, several cases appeared to be homicides, and most of the missing were long-term. The oldest case was from 1965, with others from the 1970s, 1980s, 1990s, and more recent, as well. One case was resolved even before the doors were open. Detective Stuart Somershoe of the Phoenix Police Department was one of the organizers and stated, "A call came from a mother from back East who couldn't attend the event but reported that her homeless, schizophrenic son was missing," he said. "The son was located alive and spoke to his mother on the phone."[24]

One of the families attending the Missing in Arizona Day event included the father, the father's girlfriend, the father's sister, and an uncle of Darian Nevayaktewa ("Walking on Snow"). The young Native American man had disappeared from a party on June 20, 2008, in the village of Kykotsmovi on the Hopi Indian Reservation in Navajo County, Arizona. Originally, Darian's case had been assigned to two investigating agencies—the Bureau of Indian Affairs (BIA) on the Hopi Reservation and the Federal Bureau of Investigation (FBI) in Flagstaff.[25]

Darian's family arrived in Phoenix on the morning of the event, after driving four hours from their home in northern Arizona, east of the Grand Canyon. After meeting with investigators (see figure 8.2), the young man's father explained in a conversation with the author that the journey had been very worthwhile, as, previously, no law enforcement investigator had taken the family's DNA or was receptive to the information they had to offer.[26] Without commenting on any specific cases, Detective Somershoe added, in email correspondence with the author, "A common theme was that the families had previously tried to file reports but that law enforcement wouldn't take the reports or gave them the run-around in some fashion."[27]

Figure 8.2   Family and Detectives, Missing in Arizona Day Event. Detectives at the 2015 Missing in Arizona Day event are shown meeting with a missing person's family. Attendees were given the opportunity to give their DNA, discuss the circumstances of their cases, and have their cases entered into the NamUs System. *Source:* Photo by author

In addition to receiving the attention Darian's case deserves, it is now publicly viewable in the NamUs Missing Persons database as MP-30248.[28] A poster with the man's photograph and description also has been posted on the Lost and Missing in Indian Country Facebook page, reaching thousands of new viewers. The chances of Darian's case being solved is much higher, now, than it had been before his family attended Missing in Arizona Day event. For more on the Facebook page, see "Janet Franson—Doing God's Work," in chapter 5, "Civilian Searchers."

At the daylong event, law enforcement investigators continued to meet one-on-one with families. Meanwhile, approximately two dozen family members who had already met or were scheduled for later in the day, got together in a separate room, comfortably arranged with banquet tables, coffee, and refreshments. There, without anyone else allowed in the door, they spent more than two hours visiting and talking with each other. "Many families expressed gratitude that someone had finally listened to them and felt validated," stated Detective Somershoe. "The feedback I got back from the support group was that it was a valuable experience, where families were able to share their experiences with others who have gone through something similar."[29]

In the main portion of the open ballroom were twenty or so tables staffed by various organizations with an interest in missing persons and unidentified remains. As is obvious from the list below, several of the presenters and their displays were specific to Arizona. See figure 8.3. The list is not comprehensive, but it includes the following organizations and agencies:

- Alzheimer's Aware
- Arizona Child Identification Program (CHIP, sponsored by the Arizona Masonic Foundation)
- Arizona Department of Public Safety Crime Lab, DNA Unit
- Arizona State University (information on Bachelor of Science in Forensics)
- Can You Identify Me? (a nonprofit dedicated to the unidentified)
- Coconino County Office of the Medical Examiner
- Colibri Center for Human Rights (advocates for families of persons who have died or disappeared on the Mexican border)
- Consulado General de Mexico en Phoenix, Arizona (Mexican Consulate)
- FBI
- Maricopa County Office of the Medical Examiner
- Maricopa County Public Health Department, Office of Vital Registration (provided information on obtaining death certificates)
- Maricopa County Sheriff's Office

Figure 8.3   Displays, Missing in Arizona Day Event. A Phoenix-area resident at the 2015 Missing in Arizona Day event stopped by a display prepared by the Maricopa County Office of the Medical Examiner. The panel on the left illustrates the identification of a Jane Doe as Shannon Michelle Aumock. *Source:* Photo by author

- Missal, Stephen J. (forensic artist)
- NCMEC, with child identification kits and information about Team HOPE
- NamUs and the University of North Texas Health Science Center
- National Runaway Safeline
- Pima County Office of Medical Examiner

- StreetlightUSA (serves girls 11–17 who have experienced sexual trauma)
- Various police departments from around the state[30]

Also available to the public were dog handlers, with their search dogs, giving training demonstrations, answering questions, and allowing their dogs interaction with anyone who wanted to pet them. Suggestions for next year's event included a kid-friendly area with babysitters for family members attending the support group. Also, due to the favorable attendance, the NamUs staff members were stretched thin. Next year's plans include NamUs training, in advance, for the investigators so they will be able to intake cases, if needed.[31]

Colorado

Colorado followed the states of Michigan and Arizona with its first annual Missing in Colorado Day event (and Missing in Colorado Facebook page), held in Denver on August 6, 2016. Individuals and organizations that put on displays included Families of Homicide Victims and Missing Persons (FOHVAMP), Northern Colorado Crime Stoppers Inc., Colorado Forensic Canines, Metropolitan State University of Denver Human Identification Lab, the Boulder County Coroner's Office, and Nevada Lodge #4 members of the Masonic Child Identification Program, as well as NamUs, the National Runaway Safeline, and the NCMEC. In addition, a revolving PowerPoint presentation displayed all of Colorado's *reported* unidentified persons, while forensic artist Cynthia Marsh and forensic sculptor Daniel Marion, Jr. PhD demonstrated their skills.

Members of several Colorado law enforcement agencies met privately with family members. So, too, did representatives from NamUs, including Melissa Gregory, whose duties as regional system administrator are discussed in chapter 7, "NamUs: An Investigative Tool." In email correspondence with the author, she said that one of her goals is to get a Missing Persons Day started in each of the states she represents. When asked how NamUs can assist, Melissa stated, "At a Missing Person Day event, I can collect DNA from family members, enter cases into NamUs, respond to family and law enforcement inquiries, provide information about NamUs resources, and/or essentially support the event in any way that is needed." She added, "Family members also have the opportunity to meet with others who are searching for their loved ones and discuss the unique, and heartbreaking, aspect of not knowing where someone is."[32]

SUPPORT GROUPS

As noted above in the section on Michigan, family members in that state are urged to seek support from the Missing in Michigan Facebook group. Many other social media sites reach family members, as well, but sometimes there is no substitute for meeting in person with others going through similar situations. Not all states have support groups where family members can meet each other in person, but Missouri and Colorado are ones that do.

Missouri Missing

Missouri Missing is a nonprofit organization that was formed in 2007 by two mothers after suffering the losses of their adult daughters. The group's members have several events throughout the year, and many of the participants have become close friends.

As posted on the organization's website, Missouri Missing's mission is to:

- provide a voice for the missing and unidentified who can no longer speak for themselves.
- provide support for families who have missing loved ones through an outreach program.
- educate and provide public awareness of the impact of missing persons in Missouri.
- work closely with law enforcement and provide as much assistance as possible to individuals and law enforcement agencies in the prevention, investigation, and prosecution of all cases involving missing persons in Missouri.
- distribute photographs and information of all missing persons in Missouri. Continue to restructure the organization to maximize the efficient use of resources available to families of the missing.[33]

Families of Homicide Victims and Missing Persons (FOHVAMP)

FOHVAMP is a support group for family members with a connection to Colorado, that is, either the family lives in Colorado or the family member went missing in, or was murdered in, Colorado. A handful of family members first met together, informally, in 2002, in a conference room in the Denver Public Library. For the next two years, they held potluck dinners in a café owned by one of the group's members. Eventually, FOHVAMP moved up to daylong annual meetings in comfortable facilities, complete with luncheons, presentations, and panel discussions.

The state has a backlog of approximately 1,750 unsolved murders (including persons missing under suspicious circumstances) dating from 1970, with nearly half of them in Denver. Throughout a six-year period, university students and both paid and volunteer researchers assembled background information on each case. The data came, primarily, from newspaper reports and has been compiled into a searchable database.[34]

NCMEC's Team Hope

NCMEC's Team Hope, established in 1998, is part of the National Center for Missing & Exploited Children® (NCMEC). Team HOPE's volunteers are mothers, fathers, siblings, and extended family members who have had, or still have, a child who is missing, recovered, or has been sexually exploited. According to the NCMEC's website, "These volunteers have demonstrated the ability to turn their personal tragedies into vital lifelines of support for other families. Team HOPE volunteers are passionate about extending their hearts, time, experience, knowledge and wisdom to those who have a missing or sexually exploited child."[35]

After Team HOPE volunteers go through training, they:

- help families in crisis with a missing, sexually exploited or recovered child as they handle the day-to-day issues of coping and/or searching for their child.
- help provide peer support, emotional support, compassion, coping tools, empowerment, and resources to families with missing, sexually exploited, and recovered children.
- help instill courage, determination, and hope in parents and other family members.
- help alleviate the isolation so often resulting from fear and frustration.
- remain honest, trustworthy, nondiscriminatory, and fair.
- respect the privacy of those with whom they are working.[36]

NCMEC also provides support through its Family Advocacy Division. The Division's services include:

- Intervention when a family is in crisis and needs immediate help with a missing, sexually exploited, or recovered/located child.
- Support for families of abduction and sexual exploitation survivors including helping them connect with other victims.

- Support, especially of an emotional nature, for endangered runaways and their families.
- Referrals to appropriate agencies and mental health professionals.
- Assistance with reunification from skilled mental health professionals to help reintegrate a recovered child back into the home during each stage of reconnecting and rebuilding.
- Support for siblings of victims.
- Assistance in locating federal, tribal, state, and local organizations available to help sexually exploited children.
- Support for law enforcement if local services are not able to meet a family's needs.[37]

WHEN IS IT TIME TO GO TO THE MEDIA?

When to go to the media is a question all families of missing persons, as well as law enforcement agencies, should ask. In its broadest definition, media refer to all forms of mass communication, from traditional newspaper articles and television broadcasts to innovative information-sharing and investigative techniques that include social media and websites. In cases of long-term missing persons, someone may know something. In those cases, the goal of media is to reach that person and convince him or her to contact law enforcement.

Print and Broadcast Media

A family member with a good working relationship with an investigator might want to discuss the idea of asking a crime reporter for a local newspaper or television network to cover the family's missing person's story. Getting the law enforcement agency's involvement is common courtesy and also gives the investigator and/or the agency's Public Information Officer (PIO) the opportunity to contribute. But, families can also make the contacts themselves.

Tie the story, time-wise, with the missing person's birthday or the anniversary of the date that he or she went missing. Some families like to hold a candlelight vigil on the anniversary and invite the press. Practically all print and broadcast news stories get out, and stay out, on the Internet, as well, continuously keeping the missing person's case in front of the public. Keep in mind the following:

- Contact the media several weeks in advance of an anniversary date.
- Mention the availability of photographs.
- Refrain from criticizing law enforcement.
- Share the family's perspective and maintain control. Not all of the reporters' questions need to be answered.
- To ensure accuracy, ask the reporter to confirm quotes.

If possible, develop a rapport with the reporter. An email request may initially be met with enthusiasm, but it may need to be followed up with a telephone call or a request to meet in person. When dealing with the press, family members need to walk the fine line they do with law enforcement, that is, be the squeaky wheel, but do not be a pest. If the story is a major one, some reporters may not keep the families' best interests at heart. Their bottom line is to sell newspapers, so it is important to only share the information that others should see. "Off-the-record" requests may be ignored.

There are appropriate times for law enforcement to go to the media, too. As mentioned in "Trooper Brian Gross and the Westmoreland County Girls" in chapter 4, "Proactive Police," even before the exhumation of the two Jane Does, the Pennsylvania State Police had publicized the upcoming disinterment. As a result, a possible family member of one of the unidentified persons immediately came forward. This allowed the police to proceed right away with a DNA comparison. When authorities are willing to go in front the camera and talk about their cases, it helps to reach people who may hold the one missing piece to unraveling a long-unresolved mystery.

In another case, in 1983 in Marin County, California, the body of an unidentified man had washed up on the beach at Point Reyes National Seashore. Keys and a key fob were found in the man's pocket. On the fob was the name, address, and telephone number of a business in Erie, Pennsylvania. At the time, an investigator in California contacted the business in Erie, as well as local authorities, but no missing persons either in Erie or in coastal communities in California matched the unidentified man's description. The remains were buried, and the keys and fob put into evidence. The case was filed away and forgotten until 2004, when a new investigator gave it a fresh look.

The new investigator contacted a reporter at the *Erie Times* who agreed to write a story. The resulting article "Keys Could Unlock Mystery Death" became a turning point in solving the case. Only one reader responded to the story, but that one man had been the missing man's college roommate. As he related, he and the man had been photographing on the rocky coast in

Monterey County, California, and the man fell off some rocks and was swept into the Pacific Ocean. According to an accident report filed with the Monterey County Sheriff's Office, members of the United States Coast Guard had spotted him floating lifeless in the water but were unable to recover his body. Although the "accident" was documented, the man had never been reported as a missing person. Today, his remains are back on solid ground, and he is buried with his family in Pennsylvania. Thanks to an investigator who took his case to the press, the man's own name, Joseph Coogan, is now on his grave.[38]

Social Networking

In addition to getting tips from law enforcement and from the public, newspaper reporters often pick up stories on missing persons and unidentified remains from social media. But the field of social media, itself, is exploding. Social media has become, perhaps, the single most effective strategy to reach as many people as possible. And, as shown in the solution to finding the identity of Grateful Doe (see "Communicate with Law Enforcement" earlier in this chapter), the people who are reached by social media may be the people with the answers.

In 2004, the same year that the *Erie Times* article led to the identity of Joseph Coogan, a student at Harvard University designed a networking tool that quickly spread to other schools. Named Facebook, the tool was opened to the public in 2006. By January 2015, the popular social media site had 1.59 billion global monthly active users.[39] According to the most recent demographical statistics compiled by the Pew Research Center, 62 per cent of the entire adult population in the United States uses Facebook, the most popular of the social media sites. This translates to 72 per cent of all adult Internet users. There are slightly more women than men on Facebook, and, as expected, more younger users than older users.[40]

Facebook is user-friendly, making it easy for anyone to start up a "Page" or a "Group." ("Pages" are public and available to anyone on Facebook, while "Groups" have more privacy settings.) As shown in chapter 5, "Civilian Searchers," Janet Franson, Ashley Kroner, and Megan McWilliams have been immensely successful with their Facebook page, Lost and Missing in Indian Country. So, too, has Jody Ewing with Iowa Cold Cases. Both pages have corresponding websites, as well. Some other state-oriented missing person Facebook pages include Wyoming LostNMissing, Missing in Arizona, and Missouri Missing. Another popular Facebook page is Coconino County Sheriff's Office Cold Cases & Missing Persons. Groups include "Missing in Michigan" and "Unsolved & Missing in Texas."

The NCMEC launched a Help ID Me page on Facebook which has a very large and engaged audience.[41] Awareness through social media is working, as children are being found and identified based on people coming forward after seeing facial images and descriptions. As NCMEC's Senior Forensic Case Specialist Carol Schweitzer stated in email correspondence with the author, "Social media is equipping the public to stand behind missing and unidentified child cases. We are constantly hearing from people asking how they can get involved in NCMEC and help on our unidentified child cases. We direct them to the Help ID Me Facebook page and ask them to read our stories, to share the photos and stories, and to help push them out to different sites on different social media platforms. Someone out there knows these children, and we just need to find that person."[42]

In addition to individuals, law enforcement, and federal agencies, family members are encouraged to launch Facebook pages and groups, as well, presenting a personal perspective as they raise awareness of their own missing loved ones. An example is "Angie Yarnell Still Missing and Loved." The Facebook page keeps the young woman in the public eye and was created by her mother, one of the founders of the support group, Missouri Missing.[43] Similarly, a Facebook group titled "Where is Gloria Jean?" was started by the daughter of a missing woman, Gloria Jean Baird, as discussed in "Undetermined," in chapter 2, "Categories of Long-Term Missing Adults."[44]

Other families may prefer to ask a non-immediate family member or trusted friend to be the Facebook "administrator." Some rules of thumb for whomever is in charge is set the privacy settings to "public" and to ask friends to "share" the posts and/or page or group. It is also important to avoid negativity and remain committed. If, for instance, a misguided person posts a negative message, the message can be "hidden" from the group or page and/or the person posting the messages can be banned via Facebook settings. Staying committed means keeping up with page discussion and messages and posting new information at frequent intervals.

Another popular social media site is Reddit. According to its Frequently Asked Questions page, "Reddit is (sort of) a play on words—that is, 'I read it on Reddit.'" The site is made up of many individual communities, also known as "Subreddits." Each community, such as "Unsolved Mysteries," has its own page, subject matter, users, and moderators. Users post stories, links, and media to these communities, and other users vote and comment on the posts. Through voting, users determine which posts rise to the top of community pages and, by extension, the public home page of the site.[45]

Similarly the online "bulletin board" Websleuths also contains several broad categories, with forums (specific subject areas), and threads or sub-forums (conversations on a topic), and individual posts. For instance, under the forum titled "Missing" are dozens of sub-forums from "Missing Person Resources" to "1970s Missing." At the time of this writing, the 1970s Missing sub-forum has more than 450 individual threads.[46]

Both Reddit and Websleuths have corresponding Facebook pages, and many of the Facebook pages and groups have their own websites. The Internet truly has created a worldwide web, as so many resources overlap and are interconnected. For the computer-savvy, individual websites on missing persons and/or cases of unidentified remains can also be an excellent way of organizing and sharing information.

In cases of recently missing teenagers, social media is one of the first places investigators will look. Parents should, too, as social media may be the only way to attempt to keep up with the whereabouts of their children, as well as their friends. Often, an accompanying photograph is the most recent one taken of the missing person. (If parents are not familiar with social media and do not know if their missing teenager has one of these social media sites, they might want to ask for guidance from one of the teenager's friends.)

Some investigators even have had luck creating Facebook accounts for fictional individuals and then attempting to "friend" that person in order to access his or her "wall" (the portion of a Facebook page that displays user updates and comments). Then, once on the wall, the investigators can read the same "chatter" that anyone else can read, which may include bragging about crimes committed, statements about conflicts between people, or threats of future crimes.[47]

While social media should be considered a resource for the public, law enforcement investigators actually consider it an investigative tool. Consider the case of a graffiti tagger apprehended a few years ago by the Bowling Green Police Department in Bowling Green, Kentucky. The tagger took photographs of his artwork and then posted them on his Facebook page. As Bowling Green Detective Tim Wilson stated to a reporter, "Solving crime is like putting together a puzzle, and sometimes Facebook might have an outside piece of the total picture of the investigation."[48]

DO I NEED A PRIVATE INVESTIGATOR?

At some point during any long-term missing person investigation, family members may consider hiring a private investigator. Like any other profession, there are very good private investigators and very bad ones, as well. The good ones will work hard on the families' behalf, while the bad ones will prey on the emotions of the vulnerable and promise work that they cannot deliver. A few words of advice include researching an investigator before hiring him or her. Make sure the investigator is licensed. Ask for references and check for unfavorable reviews with the Better Business Bureau and related agencies. There is no need to pay for services already being performed by the police.

The bottom line is that if families have kept open their lines of communication with law enforcement and have become their long-term missing person's advocate, they do not need anyone else.

Chapter 9

Gather Information, Document, and Do the Research

Often, after many years, a sibling or grown child of a long-term missing person will take up the search, only to find that once clipped and carefully preserved newspaper articles have, too, become lost. Maybe the family's only documentation of possible suspicious circumstances surrounding a loved one's disappearance was thrown out in a move. Or, maybe, one person lent a bulging envelope or box of papers to someone else and forgot to keep track of it. Maybe new questions are being asked about historic context, such as what else was going on at the time? Did a teenager disappear during the weekend of a rock concert? Did a recently named suspect show up in the police notes at the time?

Perhaps ten, twenty, or more years ago, someone was interviewed, but the new family member searching today does not remember, or never knew, the person's name. These names and the whereabouts of these people are worth looking up again. In cold cases, the passage of time often brings with it a change in relationships, as was seen in the case of Surette Clark in "Lost, Injured, or Otherwise Missing" in chapter 3, "Children: Helping to Bring Them Home." A former suspect's girlfriend, for instance, may talk more freely today than she would have years ago. For these and a myriad of other reasons, families will find it beneficial to reconstruct—and add to—their own case files. Sometimes all it takes to uncover a key piece of evidence is a fresh pair of eyes. Readers should be warned that historical research can be addicting, and, for many, the research is fun—like taking a trip back in time.

Included in this chapter are cold case resources that anyone can use in his or her research. The first step is to gather whatever is available. If information on the missing person is sitting on a shelf, open up the folder or file and see what it contains. Hopefully, there is a missing person report and/or other police reports, but there may also be newspaper clippings, lists of contacts, and photographs. Ask other family members what information they have. Write down or record their comments on whatever device is handy. Start a notebook or, if nothing else, take notes, make multiple photocopies, and spread whatever is collected among family members. Better yet, scan the documents and email them to others in the family. Put one person in charge of keeping everyone informed.

Then, start supplementing whatever is available by piecing together a paper trail. The process relies heavily on computers and the Internet, and not everyone has this access. But, in today's technological age, that is not an excuse. Everything on the following pages can be done on a computer in a public library. And, for those who need instruction, most libraries have classes, as well as helpful librarians.

First, however, is a note on genealogical research. Limited editions of some genealogical databases are available in public libraries. And, researchers with paid subscriptions, for instance, to Ancestry.com, already know that resources including some (but not all) city directories, newspapers, and obituaries are available to them online. Some of this same information is also obtainable on free genealogy websites including RootsWeb.com and FamilySearch.org.

Additional free resources are discussed on the following pages. Places to start include:

- people searches.
- ruling out proof of death.
- published records.
- public records.
- newspapers and obituaries.

PEOPLE SEARCHES

It would be ideal if family members and others could find their missing persons (or even the person's former associates) with a click of a mouse. With searches in the NamUs database, some, including the sisters of Paula E. Beverly, actually do. For more on her case, see "Paula E. Beverly: Found by Her Sisters" in chapter 7, "NamUs: An Investigative Tool."

Another missing person database that should be part of everyone's search is the Doe Network. The volunteer nonprofit organization was founded in 2000. It lists both missing persons and unidentified remains and is searchable geographically (by location), as well as chronologically (by year). As stated on the organization's website, "It is our mission to give the nameless back their names and return the missing to their families. We hope to accomplish this mission in three ways: by giving the cases exposure on our website, by having our volunteers search for clues on these cases as well as making possible matches between missing and unidentified persons, and lastly through attempting to get media exposure for these cases that need and deserve it."[1]

Sometimes the solution is as simple as Google. This search engine is so commonly known that it is easily overlooked when looking for missing persons. Consider, though, the case of Twylia May Embrey, a spunky and independent 17-year-old who left North Platte, Nebraska, in 1952. According to a researcher who contacted, years later, one of Twylia's closest friends and classmates, Twylia had confided (to the classmate) that she had been raped by her father. She had told him that that once she graduated from high school, he would never see her again. He never did, nor did anyone else in her family.[2]

After Twylia left, no one filed a missing person report. As is often the case, her parents simply assumed the teenager had run away and, one day, would return home on her own. When, after a few years, she had not returned, her parents sold their midwestern farm and drove to California to look for her. Eventually, but still before the days of the Internet, one of Twylia's sisters hired a private investigator who physically thumbed through telephone directories in hopes of finding her name. Two decades later, the young woman's great-niece and a team of online researchers continued the quest. During this third-generation search, a few selective keywords typed into Google revealed Twylia's past. But the discovery came three weeks after her death, so there was no long-hoped-for reunion by the woman's then-elderly sisters.[3]

Previously, and for more than a year, the researcher, Virginia resident Micki Lavigne, had creatively chosen various combinations of keywords which she repeatedly plugged into Google. In April 2006, when she typed in—only—Twylia's mother's maiden name, up popped an online obituary of a recently deceased woman. The deceased had Twylia's date of birth, but completely different first, middle, and last names. It did list, however, both parents' correct first names, as well as "Enberey," a misspelling of the family's last name. Included in the obituary was a photograph. When the woman's surviving sisters were shown the image, they saw a family resemblance.[4]

A sheriff's office detective then contacted the obituary informant and learned that the woman, who lived out her life in Boston (not California as the family had believed), had lived under a different identity for more than fifty years. Only on her deathbed did Twylia reveal her parents' names and state of birth to the informant, a close friend. Even that friend, though, did not know Twylia's real name.[5] Needless to say, the friend was very surprised, and the revelation of the missing young woman's half century with a changed identity and secret life answered many of her family's questions.

Google is free and is one of several, also free, search engines. (When using it, be sure to keep search terms focused, in quotes, as noted under "Online Research" in the section on "Newspapers and Obituaries" later in this chapter.) In addition, there are many databases that give names, ages, and cities and states of any name that is entered. Access to some of these databases is free and some charge a fee. Look up yourself to determine how much information is given and whether or not you believe the representative sample (i.e., your information) is accurate.

A free people-search website that often is helpful is Veromi, as it gives possible relatives of the person being searched and can aid in establishing family relationships.[6] One technique is to plug in search names, then figure out how the names of the people being searched overlap with others who are associated. The results can narrow down the names of people who share the same residence, particularly when a woman with a specific first name is "related to" or "associated with" a woman with the same first name and a different last name.

For example, if all that is known about the name of a married woman is her maiden name (i.e., "Emily Jones"), then entering that woman's maiden name will often reveal her married name (i.e., "Emily Smith"), as well. The opposite also is true. Entering a married woman's name (i.e., "Emily Smith") can reveal her maiden name (i.e., "Emily Jones"), which can lead to parents and siblings with the same (i.e., "Jones") name. Once names are sorted into family groups, they can be correlated into lists that may even include aliases. These names can then be traced through published and public records, as explained on the following pages.

Figuring out family relationships can also be attempted on social media sites such as Facebook, if the social media site of the person one is searching is public. People often list their family members under their "friends." And, if their "timelines" and comments are public, the family members' locations and activities can be revealing. In a recent cold case, the author participated in a search for an elusive witness for a possible upcoming trial. The family had used aliases and had moved nearly every year for two decades. But Reunion.com proved to be a gold mine, as the potential witness listed current contact information for herself and her husband, as well as the couple's grown children.

RULING OUT PROOF OF DEATH

When law enforcement investigators begin their searches for long-term missing persons, they first try to find the persons alive. If they cannot, then they attempt to determine if there is proof that the person is deceased. This hit home a few years ago when a detective friend of the author's was trying to track down a long-lost fugitive in a homicide investigation from 1970. The case had gone cold, and there was enough evidence to arrest the alleged murderer, but no one who had worked the case had been able to find him. In light of the man's criminal history, they speculated that he might be participating in a witness protection program. The author plugged the suspect's name and date of birth into the genealogical database Ancestry.com, and, two minutes later, found data that had been extracted from the man's Oregon death certificate. The new information led to more questions, but it allowed the investigation to move forward. Today, the case is closed—labeled "Exceptionally Cleared; Death of Offender."[7]

There are, however, more conventional ways to try to find proof of death of a long-term missing person. One place to start is with the Social Security Death Index (SSDI). FamilySearch.org, the genealogical website run by The Church of Jesus Christ of Latter-Day Saints, is (at the time of this writing) free and includes a name index to the database of the SSDI.[8] These are deaths recorded by the Social Security Administration beginning in 1962 and are current to within three years of one's search. Information provided includes the person's full name, date of birth, state where the person applied for his or her Social Security card, last place of residence, and date of death.

Obviously, members of a close-knit family would inform each other if they knew their missing person was deceased, but some families are estranged. What if someone in one side of the family is trying to find a person missing from another side of the family? If the missing person is known to be deceased, a date of death and last-known address can be very helpful in tracking down an obituary which often will lead to the names, addresses, and relationships of additional family members or friends. (See "People Searches" for the case of Twylia May Embrey and "Newspapers and Obituaries" for hints on accessing obituaries.)

If a person's name is not found in the Social Security Death Index, however, it does not necessarily mean that he or she is still living. For instance, the entered name has to match the SSDI records, so a search for "James T. Smith" could be under "James Smith," or "J. T. Smith," or even "Jim Smith." All combinations of proper-versus-informal names, and middle-initials versus no-middle-initials, may need to tried in a name-only search. However, if the date and/or place of death is known, or if the Social Security number is known, then just a last name and another piece of identifying information may be all that is needed to find the records of the deceased person.

In addition to the need to try name variations, the SSDI has some other limitations. Names can be missing if a funeral home or a relative failed to notify the Social Security Administration of a person's death, or if a spouse and/or dependents were not, or are not, receiving survivor death benefits. Keep in mind, too, that the index is of no use at all if the person one is searching for, like Twylia May Embrey, changed his or her name or identity. It is also of no use if no body has been found or, even if it has been found, not identified. And, as mentioned under "People Searches," it is important to repeatedly access the NamUs Unidentified Person database. Still useful, too, are coroner websites, the only resource available to Celeste Shaw, as discussed in chapter 6, "Celeste's Sister Sara: Found Alive in Mexico," in her pre-NamUs-day search for her sister.

Another reason that the Social Security Index may not reveal a missing person is if that person changed his or her Social Security number. This is practically unknown today but was more easily done in the past. In Twylia's case, her Nebraska family had retained possession of her original Social Security card. A check by law enforcement with the Social Security Administration did not show any activity on her number, leading to the possibility that she was deceased. But, no one, at the time, was aware that the young woman had applied for and was using a second card, with another number. After her death, a request for the second application to the Social Security Administration revealed the truth. In 1955, three years after Twylia left Nebraska, the young woman created her new identity with fictitious first, middle, and last names, as well as a false date and place of birth. Following a question that asked if she had ever applied for, or had, a previous Social Security number, she simply marked the box labeled "no."[9]

How do people searches and ruling out proof of death help in an investigation?

- First try to find the missing person alive.
- Then try to rule out proof of death.

PUBLISHED RECORDS

For the purpose of this book, *published* records are defined as items such as telephone books and city directories, that are privately published but available to the public in public libraries. (*Public* records, however, are documents created by government entities that receive public funds. Public records will be discussed on following pages.) Together, published and public records can establish and supplement a paper trail on the missing person and his/her associates, be used to obtain new information, and are helpful in placing the missing person (and associates) in historical context.

As to the telephone books, a whole generation has grown up without them. Not long ago, the way to find a telephone number, or order a pizza, was to flip open a telephone book. Most people, today, look up current numbers on the Internet. But what if the contact information for the person being searched is from twenty-five or thirty years ago, and modern search engines show that the number either does not exist or has been assigned to an unrelated party? The place to begin a paper trail is the old-fashioned way—by opening a telephone book or city directory and starting from the year being researched.

Reference sections of most public libraries have both telephone and city directories for their communities. Usually, these directories were issued annually and go back many decades. In addition to the telephone directory listings for residents and businesses, they include "yellow page" advertising, which aids in determining a business's location and whether it was open during a certain time period. When searching telephone numbers, keep in mind that widows often kept the names of their late husbands, both for continuity (the wife may never have been listed in first place) and for safety, so that it would appear that a man was living in the home.

Along with alphabetical listings of individuals, city directories often go a step further by including occupations and places of employment. Individual and business names are cross-referenced by telephone numbers and street addresses showing, for instance, every address in sequence, or in a city block or suburban subdivision. City directories provide the only way, prior to the beginning of the Internet era (mid-1980s), to figure out the names and addresses of everyone who lived in a particular neighborhood or on a specific street. This can be helpful, for instance, if a researcher wants to know who used to live next door, or what was the name of that long-gone burger restaurant/teenage hangout two blocks away from the missing person's home? The city directory will give the owner's or manager's names. By using one's people-searching skills, that person may be able to be tracked down and interviewed. There is no reason to fret about not remembering someone's name when the simple solution is to look it up.

If a personal library visit is inconvenient, or if the desired information is in another city or state, an online search for the website of a public library in the desired location will bring up a telephone number or an email option titled, "Ask a Librarian." When calling (or emailing) a library, the answer to "What was Brian Leopold's address in Seattle, in 1985?" would, most likely, be given immediately, while a printout of all Leopolds in the 1985 Seattle telephone book or city directory probably would require scanning and emailing or photocopying and mailing. What is important to remember is that the information still exists and is easy to obtain.

When contacting a librarian, it is important to:

- Make an appointment if the research is extensive. Assuming the library is local, introduce oneself and explain, firsthand, the information being sought. Some public libraries now offer "Book a Librarian" services for this very reason—to discuss research needs.
- Put as much information as possible into one's request, either in person, by email, or on the telephone. For instance, if all that one gives is a search name, and if there is a possibility that the name might be misspelled, then a cursory search by a librarian would not find it. Give enough details to make the librarian feel invested in the request and to allow him/her to expand the request, if needed.
- Remember that libraries have other patrons and budgets are tight. Be patient and offer to pay for research time and/or photocopying and postage costs. (At most libraries, however, at least one hour of a librarian's research time is free.)
- Try again, if one's request does not provide the results hoped for.
- Be sure to thank the librarians. They will appreciate it, and their help may be needed again in the future.[10]

PUBLIC RECORDS

It is easy to envy law enforcement investigators in their work, as they can access more specialized databases than are available to the general public. But, it is important to remember that the rest of us still have access to much of the same information, as most of it comes from public records, financed with public funds. For the investigators, data aggravators assemble the information and make it available, but savvy members of the public can find the same information on their own. It is just a matter of knowing where to look.

Public records can be found on the federal, state, and local levels, but they are not as public as they used to be. Drastic changes have occurred since the terrorist attacks on the World Trade Center, in New York City, on September 11, 2001. And, with additional concerns of identity theft, many government offices have redacted Social Security numbers and other previously available data. In situations where there has not been enough staff to remove the information, some of these records (including many divorce records) are no longer available to the public, at all.

Federal Public Records

Requests for information from the federal government can be made through the Freedom of Information Act (FOIA). When a FOIA request is made to the FBI, information can be obtained on organizations, businesses, investigations, historical events, incidents, groups, and even deceased persons.[11] Another federal agency is the National Archives. Divided into regions, this huge repository of information preserves and makes available federal records and files on court cases, employees, prisoners, and nearly everything imaginable that pertains to the federal government.[12]

As stated on the National Archive's website, only 1–3 per cent of its holdings are so important for legal or historical reasons that they are kept forever. However, the sheets of paper in the agency's holdings, laid end to end, would circle the earth more than fifty-seven times. In addition to paper documents, the archives has:

- more than 93,000 motion picture films.
- more than 5.5 million maps, charts, and architectural drawings.
- more than 207,000 sound and video recordings.
- more than 18 million aerial photographs.
- nearly 35 million still pictures and posters.
- and more than 3.5 billion electronic records.[13]

FOIA requests to the National Archives can help in the search for missing persons, as Colorado resident Roland Halpern discovered when searching for his uncle, Joseph Halpern. As discussed in "Natural or Accidental Deaths Most Likely" in chapter 2, "Categories of Long-Term Missing Adults," the 22-year-old graduate student from Chicago, Illinois, disappeared on a vacation with a his parents and a friend in 1933, while climbing a mountain peak in Rocky Mountain National Park.

Roland (Joseph's nephew) picked up the search after the deaths of the missing man's parents. And, he discovered that the Rocky Mountain Region keeps files on "Accidents in National Parks." When Roland submitted his FOIA request, the agency sent him "A Report on the Disappearance of Joseph Laurence Halpern," written on August 23, 1933, by John S. McLaughlin, former chief ranger of the Rocky Mountain National Park. The file also contained information on the Park's initial search, a photo of Joseph submitted by his parents, and a detailed colored map of six days of search routes.[14]

Included, too, was some of the Halpern family's correspondence, as well as new and startling information that Joseph may have walked away from the Park. The new information included a letter from an Iowa resident, in 1933, stating that Joseph had been part of a "rough crowd," as well as a statement from a family friend indicating that Joseph may have been seen in Phoenix, Arizona, in 1934. Additional references tied Joseph to the Civilian Conservation Corps (CCC) and hobo camps. Although not likely credible, Joseph was said to have worked for the Lewis Brothers Circus in Michigan in 1935. The FBI file also included his fingerprints from a postal savings account.[15]

In correspondence with the author, Roland stated, "Advances in technology have made old and almost forgotten documents available with a few clicks of the mouse. I have been amazed at what we have been able to uncover and hope that with today's resources our family will finally get closure so that my son doesn't have to wonder what happened to Joe."[16] At the time of this writing, Roland is still trying to solve the mystery of Joseph's disappearance, but the information that this family member has learned—by doing his own research—has stirred up new questions. Did Joseph fall to his death in the Park, as the park rangers believed? If so, why has no shred of clothing or any of his remains been found? Or, did he choose to walk away? If that was the case, did he tell his (now deceased) friend and hiking partner of his plan? If Joseph left on his own, where did he go, and why? What did he do with his life, and where did he spend his last days? These and other questions—for the families of the missing—do not go away.

State Public Records

Using Colorado as an example, the Colorado Open Records Act (CORA) defines public records in the Colorado Revised Statutes, 24-72-202 (6)(a) as all writings that are made, maintained, kept, or held by entities that are "for use in the exercise of functions required or authorized by law or administrative rule or involving the receipt or expenditure of public funds." Criminal records, however, are excluded. A "writing" is defined as "all books, papers, maps, photographs, cards, tapes, recordings, or other documentary materials, regardless of physical form or characteristics." Data that is stored digitally, including email, is included in the definition.[17]

Secretaries of states, departments of consumer affairs, and related statewide licensing boards and agencies (as well as locally recorded documents, see below) can be helpful when tracing people with name variations and/ or aliases, allowing investigators to compare signatures. Some states have searchable records, with PDF files of signed documents, viewable online. Some searches require a fee, while others do not. Documents that can be searched include:

* business licenses.
* trade name renewals.
* uniform Commercial Code (UCC) filings that include finance statements, security instruments, and tax liens.

Not to be overlooked are state archive collections, where Robert Gates (as shown in "John William Gates" in chapter 2, "Categories of Long-Term Missing Adults") found an obscure, but helpful, document. The archives vary from state to state, but their missions are similar, that is they preserve and make available records and information created by state (and local) governments. District court records of closed cases are public record, and they can contain a wealth of information including copies of arrest warrants, search warrants, and even the name of a person who bailed a prisoner out of jail. More recent court records can best be obtained by contacting the individual court where the original documents were filed, but older records usually are transferred to state archives. When researching serial killer Harvey Glatman, the author obtained Glatman's case file that covered court appearances from 1945 through the early 1950s. In the files were legal correspondence and even psychological assessments, as well as witnesses' names. One of those names led to an interview, in 2007, with one of Glatman's now-elderly assault victims.

Also publicly accessible are penitentiary and reformatory records. Colorado has records of its state convicts from 1871 through 1973, with additional mug shots to 1992. The Records of Convicts in the Colorado State Penitentiary Records collection makes for interesting reading and includes:

- name.
- date when convicted.
- date when received.
- crime.
- sentence.
- county.
- description (age, height, complexion, color of eyes, color of hair).
- occupation.
- place of birth.
- next of kin (names of parents and residence, marital status, name of wife or husband and where living).
- ability to read and write.
- signature.
- scars.
- additional remarks.
- mug shots.[18]

Local/County Recorded Documents

Recorded documents tie individuals and businesses to dates and places. A last name entered into the search field on a county recorder's website, for instance, can lead to new information on dates, addresses, family relationships, and even a woman's former name. Traditionally, the offices that housed recorded documents were located in courthouses, but where they are now and what they are called varies widely by locality. In some states, the offices use the name "register of deeds" or "clerk and recorder," but their functions are basically the same. Small rural communities may not have any online records at all, but access to their records can be obtained by telephoning, emailing, or walking in the door. Unless a previous courthouse building burned to the ground (and some have), the information, most likely, is still there.

Some local government websites are easy to navigate, while others leave plenty of room for improvement. One of the more user-friendly websites is the Maricopa County Recorder that encompasses Phoenix, Arizona. Its recorded documents date all the way back to 1871. The county has more than a hundred search types that include:

- bankruptcy.
- child support.
- divorce.
- medical liens.

- power of attorney.
- property.[19]

Name changes can be traced in the same way that title companies follow transfers of titles from grantors to grantees. For instance, entering a name in a document search can bring up all documents (depending upon the setting of parameters) that contain the same name. In many cases, a PDF file of the actual documents can be viewed online—complete with the names and signatures of both a husband and wife, or whoever signed the documents—as well as the names and dates of parties involved in related transactions. If "Delores H. and Gregory M. Abernathy," for example, owned property in joint tenancy, and then, a few years later, "Delores H. Manning" is the owner of the same property, chances are that Delores H. Abernathy changed her name to Delores H. Manning.

Many county clerks also keep records of marriages (and even premarital agreements), which is the most obvious way to search for a woman's maiden, former, or married name. These online listings, however, vary by state and even county. Marriage records in some local governments can be searched online. In Arizona, marriage records are kept by superior courts in the counties where the marriage licenses were obtained. Even if the records are not online, though, the local-level governmental offices are the designated repositories for these records, and their records remain in their books. The process for obtaining the information can be initiated with a telephone call or an email, although names of these offices vary by state. The best way to find them is with a Google search for a specific county, along with "recorded documents."

Police and Sheriff Records

Law enforcement records are preserved in various formats—from accordion files and notebooks, to microfiche and microfilm, to historical data that can be searched via computer through scanned images on DVD and/or new computerized records management systems. Members of the public can access closed cases by filing Open Records Requests with the specific law enforcement agency.

Families of long-term missing persons may want to submit an Open Records Request for the missing person report and case file with the investigating agency. Laws vary from state to state. Some law enforcement agencies will not honor a request if the case is unsolved, while others will redact portions of the file. Some information, however, is better than none, and family members can learn a lot about their loved one's case by achieving a sense of what has and what has not been done. This is particularly important if the family is considering hiring a private investigator, so the investigator does not waste time duplicating law enforcement's efforts. As in any records request, expect to pay a per-page fee for copying.

Coroner and Medical Examiner Records

Both coroners and medical examiners investigate suspicious deaths and establish cause of death and perform similar services, but a medical examiner also is a physician. Either way, their offices maintain autopsy reports, death certificates, photographs, information on next of kin, and tissue samples and slides. In some states, some of these records are open to the public, and in some states they are not. Coroners' and medical examiners' records are not protected by Health Insurance Portability and Accountability Act (HIPPA) privacy laws, as they would be if the records were filed in a hospital.

Probate Court Records

Probate Court records can be helpful in determining a person's heirs, along with the last-known addresses of the heirs. Sometimes, however, they include surprises. In research of convicted felon Harvey Glatman, the author came across a reference to the Harvey M. Glatman Memorial Scholarship, at Denver University. The motivation for the bizarre bequest (a scholarship named for a serial killer) was revealed in Glatman's mother's (Ophelia Glatman's) probate file, found in the Denver Probate Court. Ophelia had died in 1968 and left most of her estate to "memorialize" her only son, Harvey M. Glatman. The mother was well aware of her son's criminal record, as she wrote her will in 1960, one year after Glatman was executed for murder at the California State Prison at San Quentin. The probate file also revealed that Ophelia Glatman's nephew, now deceased, was the executor of Ophelia's estate, and he was the person who actually carried out the mother's wishes and initiated the scholarship.[20]

NEWSPAPERS AND OBITUARIES

Newspapers today are a lot different from the newspapers of twenty and thirty years ago. Back then, most people picked up a rolled paper copy from their front porch or driveway. The pages were bigger and there were more of them. In addition, the articles often were longer and more detailed. Today, many of us skim the online newspaper websites and may only read headlines or listen, on the Internet, to online video sound bites. Either way, though, newspapers are well-worth accessing when researching the time period in which a person went missing or when gathering data on a suspicious circumstance that might be related to the missing person's disappearance.

Some people mistakenly believe that the Internet is all-encompassing and that it can be used to access all newspapers. This is not true. Most of the freely accessed online newspapers only cover the recent years (those from the late 1980s or early 1990s, or later) to the present day. And, even to access them, requires some research skills. Practically all of the older issues are available through local libraries and on microfilm. Both ways to access newspapers are discussed, below.

Newspapers and obituaries aid the family member/researcher in the following ways:

- New information adds to historical context.
- Criminal cases of the past can be read as they unfolded.
- New witnesses (such as retired police officers and witnesses) and newly found next of kin can be found to contact and interview.

As previously noted, newspapers and obituaries can be accessed on genealogy websites, some of which require payment. But some of this online research can also be done for free. The easiest way to find newspapers from the past fifteen or twenty years is via "NewsBank: America's News," available through most local libraries. All that is needed is a library card for remote access from one's home or other location. The initial procedure is as follows:

- Access one's local public library's website.
- Click on "elibrary" or "research," or a similar listing.
- Find a list of databases.
- Click on "NewsBank: America's News." At this point, most libraries will request the card holder's name and library number. To keep the number handy, researchers have found that it helps to type it on a folder easily visible on the desktop of their computers.

If researching within a particular state, click on "USA" and then the state's name, either from the list or from the map. For illustrative purposes, consider the state of Tennessee. Clicking on "Tennessee" reveals (at the time of this writing) databases of twenty-eight publications, with the oldest, *The Commercial Appeal* from Memphis and the *Knoxville News Sentinel* from Knoxville, online from 1990. By clicking on the *Knoxville News Sentinel*, one can browse the newspaper on any specific date and also search for specific text, such as a person's name. Custom dates can be set to "before" a specific date or "after" a specific date, with the most recent or the oldest matches first.

An important rule of thumb that should also be used in Google searches and with other search engines is keep the search focused by using quotes. For instance, a search in the *Knoxville News Sentinel* for unidentified remains for all dates and without quotes yields a total of 184 articles. Showing up are all articles with the words "unidentified" and "remains" within the same story. In many instances, the words have completely unrelated meanings, such one sentence that reads, "An unidentified Oak Ridge teacher remains on unpaid leave."

Putting "unidentified remains" in quotes, however, narrows the number of results to only fifteen. But all of the articles, such as one with the phrase "unidentified remains were exhumed on July 10" relate specifically to the remains of unknown deceased persons. The same technique should be applied to a search for "Jim Jones." In order to search for people named "Jim Jones," it is important to put quotes around his name. Otherwise, every article with both "Jim" and "Jones" in the text will show up, not necessarily those specific to "Jim Jones."

If, however, a newspaper to be searched predates NewsBank listings or is not in NewsBank at all, then there are two solutions. When the author needed to access the *Blue Earth Post* from June 5, 1980 (as discussed in "The Unidentified Woman," in chapter 11, "Retrospect: Inside a Previously Cold Case"), all it took to obtain a scan was an email to a kind librarian at the Blue Earth (Minnesota) Community Library. Most librarians will do their best to honor these types of requests for people located outside of their service areas.

When a quick call or an email to a library, in reference to a specific news item and date, does not provide an answer, the alternative is to send off for newspapers on microfilm. Depending upon the size of the newspaper, a reel of microfilm will cover a couple of weeks or, perhaps, a month. Day-by-day accounts of a story, as it unfolds, can make for interesting reading. All that members of the public need to do is to contact their own local libraries and, through interlibrary loans, make their requests. They do not even need the name of a newspaper, as long as they give a location such as "Minneapolis, Minnesota" and a range of dates, such as "May 1 through June 30, 1980."

Figure 9.1 Microfilm Scanner and Computer. State-of-the-art microfilm scanners are available to patrons of many public libraries, including this one in Denver, Colorado. Images are displayed on the reader/scanner on the left, then individual pages can be scanned, for downloading or emailing, to the computer monitor on the right. *Source:* Photo by author

The reels of microfilm will then be sent to the library where the request originated. This can take a week or two, but it is worth the time when there is no alternative. Most libraries require that the microfilms be read on the premises, but some of these research facilities provide twenty-first-century microfilm readers/scanners, as shown in figure 9.1, that allow the content to be read, scanned, and then either placed on a thumb drive or emailed to one-self. An added plus is that unlike the articles in NewsBank, the microfilmed newspapers include accompanying photographs. The microfilmed newspapers also give all-important historical context as to what else was going on at the time that a person went missing or a crime was committed. This includes the weather, police notes, and items of interest such as notices of movies playing in local theaters.

New People to Interview

As the Virginia researcher learned when she found the obituary for Twylia (the Nebraska woman who changed her identity), these end-of-life stories can provide a wealth of information. For Twylia's family, the obituary opened up a secret life, but in most instances an obituary reveals names and contacts for the deceased person's next of kin. Finding an obituary, for instance, for a distant family member, can bring up contact information for that person's close friends and relatives. Perhaps one or more of them could provide insight into the missing person being sought.

Recent obituaries may be found online in a Google search, but they also are accessible along with articles on NewsBank. Obituaries also are included in microfilmed newspapers and often can be obtained through direct library contacts, all for free. An important distinction to be made, however, is that traditional obituaries were written by newspaper reporters who followed a formula-style of writing. The information on the deceased came from a funeral home where an employee obtained it from the person listed as the informant on a person's death certificate. Today's obituaries are treated by newspapers as paid advertisements. They print what people pay them to print. The good news is that these newer obituaries usually are written by family members and may include much more detailed information than in former years. But, they can also contain errors or emissions.

What else can be gained by this time travel into the past? If a family member and/or investigator wants to follow up on a crime involved in a missing person's disappearance and has found one or more newspaper articles on the case, it is important to make a list of all names that are noted. The list should include any police officers or detectives on the scene, as well as the reporter who wrote the story. It is equally important to add everyone who was mentioned in the article, then access databases and websites, as well as published and public records, to find current contact information. All of these people including the detectives and the reporters can then be contacted, as they may have additional information or something new to add that will aid in finding the missing person.

Chapter 10

Pitfalls and Legalities

Throughout time, people have been fascinated with the unknown. According to *The Encyclopedia Britannica*, however, "Modern spiritualism" began in Rochester, New York, in 1848, when two sisters were said to have heard knocking sounds in their home. The women then claimed to "communicate," as mediums, with the originator of the sounds, whom they professed was the spirit of a murdered peddler. Before long, Spiritualism spread all over the country and even overseas, with men and women alike who "channeled" conversations between the living and the dead.[1]

For some, the spiritualist movement became a parlor game, and the "medium" was replaced with the Ouija Board. This was (and is) a board game with letters of the alphabet and a "planchette" (a small indicator) on which each player alternately places his or her finger. When a player asks the board a question, that person's unconscious mind supposedly causes the indicator to glide from letter to letter, spelling out the answer. The author briefly owned a Ouija Board as a child, until her father, a scientist, banned it from the family home.

PSYCHICS: A PITFALL TO AVOID

The nineteenth-century medium became today's psychic. The *Merriam-Webster* dictionary defines a psychic as "a person who has strange mental powers and abilities such as the ability to predict the future, to know what other people are thinking, or to receive messages from dead people."[2] Those who are skeptical of psychics may see them as entertainment, at best. Others, however, including most law enforcement investigators (as well as the author's father), consider them time-wasters and even exploitative shysters.

Although there may be some self-professed psychics who sincerely want to help families find their missing persons, police say to let law enforcement officials handle the investigations. A word of advice is to avoid publicizing one's own contact information on a missing person's flier or when seeking tips. Refer anyone with information to contact law enforcement and give the detective's telephone number instead. That way, family members will be shielded from people who may ask for exorbitant amounts of money while, in most cases, delivering little in return.

It should be noted that the registration materials for the 2015 Missing in Arizona Day event stated, "We remind you that the Missing in Arizona organization does not condone the use of psychics, mediums, or supernatural communicators in missing person cases." Pertaining to this discussion, Detective Stuart Somershoe, with the Phoenix Police Department, added in email correspondence with the author, "A secondary category can be 'search groups' that claim to be nonprofit but then start hitting up the families for 'expenses' for the search. Some of these groups are populated by the mentally unstable, wannabees, and criminals who put families through unnecessary grief and financial expenditure. It's important to note that the members of these groups are not background-checked and can pose unforeseen dangers."[3]

DON'T GO NEGATIVE

Another pitfall to avoid is allowing one's relationship with law enforcement to become toxic during the investigation. Families are stressed and overwhelmed and this sometimes translates into anger and hostility toward officers and detectives. According to Detective Somershoe, "Families are desperate for answers and often feel the investigator doesn't care or isn't doing enough. I've seen a number of investigations get derailed when a family turns against law enforcement and expends time and energy complaining to media or politicians about the case. This rarely results in anything positive."[4] For more on this topic, see "Communicate with Law Enforcement" in chapter 8, "Become Your Long-Term Missing Person's Advocate."

LEGAL ACTION

The learning curve for families dealing with long-term missing persons is huge. First, family members have to get through the initial phase of filing a missing person report, communicating with law enforcement, and, if the missing is a child, communicating with the National Center for Missing & Exploited Children® (NCMEC). Then they just have to try to emotionally hold the rest of their family together. After that, family members join search parties, make telephone calls, and get the word out with fliers or social media. Before they know it, they have become their missing person's advocate—searching databases, getting their DNA into NamUs, and sharing experiences with other families in similar situations.

But what happens if years go by and the missing person is thought to be deceased? What happens to a missing person's property? Can a spouse remarry, and who is legally responsible for the missing person's children? These and other questions fall into uncharted territory, and most families are at a loss on how to proceed. The remainder of this chapter discusses:

- Legal Presumption of Death
- Civil Lawsuits

Legal Presumption of Death

When a person has been missing for several years, his or her family is left in limbo. Depending upon the circumstances of the person's disappearance, it may be time to face the possibility that the person is deceased. As noted in chapter 6, "Celeste's Sister Sara: Found Alive in Mexico," after years of searching for her sister's remains, Celeste stated, "At some point I had to stop and just admit that maybe Sara was in Mexico and fell off a cliff." Celeste was, in fact, in the process of obtaining the final document she needed for her sister's legal Presumption of Death when she received word that Sara had been found alive. Also see chapter 6 for more on guardianship of the mentally ill.

A medical examiner/coroner must issue a death certificate for the long-term missing person in order for his or her family to collect on life insurance policies, to remarry, and to settle legal issues such as disposition of property. The certificate will not be issued without a Presumptive Death being established first by a formal legal proceeding which can only be commenced after a period of years that varies from state to state. This proceeding requires submission of evidence to a court of all efforts to locate the missing person.[5]

Another advantage of the court order and the death certificate is the ability for family members to file for survivors' benefits with the Social Security Administration. According to Administration policy, families are urged to file a claim shortly before a person has been missing for seven years. The Social

Security Administration's requirements for Legal Presumption of Death state that:

- the evidence establishes that the missing person has been absent from his or her residence and has not been heard from for seven years.
- the presumption arises without regard to the reason for the absence. (In some cases, however, such as proof that the missing person is a fugitive, presumption of death can be rebutted in court.)[6]

To open a presumptive death case, a formal legal proceeding must be brought before a court with jurisdiction over probate matters, that is, the segment of the judicial system primarily charged with handling wills, estates, conservatorships, and guardianships. In an interview with the author, Denver probate attorney Joseph K. Reynolds stated, "The objective in a presumptive death case is to present the court with sufficient evidence that all reasonable efforts have been made to find the missing person." He added that families do not need to engage an attorney, but, if they do, having an attorney can help to assure a judge that a thorough and reasonable search has been conducted.[7]

One of the first tasks in the search is to identify and contact all of the missing person's next of kin, friends, and acquaintances. Other contacts to be made include previous employers, co-employees, landlords, health care providers, and law enforcement, as well as county coroners/medical examiners. This is where people-searching skills come into play, as the names and current contact information of all of these people, as well as the information they may, or may not, have, needs to be documented.[8]

Obviously, filing a missing person report with law enforcement helps to satisfy the court that the missing person "cannot be located by diligent search and inquiry." It also documents that the missing person's absence was continuous and without explanation, and that those most likely to hear from the missing person have heard nothing during the time he or she has been missing. Once the process is complete, the missing person's estate can then be distributed as if the person was deceased.[9] Specific laws on inheritance and remarriage, however, vary from state to state.

"Imminent peril," such as a plane crash in which all on board are presumed dead (as in the September 11, 2001, attacks on the World Trade Center in New York City), expedites the issuance of death certificates for those whose remains have not been found. What happens, though, if the missing person is declared dead and then returns? It does not occur often. But, as noted in "Voluntary Disappearances," in chapter 2, "Categories of Long-Term Missing Adults," after the requisite number of years the husband of Brenda Heist had her declared dead, then he collected on her life insurance, moved on with his life and remarried. His remarriage likely is valid, but initial news reports were unclear as to whether or not the insurance company will sue (or has sued) to collect the life insurance money from Brenda.

There are other documented cases that do illustrate the complexities of a missing person declared dead who then returns. One was John Burney, a Helena, Arkansas, man on the brink of financial collapse. He was involved in a head-on collision on a bridge. Without anyone seeing him, he slipped over the bridge railing, climbed down a piling, and swam downstream. Then he walked into the state of Mississippi and took a bus to Florida where he assumed a new identity, remarried, and had a child. His first wife and his company collected on a large amount of life insurance.[10]

After a stated amount of time had elapsed, Burney returned to Arkansas to visit his father. According to the *Straight Dope Science Advisory Board's* article "What Happens When Someone 'Legally Dead' Shows Up Alive?" the court found that the man's beneficiaries did not have to return the money. But, Burney himself was not so fortunate. The court ruled his actions were fraudulent and entered judgment against him for $470,000.[11] Some well-known people who have been declared dead include trade union leader Jimmie Hoffa who has been missing since 1975 and American teenager Natalee Holloway, missing in Aruba since 2005.

In some cases, family members may have reasons to believe that their long-term missing persons are still alive, even though they are nowhere to be found. In those cases, and if the persons left behind estates, conservators can take legal actions to manage the missing persons' properties.[12]

Sometimes the lengthy court proceedings can bring resolution to family members, but they can also be emotional letdowns. A few years ago, after the finalization of a declaration of death for a woman who was missing for eleven years, a victim advocate related that the victim's mother and sister broke down sobbing in the courtroom.[13]

Civil Lawsuits

Chapter 3, "Children: Helping to Bring Them Home," "The Case of Curtis Huntzinger" relates the recovery, in 2008, of the 14-year-old boy's remains. His killer was tried, convicted, and sentenced to Folsom State Prison in Folsom, California. But, even in prison he was not immune from further legal action. A few months later, Curtis's mother, Nancy Huntzinger, filed and won a wrongful death judgment against her son's murderer. Unlike the criminal case that punished the killer for his crime, Nancy's civil case sought monetary compensation. Whether or not the prisoner or his eventual estate will be able to pay, however, remains to be seen.

In making the case for Nancy's damages, her attorney told the court that she had spent more than eighteen years not knowing what fate had befallen her son, not knowing whether he was alive or dead. Damages were estimated at $200,000 for each of those years, for a total of $3.6 million and attorney's fees. That estimate, the attorney told the court, was conservative. In offering his condolences, Judge John E. Feeney, stated, "Clearly, no monetary judgment can compensate you for the loss of your son."[14]

Collecting on much or all of the judgment is unlikely, but Nancy took an appropriate action. Most members of the judicial system agree that this civil remedy is underutilized, even though there are strict rules on who can seek recompense. In broad terms, wrongful death lawsuits may only be brought by a personal representative of the decedent's estate. These include the surviving spouse, domestic partner, children, and issue of deceased children "who would be entitled to the property of the decedent by intestate succession."[15] Filing of these civil suits also have short time limits, called statutes of limitations. The procedures, as well as the statutes of limitations, vary from state to state, and families will need an attorney.

Some cases directly apply to persons still missing, even long-term. Normally, statutes of limitations are only two or three years, but there are ways to delay the date that they begin. Children, for instance, cannot use up their specified time limit while they are still minors. Consider the hypothetical case of a 5-year-old child whose father kills the child's mother and causes her to go "missing." The clock will not start ticking on the statute of limitations until thirteen years later, when the child turns 18. Then, and only then, can the "child" bring a wrongful death lawsuit against his or her father.[16]

If, in this hypothetical case, the child's mother was still missing when the child reached the age of 18, crucial information to help find the missing mother could potentially be revealed during the discovery process of the civil proceeding. In addition, information learned through depositions (when witnesses are compelled to testify) would be evidence in subsequent criminal proceedings.[17]

Even in cases where criminal acts are strongly suspected but trial evidence does not rise to the level of prosecution, families can pursue civil action. Most people are familiar with the criminal trial of former actor and football star O.J. Simpson, charged with the murder of Nicole Brown Simpson (his wife) and Ron Goldman. In 1994 and 1995, the daily courtroom drama captivated television audiences for eleven months, as witnesses and a high-profile defense team became household names. Lead attorney Johnnie Cochran made the often-quoted remark, "If it doesn't fit, you must acquit," after handing Simpson a pair of gloves similar to one found at the murder scene.[18] Although many other variables also were under deliberation, the jury did acquit Simpson of both murders.[19]

But, the verdict did not stop the Brown and Goldman families from seeking justice for their loved ones. After the conclusion of the criminal trial, they filed a wrongful death lawsuit in civil court in Santa Monica, California. Unlike criminal court, in which the burden of proof—beyond a reasonable doubt—has to be unanimous, a civil court decision only has to show a preponderance of the evidence. In the civil case against Simpson, only nine of the twelve jurors needed to agree to the verdict. All twelve jurors, however, found him liable in the two murders.[20]

Although Simpson was freed on the criminal charges for murder, he has since been charged for other felonies and is currently serving time in the Lovelock Correctional Center, a treeless prison in the Great Basin desert of Nevada.[21]

Chapter 11

Retrospect

Inside a (Previously) Cold Case

For thirty-five years, the family of a missing teen from Bay City, Texas, had no idea where she was, or even if she was alive. Then, in March 2015, the long ordeal was over when a previously unidentified homicide victim, buried in Blue Earth, Minnesota, was identified as Michelle Yvette Busha. As her father, Don Busha, told a television reporter a few months later, "She was the rebellious type. She wanted her freedom, and she left." Meanwhile, Don had kept his same address and telephone number, in hopes that his oldest daughter would find her way home.[1]

According to the news report, Don wanted to live with that hope, but when his daughter stopped calling, he feared that something had happened to her. On May 9, 1980, he filed a missing person report with the Matagorda County Sheriff's Office (in Bay City, Texas) and began grieving. "Originally I was a wreck," he said. "And, one day I woke up to the fact that I still had a wife and I had other children that needed me."[2] Michelle's six siblings grew up, and life went on.

In 2007, Don and his second oldest daughter were asked by an officer at the Matagorda County Sheriff's Office if they would give their DNA. Lab technicians swabbed saliva from inside their cheeks. The family's willingness to be proactive led to the resolution of this long-term-missing-person case.[3]

BLUE EARTH JANE DOE

Meanwhile, 1,200 miles to the north, in the small town of Blue Earth, Minnesota, efforts were being made by a caring community to identify an 18-year-old woman whose body had been found in a drainage ditch on May 30, 1980. Her remains, which would eventually be identified as Michelle's, lay in Riverside Cemetery, under a stone that read:

UNIDENTIFIED WOMAN
FOUND MAY 30, 1980 NEAR
INTERSTATE 90, EAST OF BLUE EARTH

Family members of long-term missing persons need to know that when an individual (often a member of the public) takes so much of an interest in a John or Jane Doe that solving that person's identity becomes part of, and a priority in, their lives, the unidentified person *will*, eventually, regain his or her name. Some refer to these dedicated volunteers as victim advocates, while others may use the term guardian angels. In Blue Earth, Deb Anderson was that person, but the "unidentified woman" would lie in her grave for nearly two decades before Deb moved to the Minnesota town. Families of other long-term missing persons may, too, have an advocate watching over their loved one right now.

But, what brought the Texas teen to Minnesota? What led to her homicide and the confession of her "killer?" Most importantly, has justice been served? The case is closed, but these questions may never fully be answered. The case file, however, is now an open record, allowing the public a glimpse into its past. It is hoped that by reflecting on the Blue Earth/ Michelle Busha case, families with other long-term missing persons will have a better understanding of the changes in technology, as well as the challenges of unidentified-person cases that overlap several decades.

Prairies of Minnesota

The prairies of southern Minnesota typify the Upper Midwest. One by one, small cities and towns stretch out over an agricultural landscape connected by an asphalt ribbon—Interstate 90—that passes south of Rochester, on to Alberta Lea, and then to smaller communities to the west. One of these, in south-central Minnesota, is Blue Earth, the seat of Faribault County. The county's population of approximately 14,000 has dropped significantly in recent years as large farms are being swallowed up by family farms, and the younger generation is moving away.

The town of Blue Earth is home to 3,300 of the residents and was named for the blue-black clay in surrounding riverbanks. Also setting the town apart is a nearby section of Interstate 90—the very last portion of the entire 3,081-mile coast-to-coast highway between Boston and Seattle to be completed. To commemorate its formal opening in 1978, a golden stripe was painted from shoulder to shoulder. Crowds of national, state, and local officials, as well as area residents, gathered for a ribbon-cutting and a flyover by the Minnesota Air National Guard. To capitalize on tourism, the town's businesses erected a fifty-five-foot statue of the Jolly Green Giant, mascot of General Mills. The new route also carried the promise of faster and safer travel.[4]

A Teenager Leaves Texas

The following year, in December 1979, 18-year-old Michelle left her father's home. At the time, the Eagles and Waylon Jennings topped the music charts, and the Broadway musical *Hair* had just been released as a movie. Fifty-two Americans were held hostage in Iran, Jimmy Carter was the US president, and double-digit inflation had spiraled out of control. Michelle continued to travel, and she telephoned her family from places as far north as Indiana. But Michelle's call in early May 1980 was her last. In Texas, at the Matagorda County Sheriff's Office, investigators checked a number of leads, but none were successful in discovering the young woman's location.

It is not known if Michelle was a Grateful Dead fan, but *if* she, like many runaways from the era, had been following the rock band, it, too, worked its way north. Early May 1980 concerts included Ithaca, New York (south of I-90), Glens Falls, New York (north of I-90), and Boston, Massachusetts (on I-90). According to the Blue Earth Jane Doe case file, Michelle's "killer" claimed to have watched her, at the Bricelyn exit, get out of a blue van that was heading west.[5]

Perhaps the driver and the van's other passengers intended to camp nearby, then head south to the next Grateful Dead concert on May 29, 1980, in Des Moines, Iowa. Or, the concert-goers could have been on their way to the June 7 and 8, 1980, concerts in Boulder, Colorado. Also likely, Michelle could have been riding with "Deadhead" fans who planned to follow I-90 all the way to Spokane and Seattle, Washington. Concerts were held in both of those cities, that year, in mid-June. All that is known for certain is that the body of the young woman, now identified as Michelle, was found strangled to death near I-90, east of the town of Blue Earth.[6]

The Unidentified Woman

When the town's residents opened the *Blue Earth Post* (their local weekly newspaper) on June 5, 1980, they were shocked to read that a farmer had found a young woman's nude body in a drainage ditch, close to the Interstate. In the quiet farming community, murders were few and far between. "Who Was She?" asked the headline. The story continued:

> A macabre tale of death has been unfolding in Faribault County throughout the past week. It began, according to daily newspaper, radio, and TV reports, with the discovery of the naked body of an unknown woman in a drainage ditch in rural Blue Earth last Friday.
>
> Just who the woman is, or was, remains a mystery.
>
> We're still at a dead end right at this moment," remarked a spokesman for the Faribault Sheriff's Dept. Wednesday morning, who admitted efforts to identify the victim were getting a bit frustrating. "We're sitting here with a body and nowhere to put it," he said.
>
> Gilbert Schewe of rural Blue Earth found the body Friday morning, May 30, in a ditch near his farm on County Road 109 east of Blue Earth. It had a small rope around its neck and the head appeared to be shaved except for a small patch of hair.
>
> The woman was thought to be between 25–35 years old, about 5'3" and 128 pounds. The body was badly decomposed and was taken to Ramsey County for an autopsy.
>
> Strangulation was cited as the cause of death. The body was probably dumped, officials say, between May 25 and May 28, either directly from County 109 or directly from I-90 into the ditch, and then it floated the three-fourths of a mile downstream after heavy rains last week.
>
> Officials are using fingerprints and dental records in attempting to make positive identification.[7]

The weather had been hot and humid, with recent heavy rains. On May 30, as soon as the farmer reported the body, Faribault County Sheriff Roger Fletcher and deputies Jerry Kabe and Jerry Anderson arrived on the scene, along with Captain Vergil Karl and Trooper Richard Hull of the Minnesota State Patrol, see figure 11.1. They called the Minnesota Bureau of Criminal Apprehension (MNBCA), as well as five members of the Blue Earth Fire Department who carefully extracted the victim from the debris. The small rope or cord was still around her neck. Because of the decomposition, visual

Figure 11.1 Crime Scene, "Blue Earth Jane Doe." In 1980, near the town of Blue Earth, Minnesota, a farmer found an unidentified woman's body in a drainage ditch. Shortly afterwards, members of the Minnesota State Patrol and the Faribault County Sheriff's Office arrived on the scene. *Source:* Photo courtesy of Sheriff Michael S. Gormley, Faribault County Sheriff's Office

identification was unlikely, and investigators were only able to obtain one fingerprint.[8]

No one had a clue as to where the young woman had come from or who she was. Her body was transported to St. Paul, Minnesota, where, on June 2, 1980, Dr. Michael B. McGee performed an autopsy at the Ramsey County Medical Examiner's Office. Medical Examiner McGee also prepared a dental chart, noting that the victim's wisdom teeth were in the process of erupting, and two of her teeth had, at one time, been extracted, most likely to provide space for braces. The autopsy report also stated that samples of the victim's pubic and scalp hair were collected and turned over to the MNBCA.[9] (The MNBCA, a statewide agency, assists local law enforcement in Minnesota with criminal investigations.)

In an attempt to make an identification, the Faribault County Sheriff's Office highly publicized the story. News of the victim spread from the local newspapers, radio, and television to media outlets in the cities of Minneapolis and St. Paul. The *Associated Press* even ran a story that was read across the country, although it is unknown if it was seen by anyone in Bay City, Texas. As a result of all the publicity, the Sheriff's Office received dozens of reports from other jurisdictions, as well as calls from concerned parents who were unaware of the whereabouts of their daughters.[10] Chief Investigator Kabe, who had been with the Sheriff's Office since 1963, stated in a telephone conversation with the author that he had ruled out each lead with comparisons of dental records.[11] Meanwhile, Medical Examiner McGee refrigerated the young woman's body in the Ramsey County Morgue until August 1980, when her remains were returned to Blue Earth, then buried, at county expense.[12]

During the early 1980s—and long before the forensic use of DNA—occasional reports of missing young women continued to trickle in to the Sheriff's Office. Investigator Kabe recorded some of these names in his reports, but others got jotted down (probably by whoever answered the phone) on scraps of paper and backs of envelopes. No master list or spreadsheet, if there was one, has survived in the case file. At the time, dental records and the one fingerprint were the only tools at Kabe's disposal.[13]

Investigator Kabe also sought the young woman's killer. In 1983, he followed what appeared to be a good lead when he traveled to Montague County, Texas, to interrogate jailed inmate Henry Lee Lucas. Now-deceased, the serial killer had admitted to murdering many women, including a young female hitchhiker on I-90. Lucas, however, told Kabe that if the victim did not have twenty or thirty stab wounds, then she was not one of his.[14]

At the same time that Investigator Kabe was in north central Texas, investigators at the Sheriff's Office in Matagorda County, along the Gulf Coast, were actively working Michelle's missing person case. In 1984, they compared the teen's dental records with two sets of unidentified remains—one from a body found in New York State and another from Frederick, Maryland. As noted in a timeline prepared by investigators in Matagorda County and incorporated into the Faribault County Sheriff's Office's Blue Earth Jane Doe case file, neither was a match.[15]

Back in Blue Earth, leads on the victim's identity continued to trickle in. In 1986, Investigator Kabe was contacted by the NYPD concerning a missing young woman named Jackie Lerman. According to her half-brother Phil Lerman, in a telephone conversation with the author, she suffered from schizophrenia and had run out of her Rockaway, New York, home, with no coat and no money on a cold winter night in 1979. She was last seen boarding a train bound for Manhattan. Her family never heard from her again.[16]

Investigator Kabe then requested Jackie's dental records to compare with his victim's. Two dentists concluded that they, likely, were a match. Kabe believed that Jackie was the Jane Doe, but a Medical Examiner pointed out some minor differences. As a result, Jackie Lerman was ruled out as Blue Earth's Jane Doe.[17] For many of the residents of Blue Earth, the unidentified victim was simply forgotten. Yet, her death touched the hearts of a few, including a woman who wrote to the Faribault County Sheriff after reading her local newspaper. She stated:

> I am just a mother with a daughter of my own, and after reading last night's *Free Press*, I couldn't sleep well. But for the grace of God it could be one of mine being laid in an unknown grave. She was *someone's* daughter. Please take this $10 and put a simple bouquet on her grave. Maybe one red rose, white daisies, and baby breath. May her soul rest in peace. Thank you.[18]

AN UNLIKELY CONFESSION

Whether or not the new Interstate highway made travel safer remained to be seen. Ironically—and tragically—the very person whose job it was to keep the highway safe was Minnesota State Trooper Robert Leroy Nelson. In 1988, in an interview with Special Agent Robert Berg of the MNBCA, Nelson confessed to the young woman's murder.[19]

Nelson told Special Agent Berg that he had joined the patrol in 1970 and was assigned to Blue Earth, where he remained until 1981 before transferring to another part of the state. He also acknowledged that after officials had discovered the victim's body, he had "conversations" with another State Trooper (likely Captain Vergil Karl or Trooper Richard Hull, who were at the scene) "and with other deputies from the Faribault County area regarding the homicide."[20]

One wonders if he listened with interest to all of the details, hiding the fact that he was to blame? Or, if, for whatever reason, he made a false confession, did he simply remember those details at a later date to collaborate his story? There was no evidence to connect him to the scene. The only facts recorded in the Blue Earth Jane Doe case file, are as follows:

- On the night of the murder, Nelson was on duty, in uniform, in a patrol car, and in the vicinity of Blue Earth.
- A few years later, he joined the religious group, "Into the Light Ministries."
- In 1985, citing incompatibility between his job and his religion, he quit the State Patrol and followed the religious group's move to Texas.
- There, in 1988, after owning up to prior sexual abuse of one of his own children, he was convicted of sexual assault on a child and sentenced to life in prison.
- During the MNBCA's 1988 interrogation of Nelson (at the Texas State Penitentiary), he stated that he had no independent memory of committing

Jane Doe's murder, but he "knows" he did it because of "images" that he had.[21]

The MNBCA report also noted:

The "image" that he [Nelson] sees is a Caucasian female on her knees nude with someone standing alongside strangling her with some type of cord or rope. He advises that he cannot see it very clearly, and, as a result, can give no physical description of this female or recognize what her face looks like. He states that his "image" [i.e., the murder] occurred in a field, and that her body was placed in some type of ditch with water in it. He goes on to advise that the area where the body was disposed of was along I-90 approximately 3 miles east of the Blue Earth, or 169, exit. When specifically asked if he believed that he was involved in the death of Jane Doe, Mr. Nelson stated that he "may have had something to do with her death," however he is not sure if he did it, whether he is watching someone do it, or someone told him that they had killed her.[22]

In a follow-up telephone interview by the MNBCA on April 15, 1988, Nelson stated that he had asked the victim for her identification. He believed that her middle and last names were "Marie Jacobson," and that her first name was either "Christina, Christine," or "Carolyn." He also said she was born in 1958 and was from the Milwaukee, Wisconsin area. In addition, Nelson explained that he had hidden the young woman's purse (with her identification) in his barn at his home near Blue Earth.[23] Sheriff officials extensively searched the barn, but they never found her purse or identification. (In addition, neither the victim's name, age, or location proved to be true.)

The public was kept informed. A May 27, 1988, press release issued by the Faribault County attorney concluded, "County officials have no plans at the present time to extradite Mr. [Robert] Nelson, as the new evidence is insufficient to support criminal charges. The investigation continues."[24] The lack of evidence then was discussed at the state level in the case, "State of Minnesota vs. Robert Leroy Nelson." In a Memorandum to the Faribault County Attorney, on August 19, 1988, the State ruled that its only concerns were:

- "The death of the victim."
- "The fact of killing by the defendant."

To satisfy "the fact of killing by the defendant," the State concluded: "We only need to prove that the death here was a homicide. We do not need proof that the defendant committed the homicide."[25]

In 1989, Nelson was brought to Minnesota to answer additional (but unrelated to the homicide case) sexual assault charges. While in Blue Earth, he took sheriff officials to the scene of the young woman's murder. According to former chief investigator Jerry Kabe, Nelson gave a more complete confession under hypnosis. He also submitted to a polygraph test, and he allowed his interrogators to question him under sodium pentothal (truth serum). In a telephone conversation with the author, Kabe stated that Nelson had provided information that he and former Sheriff Roger Fletcher had withheld from the press, that is, information that only the killer would know.[26]

So, what did Nelson say about that night, that he believed was May 24, 1980? According to his July 1989 statement, he watched the young woman get out of the blue van at 9:30 p.m. She was dressed in a T-shirt, blue jeans, and a light jacket and carried a black purse. After the van left, he drove up, asked her to get into his patrol car, and asked to see her identification. She must have, initially, felt relieved. Instead of being on her own in the dark, she was in the company of a uniformed law enforcement officer.[27]

As Nelson relayed in his statement, he began to drive toward Blue Earth. His passenger explained that she had been hitchhiking and was kicked out of the van because she refused to comply with a request by one of the other passengers for a sexual favor. Instead of driving the young woman into town, however, Nelson turned onto a gravel road, stopped the car, and made sexual advances of his own. When she resisted and threatened to turn him in, he pulled her out of the car, stripped off some of her clothing, handcuffed her, and forced her to perform the same sexual favor on him that she had been asked to do in the van.[28] In his confession, he stated:

> It all happened in a few minutes' time. And I was in so deep and so far and the anger and the hurt and all the fear that was inside me that she was going to do exactly what she said, and she's right. She would have been right in everything she said. All that kind of snapped and I grabbed the cord or the string or whatever it was, the pull-string, the drawstring in the bottom of her jacket, which was an Army-type field jacket with a drawstring bottom. I pulled that out, [and] tied it around her neck from behind.[29]

After Nelson strangled the young woman—now identified as Michelle—he said he removed the rest of her clothing (which he said he dumped in a landfill) and rolled her body into the drainage ditch.[30]

A joint press release issued on August 25, 1989, by the Faribault County Attorney's Office and the Faribault County Sheriff's Office stated:

According to Faribault County Attorney, Arvid Wendland, the investigation of the case had lain dormant for some time for lack of evidence when Nelson, who was incarcerated in the state of Texas on criminal sexual conduct charges in 1988, began making statements incriminating himself in the "Jane Doe" case. Faribault County Sheriff Roger Fletcher and then-Deputy Sheriff Gerald Kabe interrogated Nelson in Texas. Initially, his admissions regarding "Jane Doe" were too nebulous and vague to justify prosecution. Nelson was then charged with criminal sexual conduct involving the same family members in Faribault County and brought back to answer to those charges. While he was in the Faribault County Jail, Nelson gave Deputy Sheriff Gerald Kabe a full confession of his involvement in the "Jane Doe" matter. He was then charged with first-degree manslaughter. According to County Attorney Wendland, the prosecution could not have gone forward without Nelson's confession because of the lack of other evidence implicating him.[31]

That same day, Nelson pled guilty to, and was convicted of, first-degree manslaughter (along with the additional and unrelated sexual assault charges of a family member), then sentenced to 86 months on the manslaughter charge (along with 108 months on the additional sexual assault charges) to run concurrently with his life sentence, in Texas.[32] Nelson did not receive Minnesota's maximum charge for first-degree manslaughter, nor did he receive his request to be transferred to a prison in Minnesota. After sentencing, Nelson was returned to the Texas State Penitentiary at Huntsville, where he currently remains.[33]

For Sheriff Roger Fletcher and Chief Investigator Jerry Kabe, having a conviction in their Jane Doe case was not enough. They still were determined to identify their victim. In 1991, however, Fletcher lost the election to a new sheriff, Scott Campbell. And, that same year, Kabe retired. By then, the case file filled a box with approximately thirty pounds of paperwork.[34]

In the Faribault County Sheriff's Office, at the time, little or no progress was being made on the case, but big changes in technology were on the horizon. The first US application of a DNA profile in a criminal trial occurred in Florida in 1987. By 1995, the forensic use of DNA had become well known to the general public, particularly during the criminal and civil trials of O.J. Simpson. Blood evidence had put him at the scene of two murders, as discussed in "Civil Lawsuits" in chapter 10, "Pitfalls and Legalities."[35] Three years later, in 1998, DNA made the news again when US president Bill Clinton's semen was found on intern Monica Lewinsky's blue dress.[36]

By the turn of the twenty-first century, two decades had passed since the disappearances of Michelle Busha and Jackie Lerman. Jackie's half-brother,

Phil Lerman (a former producer with the television show "America's Most Wanted") later wrote of the importance, in long-term missing person cases, of never giving up. "My family was not one of those brave, strong families I would meet years later," he stated in a 2013 article for Cable News Network (CNN). "Jackie's disappearance tore our family apart. Her mother was driven to madness by the not-knowing; my father driven to depression and attempted suicide by a life that had become a lonely prison, caged in by his wife's grief. They became, thoroughly and utterly, hopeless."[37]

JANE DOE GETS AN ADVOCATE

In the late 1990s, Deb Anderson had become a Blue Earth resident. A few years later, she had a friend who was a cop. "I kept bugging him about cold cases," the human resources worker at Minnesota State-Mankato said in a telephone interview with the author. "He told me about the unidentified woman, so, in 2002, I went to the cemetery to see for myself."[38] Then she contacted the Faribault County Sheriff's Office and started asking questions, but she was not given a warm welcome.[39]

Changes in the Twenty-First Century

The Sheriff's Office's response, at that time, was not unusual and was not limited to Faribault County. The Internet era was in its infancy, and law enforcement agencies were not always the first to jump on board. However, media coverage of DNA successes, combined with television shows on cold cases, likely inspired members of the public to surf the Internet on their home computers. These citizen volunteers cultivated advanced research skills and were not afraid to question authority. Deb simply wanted to help identify the victim, but her skills might have been perceived as a threat to established police procedures. Although many agencies now are beginning to accept outside assistance, researchers and advocates in other parts of the country also met the same kind of opposition.

One who initially experienced a mixed reaction was the author, when offering her assistance more than a decade ago to help identify a Jane Doe (Dorothy Gay Howard) in Boulder, Colorado. Another volunteer, a New Jersey resident (who also was the Doe Network's former assistant media director), told a newspaper reporter, in 2003, "We have received enormous help from law enforcement in several jurisdictions, but then there are some officers who don't like civilians poking their noses or treading into their turf. It's mostly an ego thing with some cops."[40]

Determined, however, to move forward, Deb arranged for a sketch artist to create a composite drawing of "Blue Earth Jane Doe." She also entered the unidentified young woman's case into the then-new Doe Network database. In addition, she asked the sheriff's investigators to submit the case to the Minnesota Bureau of Criminal Apprehension (MNBCA) for inclusion in its "Minnesota Missing and Unidentified Persons Clearinghouse," which the investigators eventually did, but not until several years later. Deb even brought up the idea of exhuming the victim's remains to obtain DNA, but that request—at the time—went unheeded.

Deb then teamed up with a retired police chief, and, together, they searched through listings of missing young women from the late 1970s. With many new potential candidates for Jane Doe, Deb started a Blue Earth Jane Doe website, including a spreadsheet with names and information on dozens of missing young women. Unfortunately, Michelle Busha's name was not on the list.[41]

A missing woman who did turn up again, however, was Jackie Lerman. In 2004, Deb asked a Faribault County Sheriff's Office's investigator if he would take another look at Jackie as a possible match. He agreed, but Deb was the one who tracked down Jackie's half-brother, Phil Lerman. On the telephone, they discussed the possibility of obtaining a DNA sample from one of Jackie's family members.[42] The plan was to send it to the FBI to compare with hair samples from Jane Doe taken during her autopsy, in 1980.[43] In 2014, however, an investigative supplement accompanying a MNBCA report stated, in part:

> In 2004 a Mitochondrial DNA Profile had been established by the FBI in 2004 related to the investigation to Jane Doe. Apparently some hair samples that were believed to be collected at the time of Jane Doe's processing were submitted to the FBI for analysis. A review of the FBI Report on that profile indicated that the profile belonged to a male individual and therefore cannot be an accurate profile for Jane Doe.[44]

The investigation in 2004 proceeded without an accurate DNA comparison. The NYPD again sent Jackie's dental records, and this time they were forwarded to the MNBCA. On May 25, 2004, Special Agent Berg notified the Sheriff's Office that a forensic odontologist (and consultant to the Ramsey County Medical Examiner's Office), basing his opinion on the dental records, "eliminated Jackie Lerman as a possible identity of Jane Doe."[45]

Deb Anderson Moves the Case Forward

The new century had ushered in new tools for researching the missing and unidentified. Without realizing it at the time, Deb had joined a handful of victim advocates. When a local newspaper reporter asked why she had become so involved, she replied, "I can't really tell you why I got so deep into this, except that I kept thinking that this is somebody's sister, daughter or perhaps a mother, whose relatives deserve to know what happened to her."[46] In an interview with another reporter, Deb asked, rhetorically, "How long would I look for my child?" Then she answered her own question by saying, "probably forever."[47]

The reinvestigation of Jane Doe, with new technology, new ideas, new investigators—and new hope—had begun. In 2007, Michael S. Gormley replaced Scott Campbell as Faribault County Sheriff. According to the author's email correspondence with Sergeant Teresa Jeremiah, that was the same year that Michelle Busha's father and sister gave samples of their DNA to the Matagorda County Sheriff's Office, in Bay City, Texas.[48]

At the time, Sergeant Jeremiah, formerly with the Bay City Police Department, had recently taken on a new job as Identification/Records Officer for the Matagorda County Sheriff's Office. There, she learned about the use of DNA testing in reopening cold cases. Once settled in to her new position, she decided to apply her DNA knowledge in identifying and locating her agency's handful of missing persons. In her correspondence with the author, she explained that Matagorda County is on the Gulf coast, and most of their missing persons are drowning victims. Approximately forty commissioned officers serve the small county of 37,000 people, with half of the population in Bay City, the county seat.[49]

Sergeant Jeremiah related that, for her, the thought of not knowing what happened to a loved one, or where he or she might be, is both unbearable and heartbreaking. In her work, she only asks families for DNA in the event a family member is most likely deceased, but she also sees it as an avenue to bringing that missing family member home.[50] She submitted the DNA samples from Michelle Busha's father and sister to the University of North Texas, where nuclear and mitochondrial profiles were developed and submitted to the database of the FBI's Combined DNA Index System.[51] (The NamUs System was launched in 2009. It is not known why Michelle's case was not entered.)

At the time, the Jane Doe from Blue Earth had not yet been entered, either. But, in 2013, using the victim's original dental records, the MNBCA did create a NamUs case file. Again, Deb Anderson requested that the young woman's remains be exhumed, and this time her request was taken seriously. On July 9, 2014, Deb participated in a meeting with representatives that included the MNBCA and the Faribault County Sheriff's Office. Additional discussions were held at the MNBCA's offices to work out the details, followed by a District Judge's court order's authorization—"for the purpose of additional scientific examination to assist in identifying the person."[52]

Figure 11.2   Exhumation, "Blue Earth Jane Doe." In 2014, a local excavating company in Blue Earth, Minnesota, donated its services to exhume "Blue Earth Jane Doe's" remains from Riverside Cemetery. The murder victim was identified in 2015 as Michelle Yvette Busha. *Source:* Photo courtesy of Deb Anderson

The exhumation began at 9:30 a.m. on August 12, 2014—a warm summer day. Deb and her then-11-year-old daughter watched as a local excavating company (the same company that had buried the Jane Doe) donated its services in unearthing the grave. Former Sheriff Roger Fletcher and former chief investigator Jerry Kabe attended, as well. According to Sheriff Fletcher, there was a vault, but holes in the bottom had allowed water to seep inside, completely disintegrating the inexpensive wooden casket. Once the vault was lifted out with a crane (see figure 11.2), it was moved to a building on the cemetery grounds. There, the remains were transferred from an old body bag to a new one, then transported to the Southern Minnesota Regional Medical Examiner's Office in Rochester for examination.[53]

DNA analysis was conducted at the MNBCA. According to the author's email correspondence with Minnesota Department of Safety Public Information Officer Jill Oliveira, laboratory analysts obtained a complete mitochondrial DNA profile, as well as a partial nuclear DNA profile. At the MNBCA's request, the Olmsted County Medical Examiner's Office performed magnetic resonance imaging (MRI). A skull scan from the MRI, along with X-rays from the original autopsy, then were sent to the NCMEC for the organization's artists to use in producing a facial reconstruction.[54] For an example of another reconstruction, see "Trooper Brian F. Gross and the Westmoreland County Girls" in chapter 4, "Proactive Police."

Additionally, samples from a bone and tooth were collected and subsequently sent to the Smithsonian Institute for isotopic analysis. Forensic anthropologist Susan Myster also examined the remains and gave her opinion on Jane Doe's ethnicity and age. She believed the deceased was 17 to 23 years old at the time of her death [differing from the estimated 25 to 35 years at the original autopsy], that her height was approximately 5'2" to 5'9," and she was likely of mixed ancestry European/African.[55]

During the following months, DNA extracted from a femur was used to create a DNA profile which was periodically searched against the FBI's CODIS database.[56] According to the District Court's Petition For Exhumation, once the forensic analyses were complete, the victim's remains would be reinterred in the same location.[57] Quickly changing events, however, prevented that from happening.

Identification as Michelle Yvette Busha

According to a March 2015 summary prepared by the MNBCA, the DNA profile that had been created from the remains of Jane Doe continued to be searched against the FBI's CODIS database. On March 5, 2015, Special Agent Micheal Anderson was notified by the MNBCA laboratory that the DNA Profile that had been obtained from the remains of Jane Doe had an "association" with samples that were submitted by the Matagorda County Sheriff's Office.[58]

When Special Agent Anderson contacted the Matagorda County Sheriff's Office, an investigator there confirmed that the samples had come from the family of Michelle Yvette Busha.[59] The Matagorda County Sheriff's Office also supplied the MNBCA with Michelle's dental charts and X-rays which positively identified Michelle as the victim. Meanwhile, in Minnesota, the Ramsey County Medical Examiner's Office (that had conducted the original autopsy) issued a new death certificate identifying the victim as Michelle Yvette Busha, with a cause of death of "Ligature Strangulation" and a Manner of Death as "Homicide."[60]

For some families, not knowing what happened to their long-term missing persons can drive them to despair. For others, finally learning the truth undoubtedly opens old wounds. Either way, it is mind-boggling when one realizes that, for every case, there can be hundreds of people who work long hours, including some, like Deb Anderson, without pay. An increasing number of these citizens give freely of their time so that someone else's family member can be found.

Special thanks also go to Michelle's family. In a news release on March 17, 2015, MNBCA Forensic Science Services director Catherine Knutson stated, "Advances in forensic science led us to information we couldn't obtain in 1980. Key to our success was Michelle's family's decision to provide DNA samples. Without that information in the system, we would not know who she is today."[61]

Michelle's now-cremated remains have finally made their way home.

Chapter 12

Final Words

As shown in chapter 11 in the case of Blue Earth Jane Doe, each set of unknown remains belongs to someone. And, bringing home long-term missing persons provides resolution to families. In some cases, including that of Lisa Kay Kelly, as discussed in chapter 1, "Why Finding the Missing Is Important," the identification of a murder victim can aid in the arrest and conviction of criminals still at large. If there are no living suspects or even if there are no living family members, however, identifying the unknown gives dignity and justice to the victims. That, in itself, is more than enough reason to put a name on a grave.

JOHN AND JANE DOES CAN BE ANYWHERE

In the attempt to identify unknown remains, a common misconception is that John and Jane Does are an urban problem. Big cities, because of their large populations, have their share of them, but so, too, have many rural areas. Consider Leadville, county seat of Lake County, high in the mountains of Colorado. In the late nineteenth century, Leadville was a booming mining town, but it has less than 3,000 people today. Leadville's Evergreen Cemetery was established in 1879 and currently holds the remains of at least forty-one unnamed individuals. Notations in old cemetery records only give very brief information, such as "child without a name died at the poor house" and "found shot in Tennessee Park."[1] All but the three most recent lie in unmarked graves. The markers simply read, "Unidentified October 1958," "Unknown" (dates from 1962), and "Unidentified Male May 1970."[2]

Figure 12.1 Evergreen Cemetery, Leadville, Colorado. Volunteer caretaker John Piearson stands in the "Protestant Free" section of Leadville, Colorado's Evergreen Cemetery, which is being encroached upon by the surrounding forest. "Independence Pass John Doe," found in 1970 and buried in this section, was exhumed in 2013 in hopes of identifying his remains. *Source:* Photo by author

Leadville's Evergreen Cemetery is divided into several well-defined and well-cared-for sections. Some belong to fraternal organizations, including the Benevolent and Protective Order of Elks, the Oro City Independent Order of the Odd Fellows, and the Grand Army of the Republic. Others are divided by religious groups such as the Hebrews, Protestants, and Catholics. Most of the forty-one unidentified burials, however, are spread throughout what is called the "Protestant Free" section, as shown in figure 12.1. Along with a "Catholic Free" section, the area was reserved for those whose families could not afford a plot. Obviously, most of the unidentified ended up there, as well. For many years, the "free" sections of the cemetery have not been formally maintained. Once in a while, a community member will cut down a tree, but there is no grass to water or shrubs to trim. The graves, both marked and unmarked, are being taken over by the surrounding forest and are fading into the past.

Independence Pass John Doe

"Independence Pass John Doe," the unknown male found in 1970, is the most recent of the unidentified burials and is the most solvable as siblings, and perhaps even parents or children, may be missing this man. Leadville resident

John Piearson certainly thought so. In an interview with the author, he explained that he had come across the unidentified male's marker years ago while working as a volunteer caretaker in the cemetery. Like Deb Anderson (in "Jane Doe Gets an Advocate" chapter 11, "Retrospect—Inside a (Previously) Cold Case"), he talked up the importance of identifying John Doe, but his initial requests to local authorities produced no results. Eventually, John Piearson contacted the CBI.[3]

As soon became evident, the original law enforcement case file was nowhere to be found, so John searched through microfilmed copies of the Leadville *Herald Democrat* at the Lake County Public Library and supplemented what little information was available with original newspaper reports. A headline on the front page of the June 22, 1970, edition read, "Decomposed Body Found in Ditch on Independence Pass."[4] The man's left arm was missing. A few weeks later, a state highway maintenance worker found the missing portion of the body below the road on the switchback where the body had been found. Speculation was that the man's arm may have been severed by a passing snowplow.[5]

Accompanying the article of June 22, 1970, was a photograph of the man's legs, with the rest of his body covered by a rock fall. The caption read:

> What a lonely way to die. This seems to have been the fate of some unknown traveler or hiker whose body was found on Independence Pass, two miles east of the summit near the entrance to Mountain Boy Park. The body, which was found Friday afternoon, was discovered lying in the ditch alongside the road partially covered with rocks. The main possibility of identification seems to lie in the teeth and possible dental records somewhere. It was not possible to obtain fingerprints from the one arm which remained.[6]

A short article by the *Associated Press* titled "Man's Body Found," mentioned that the body was clad only in "summer clothing."[7] The road over the summit of Independence Pass reaches an elevation of 12,095 feet and typically is closed from early November to late May, so it was likely that the man's body had been buried in snow all winter. If so, the man would have died (or, perhaps, murdered and dumped) during the late summer or early fall of 1969, instead of "May 1970" as listed on his cemetery marker.

The article in the *Herald Democrat* revealed the following clues as to the man's identity:

- White male, age in the early twenties
- Height: five-feet-seven inches or five-feet-eight inches

- Dark hair
- "Quite good" teeth with gold and platinum fillings
- Pants pocket contained seven dollars and a razor[8]

In 2011, the Lake County Coroner entered the unidentified male's case into the NamUs database as UP #10738.[9] Then, in 2013 and with John Piearson in attendance, the Coroner's Office exhumed John Doe's remains to obtain DNA for comparison with any potential relative who might come forward. The male's DNA profile and dental charts are now complete.

At the time of this writing, three men missing at the time (and still unaccounted for) have been formally ruled out. One was an escaped convict from Nebraska, another a man missing from the Fort Carson Army installation near Colorado Springs, Colorado, and the third was a man missing from Chicago. Meanwhile, a March 23, 2016, *Herald Democrat* article is keeping this case in the public eye and, hopefully, will bring forward new leads and new information. For more on the media, see "When Is It Time to Go to the Media?" in chapter 8, "Become Your Long-Term Missing Person's Advocate." If "Independence John Doe" is not identified in a reasonable amount of time, the man's remains will be reburied in his former grave in the Protestant Free section of Leadville's Evergreen Cemetery.[10]

Figure 12.2 "Little Miss Nobody" Gravestone. "Little Miss Nobody" was found on the desert and then buried in Prescott, Arizona, by members of the community. When this photograph was taken in 2015, someone recently had left a stuffed animal on the child's grave. *Source:* Photo by author

Little Miss Nobody

One Jane Doe who practically screams out to be identified is "Little Miss Nobody," see figure 12.2. Rock collectors found the body of the little girl in a shallow grave on July 31, 1960. Estimated to be 6-to-7 years old, her fingernails and toenails had been painted with bright red nail polish. Her makeshift grave was a short distance from the intersection of Old Alamo Road and State Highway 93, near the town of Congress, in Yavapai County, Arizona. Highway 93, at the time, was the main route between Las Vegas, Nevada, and Phoenix, Arizona.[11]

The case fell under the jurisdiction of the Yavapai County Sheriff's Office, located in the county seat of Prescott. There, ten days later, the child affectionately referred to as "Little Miss Nobody" was laid to rest on a sloping hillside in the city's Mountain View Cemetery. The area's residents, including mortuary employees, cemetery operators, and florists donated to her burial, arranged for by a local radio station announcer.[12]

In "Prescottonians Do Care! Open Hearts to Dead Girl," a reporter for the *Prescott Evening Courier* described the scene as follows:

Little Miss Nobody was somebody today

She received the finest Christian burial this morning that kind-hearted Prescott people could provide. More than 70 of them sat teary-eyed through funeral services conducted by [Reverend] Dr. Charles Franklin Parker at the Widmer Mortuary.

The card of memorium [*sic*] at the services identified her as "God's Little Child, date of birth unknown, date of death unknown."

That is as much as anyone knows about the little body found half-buried on the desert July 31. Officials have been stumped at every turn thus far in their concentrated efforts to determine her identity. The exact cause of death never has been determined due to the poor condition of the body.

Dr. Parker conducted the services looking over the pale blue casket adorned with a large spray of pink and white carnations. Four baskets of flowers and other arrangements ringed the casket.

Dr. Parker thanked the mourners whose compassion for a little child guided them to the services. He expressed the appreciation also of "a suffering mother somewhere."

"We may never know the whys and wherefores, but somewhere someone is going to be watching the paper to learn what happened to a little girl left on the desert. If there has been a misdeed, probably a disquieted conscience will go on and on."

He said, "Here is a little wanderer who has been in our midst. We don't know her name. We can only guess her age. It occurs to me we may not know, but

God knows. There are no unknowns, no orphans in God's world. He knows most suffers most, and God is suffering today. She doesn't need a name today. She has the name of an angel somewhere in eternity. We may think how we would have welcomed and cared for her, but that was not the providence of God. We reach out in an expression of concern for those who knew her and whom she loved."

Dr. Parker, whose own eyes were filled with tears and whose words came hard after the ceremony, said, "We pause with sadness in our hearts at the calamity that befalls children. But we also know that this is not the end of life. That spot on the desert was only where mortality ended."

"With God, all things are well and in his hands her home is never to be destroyed—never to be left again along a desert road, but only to know love as only God can give it."[13]

According to the newspaper article on August 10, 1960, Dr. Parker also read a poem titled "For a Little Girl Unknown" that ended with the phrase, "But only the wisdom of God on high will someday answer the question. Why?" And, the Reverend also read an anonymous piece that stated, "Forgive us, child, for the weakness of men; and in turn, when in your final home, pray for us."[14]

A follow-up article on November 4, 1960 mentioned that the Yavapai County Sheriff's Office had received dozens of letters, telephone calls, and telegrams asking for more information. By then, officials had revealed that her brown hair had been tinted or dyed auburn, the girl was forty-five inches tall, and she weighed fifty-five-to-sixty-five pounds. She had a full and perfect set of baby teeth and no broken bones. According to the November article, she had been wearing pink shorts and a blouse with a "distinctive chain design." An accompanying photograph showed the Sheriff and the Deputy County Attorney holding man-sized rubber thong sandals that had been cut down to fit the little girl's feet.[15]

When found, the child's body was too decomposed to determine cause of death.[16] But what had happened to this little girl? Did a parent, or another adult in the car, pull over to admonish her, then discover that his or her punishment had gone too far? Did that person then hurriedly bury her on the desert and then get back on the highway and continue to drive to Las Vegas or Phoenix? Was there, as Reverend Parker supposed, "a suffering mother somewhere?" These and other questions need to be answered. Today, however, a new generation of investigators is looking at this case, increasing Little Miss Nobody's chances of identification. Now, she, too, is listed in NamUs—as UP-10741.[17]

MISSING IN THE MILITARY

The plight of the missing and the unknown knows no boundaries. *The Long Term Missing: Hope and Help for Families* focuses on the United States, but other countries also are faced with what the NIJ has called "the nation's silent mass disaster." In addition to our own unknown dead, some of these other countries also hold the unidentified remains of Americans who have gone beyond our shores. Many served in the military in times of war.

Clay Bonnyman Evans and His Grandfather

In November 1943, during World War II, both Japan and the United States suffered heavy casualties in the Battle of Tarawa on Betio Island in the central Pacific Ocean. Before moving on, surviving United States Marines buried their dead in mass graves, also erecting a hand-painted sign that read, in part, "Tender hands shall lift thee out to home soil waiting." In June 1946, after the end of the war, members of the American Graves Registration Service visited the island and exhumed some 500 Marines. But, they were unable to locate hundreds of others, including forty Marines in what had been designated "Cemetery 27." In 1949, the Quartermaster General's Office declared the bodies "unrecoverable."[18]

Family members grieved, but like "Gina and Her Dad: Returned Identities" in chapter 1, "Why Finding the Missing is Important," families were left with no tangible remains of their fathers, brothers, uncles, and sons. In the cases of the missing Marines, many years passed as wives, siblings, and children moved on with their lives. And then the parents died, followed by the wives and siblings, still without answers. Still, the men were never forgotten by their children and grandchildren.

Eventually, help arrived from behind the scenes. In 2007, History Flight, Inc., a Florida-based nonprofit organization, began its efforts to identify missing servicemen and bring them home. The organization works in cooperation with the Defense POW/MIA Accounting Agency (DPAA), the federal agency tasked with recovering the remains of missing US service personnel and is dedicated to finding, recovering, and repatriating America's war dead to American soil. In March 2015, members of History Flight's trans-disciplinary team of forensic anthropologists, geophysicists, historians, surveyors, forensic odontologists, unexploded ordinance specialists, medics, and cadaver dog handlers made an outstanding contribution in the search for "the lost graves of Tarawa." They discovered long-hidden Cemetery 27.[19]

One of the missing Marines was 1st Lieutenant Alexander "Sandy" Bonny-man, Jr., and participating in the search was Lieutenant Bonnyman's grandson, Clay Bonnyman Evans, a freelance journalist from Colorado. In email correspondence with the author, Clay stated that the Lieutenant's heroics had been well-documented in his posthumous Medal of Honor, but more than seventy years would pass before anyone could point to his grave. Shortly after Lieutenant Bonnyman's death, the military sent his parents a letter stating that he, presumably, was lost at sea. In his memory, his parents then erected a large marble headstone in their family plot atop the highest hill at Highland Memorial Park Cemetery in Knoxville, Tennessee.[20]

History Flight's founder and director, Mark Noah, first learned of the missing Marines in 2007 while searching for a downed plane in the Betio lagoon. The organization then spent thousands of research hours interviewing veterans and studying maps before heading off, in 2008, to Betio Island. There, team members searched for the graves with the latest technological tools, including ground-penetrating radar. Meanwhile, the process exposed inaccurate records and was hampered by human habitation (shanties with pig stys) on a polluted, one-square-mile island, but home to nearly 20,000 mostly poor people. The elusive Cemetery 27 burial trench, with the missing Marines, finally was discovered beneath two feet of crushed coral concrete in a local shipping yard. [21]

Clay learned of History Flight's efforts on Betio Island in 2009. He made his first visit to the island, in 2010, in conjunction with a DPAA mission to excavate sites identified by the nonprofit organization. Like most Westerners, he was shocked by the extreme heat and degraded environment on Betio, but he felt a deep connection to the island. He would return a half dozen times during the next five years to work as a volunteer for History Flight, doing everything from shoveling wet sand to cleaning bones and shooting video. Back home, he helped publicize the group's efforts and became a liaison to families of Tarawa missing.

All of the work paid off on May 28, 2015, when Clay knelt beside History Flight's lead archeologist Kristen N. Baker as she swept sand from a burnished skull in "Grave No. 17." Before long, she had exposed a telltale glint. Lieutenant Bonnyman was a decade or more older than the Marines buried with him, he hailed from a wealthy family, and his dental charts showed that he was the only man buried in Cemetery 27 to have had extensive gold dental work. After helping Kristen excavate the rest of the Marine's remains, Clay returned the following day to the empty grave, where he silently meditated on the family member he never knew.[22]

"The location of Cemetery 27 has been one of Tarawa's most challenging historical puzzles," stated Clay in History Flight, Inc.'s June 27, 2015 press release. "History Flight's discovery and recovery of the site is a testament to the tenacity and professionalism with which it has searched for all the missing Tarawa Marines."[23]

On September 28, 2015, hundreds of citizens joined more than seventy members of the Bonnyman family, including the Marine's two surviving daughters, ages 81 and 74, to bury Lieutenant Bonnyman with full military honors underneath his headstone in Knoxville. There, he rests in peace next to his parents, two sisters, and a brother.[24]

"The death of my grandfather shattered his family," stated Clay in his email correspondence. "My great-grandparents desperately wanted to bury their son, but died without ever knowing the truth. When a teary-eyed Marine general knelt before my mother and handed her a folded flag on that bright September day, I couldn't help feeling a sense of pride, even joy, that I'd played a part in bringing him home at last."[25]

The Vacant Chair

Many beautiful songs evolved from times of war, but one of the best is "The Vacant Chair." Initially written as a poem by Henry S. Washburn, it was inspired by the death of Lieutenant John William Grout of the 15th Massachusetts Infantry at the Battle of Ball's Bluff, Virginia, in 1861. According to the *History of Worcester in the War of the Rebellion,* Grout was killed while attempting to cross the Potomac River. His body was missing for nearly three weeks prior to being recovered downstream.[26]

Eighteen-year-old Lieutenant Grout was said to embody the sacrifice made by so many men and their families during America's Civil War. Washburn's poem depicts his family gathering on Thanksgiving Day and remembering previous holidays when family members were together. As "The Vacant Chair" became more well known, songwriter George Root put the lyrics to music. Although the words vary, the following is a common rendition.

We shall meet but we shall miss him.
There will be one vacant chair.
We shall linger to caress him
While we breathe our ev'ning prayer.
When one year ago we gathered,
Joy was in his mild blue eye.

Now the golden cord is severed,
And our hopes in ruin lie.

We shall meet, but we shall miss him.
There will be one vacant chair.
We shall linger to caress him
While we breathe our ev'ning prayer.

At our fireside, sad and lonely,
Often will the bosom swell
At remembrance of the story
How our noble Willie fell.
How he strove to bear the banner
Thro' the thickest of the fight
And uphold our country's honor
In the strength of manhood's might.

We shall meet, but we shall miss him.
There will be one vacant chair.
We shall linger to caress him
While we breathe our ev'ning prayer.

True, they tell us wreaths of glory
Evermore will deck his brow,
But this soothes the anguish only,
Sweeping o'er our heartstrings now.
Sleep today, O early fallen,
In thy green and narrow bed.
Dirges from the pine and cypress
Mingle with the tears we shed.

We shall meet, but we shall miss him.
There will be one vacant chair.
We shall linger to caress him
While we breathe our ev'ning prayer.[27]

Several veteran groups, including "Last Man Clubs," also dine with vacant chairs, draping them in black crepe to commemorate those who died during the previous year.

ONCE LOST, NOW FOUND

Music lovers also appreciate "Amazing Grace," a hymn written by English poet and clergyman John Newton and first published in 1779. Its message is one of personal redemption, but the line, "I once was lost, but now I'm found," has worldwide appeal and often is applied to John and Jane Does who have regained their names.

Corporal Athol Goodwin Kirkland

One recently identified man whose grave now has this epitaph is Australian soldier Corporal Athol Goodwin Kirkland. The young man died fighting in France in 1918, during World War I. For nearly 100 years, his remains lay in the Crucifix Corner Cemetery, near Villers-Bretonneux in the Somme, under a headstone reading "Unknown corporal of the 34th Battalion Australian Imperial Force (AIF)." Now, along with the epitaph, Kirkland's own name is on his grave.[28]

The soldier's identification began with an archivist in Fremantle, Western Australia, who decided to research the names of corporals of the 34th battalion in the AIF. There was only one. And, from official records, the archivist found record of a fellow soldier's statement that stated that the corporal had been buried in the same cemetery where his body was retrieved. The findings were confirmed by Australia's Commonwealth War Graves Office.[29]

A dedication ceremony in April 2015 in France was attended by Australian Prime Minister Tony Abbott, along with Cheryl Rowe, the soldier's closest family member—a great-great niece. "It's telling that we're Athol's closest family," Cheryl's husband Chad Rowe told a newspaper reporter. "He died so young that he was unable to have his own family."[30]

Carol Ann Cole

Carol Ann Cole is a former Jane Doe whose gravestone also now reads, "Once was lost but now am found." The young woman (as was the World War I soldier) was identified in 2015. She had been missing for thirty-four years. Many people, including a retired FBI agent in Arizona, a police department in Michigan, and a coroner's office in Louisiana were involved in her identification and return to her family.[31]

In 1981, as a young teenager, Carol had left her home in Michigan and traveled to Texas. A couple of months later, she called to wish her mother a happy birthday. Then no one in her family ever heard from her again. In 2015, Jeanie Phelps, Carol's sister, was searching on the Internet and thought she saw a resemblance between Carol and one of Arizona's Jane Does. On the sister's behalf, another family member contacted the Coconino County (Arizona) Sheriff's Office and ended up talking with Chuck Jones, a retired FBI agent and volunteer investigator.[32]

Carol was not the Jane Doe in Arizona, but Agent Jones agreed to help. He quickly learned, however, that no police department had ever filed a missing person's report on Carol. Jones then contacted the Township of Kalamazoo Police Department, in Kalamazoo, Michigan, and convinced the agency to take the report, as well as DNA samples from family members. Carol's case then was entered into the NamUs System.[33]

Meanwhile, the Bossier Parish Coroner's Office, in Louisiana, had just reopened a thirty-four-year-old cold case of an unidentified young woman. The 15- to 20-year-old Jane Doe's decomposing body, with no identification, had been discovered on a logging road off of Highway 157 near Princeton, Louisiana, in 1981. The victim had been stabbed several times and had been dead for approximately four to six weeks. Several attempts throughout the intervening years to identify her had been unsuccessful. A composite sketch had been made of her face, but she did not match anyone who had been reported missing.[34]

Social media is credited with connecting Carol Ann Cole and "Bossier Jane Doe." Louisiana's FACES lab, currently a part of Louisiana State University's Department of Geography and Anthropology, created a computer-generated "likeness" of Carol, which closely resembled an actual photograph of the young woman. Lieutenant Shannon Mack of the Bossier City Police Department then placed the image on a Facebook page she had created to generate leads for "Bossier Doe." A 911 operator matched a picture of Carol on Craigslist to the Facebook page. DNA testing, from the family samples collected by police in Michigan, confirmed Carol's identity.[35]

The young woman's remains are now interred in in the Maple Grove Cemetery, in Comstock Township, Michigan. The timeless epitaph and her name will forever be on her gravestone. In Carol's memory, her sister created the "Carol Ann Project." According to its Facebook page, its purpose is to "Let every Doe be identified, let every missing person be found."[36]

Wilma, Shannon, and Dorothy

Mentioned throughout this book are several former Jane Does, including Wilma June Nissen, Shannon Michelle Aumock, and Dorothy Gay Howard. Their gravestones speak for themselves as the inscriptions dignify the lives of these young women. (See figures 12.3, 12.4, and 12.5.) May their stories, as well as those of many others, both identified and still waiting to be identified, inspire and bring hope to families of long-term missing persons.

Figure 12.3 Wilma June Nissen Gravestone. The Lyon County (Iowa) Sheriff's Department affectionately chose the words "Our Girl" for the gravestone of its now-identified Jane Doe, Wilma June Nissen. For her story, see chapter 1. *Source:* Photo courtesy of Lyon County Sheriff's Department Chief Deputy Jerry Birkey

Figure 12.4 Shannon Michelle Aumock Gravestone. The "Amazing Grace" epitaph was chosen for Shannon Michelle Aumock, after the Phoenix Police Department's Missing and Unidentified Persons Unit identified the former Jane Doe in 2011. For her story, see chapter 4. *Source:* Photo by author

Figure 12.5 Dorothy Gay Howard Gravestone. Following "Boulder Jane Doe's" identification, in 2009, as Dorothy Gay Howard, family members combined her original gravestone with a new stone in Boulder, Colorado's, Columbia Cemetery. The new stone includes Bible verses from Numbers 6: 24–26:

THE LORD BLESS THEE
AND KEEP THEE
THE LORD MAKE HIS FACE
SHINE UPON THEE
AND LIFT UP HIS
COUNTENANCE UPON THEE
AND GIVE THEE PEACE
Source: Photo by author

Notes

CHAPTER 1

1. Silvia Pettem, *Someone's Daughter: In Search of Justice for Jane Doe* (Lanham: Taylor Trade, 2009), 47.

2. Vanessa Miller, "Family in Boulder for 'Jane Doe' Memorial, 56 Years after her Murder," *Daily Camera*, May 20, 2010.

3. Gina Hoogendoorn, email message to author, September 30, 2013.

4. Gina Hoogendoorn, email message to author, September 30, 2013.

5. Gina Hoogendoorn, email message to author, September 8, 2013.

6. Gina Hoogendoorn, email message to author, September 8, 2013.

7. Gina Hoogendoorn, email message to author, September 9, 2013.

8. Gene Ralston, email message to author, November 24, 2013.

9. Gina Hoogendoorn, email message to author, September 8, 2013.

10. Gene Ralston, email message to author, November 24, 2013.

11. Gina Hoogendoorn, email message to author, September 9, 2013.

12. Gina Hoogendoorn, email message to author, September 9, 2013.

13. Gina Hoogendoorn, email message to author, September 9, 2013.

14. Gene Ralston, email message to author, November 24, 2013.

15. Gina Hoogendoorn, email message to author, September 9, 2013.

16. Gina Hoogendoorn, email message to author, September 30, 2013.

17. Silvia Pettem, *Cold Case Research: Resources for Unidentified, Missing, and Cold Homicide Cases* (Boca Raton: CRC Press, Taylor & Francis Group, 2013), 21.

18. Sarah Langbein, "16 Years Later 'Jane Doe' Has a Name," *Rocky Mountain News*, January 25, 2006; and Pettem, *Cold Case Research*, 25.

19. Pettem, *Cold Case Research*, 23.

20. Pettem, *Cold Case Research*, 23.

21. Pettem, *Cold Case Research*, 23.

22. Pettem, *Cold Case Research*, 23.

23. Pettem, *Cold Case Research*, 23.

24. Pettem, *Cold Case Research*, 23.

25. Pettem, *Cold Case Research*, 24.

26. Sheriff Blythe Bloemendaal, telephone interview with author, May 25, 2015.

27. Sheriff Blythe Bloemendaal, telephone interview with author, May 25, 2015.

28. Sheriff Blythe Bloemendaal, telephone interview with author, May 25, 2015.

29. Integrated Automated Fingerprint Identification System, accessed April 20, 2016, https://www.fbi.gov/about-us/cjis/fingerprints_biometrics/iafis/iafis.

30. Sheriff Blythe Bloemendaal, telephone interview with author, May 25, 2015.

31. Sheriff Blythe Bloemendaal, telephone interview with author, May 25, 2015.

32. Sheriff Blythe Bloemendaal, telephone interview with author, May 25, 2015.

33. Sheriff Blythe Bloemendaal, telephone interview with author, May 25, 2015.

34. Sheriff Blythe Bloemendaal, telephone interview with author, May 25, 2015.

35. Sheriff Blythe Bloemendaal, telephone interview with author, May 25, 2015.

36. Sheriff Blythe Bloemendaal, telephone interview with author, May 25, 2015.

37. Dolly A. Butz, "Saying a Final Goodbye," *Sioux City Journal*, June 4, 2006.

38. Butz, "Saying a Final Goodbye," *Sioux City Journal*.

39. Butz, "Saying a Final Goodbye," *Sioux City Journal*.

40. Sheriff Blythe Bloemendaal, telephone interview with author, May 25, 2015.

41. Sheriff Blythe Bloemendaal, telephone interview with author, May 25, 2015.

42. Sheriff Blythe Bloemendaal, telephone interview with author, May 25, 2015.

43. Dolly A. Butz, "Looking for Buried Answers," *Sioux City Journal*, September 16, 2007.

44. Sheriff Blythe Bloemendaal, telephone interview with author, May 25, 2015.

CHAPTER 2

1. New York City Office of Chief Medical Examiner, accessed April 20, 2016, http://www.nyc.gov/html/ocme/html/mpi/mpi_home.shtml.

2. New Jersey State Police, Missing Persons & Child Exploitation Unit, accessed April 20, 2016, http://www.state.nj.us/njsp/division/investigations/missing-persons-child-exploit.shtml.

3. California Commission on Peace Officer Standards and Training, *Missing Persons Investigations Guidelines & Curriculum* (California Commission 2007, revised 2011), xiii.

4. California Commission on Peace Officer Standards and Training, *Missing Persons Investigations Guidelines & Curriculum*, 1–2.

5. Kimberly Matas, "Missing 30 Years, Victim was Right Here," *Arizona Daily Star*, April 14, 2012.

6. Matas, "Missing 30 Years, Victim was Right Here."

7. Matas, "Missing 30 Years, Victim was Right Here."

8. Matas, "Missing 30 Years, Victim was Right Here."

9. Matas, "Missing 30 Years, Victim was Right Here."

10. Connecticut State Police Officer Standards and Training Council, *Connecticut Police Officer Standards and Training Policy for Handling Missing Persons Investigations* (Connecticut State Police, no date), 2.

11. California Commission on Peace Officer Standards and Training, *Missing Persons Investigations Guidelines & Curriculum*, 1–3.

12. Florida Silver Alert website, accessed April 20, 2016, http://www.floridasilveralert.com/home.

13. Florida Silver Alert website, accessed April 20, 2016, http://www.floridasilveralert.com/home.

14. "Project Lifesaver Helps Law Enforcement Agencies Track Down At-risk Missing Persons," *KSBY TV*, October 28, 2015.

15. Project Lifesaver, accessed April 20, 2016, http://www.projectlifesaver.org/.

16. Center for Public Safety and Justice, "Alzheimer's Aware: A Guide for Implementing a Law Enforcement Program to Address Alzheimer's in the Community" (University of Illinois, 2015).

17. Silvia Pettem, *Someone's Daughter: In Search of Justice for Jane Doe* (Lanham, MD: Taylor Trade, 2009), Epilogue (digital edition).

18. Pettem, *Someone's Daughter: In Search of Justice for Jane Doe* (Lanham, MD: Taylor Trade, 2009), Epilogue (digital edition).

19. Pettem, *Someone's Daughter: In Search of Justice for Jane Doe* (Lanham, MD: Taylor Trade, 2009), 124.

20. Silvia Pettem, "Ellenor Hacker Took Out the Trash and Disappeared for 11 Years," *Daily Camera*, September 13, 2009.

21. Pettem, "Ellenor Hacker Took Out the Trash and Disappeared for 11 Years," *Daily Camera*.

22. Pettem, "Ellenor Hacker Took Out the Trash and Disappeared for 11 Years," *Daily Camera*.

23. Pettem, "Ellenor Hacker Took Out the Trash and Disappeared for 11 Years," *Daily Camera*.

24. Pettem, "Ellenor Hacker Took Out the Trash and Disappeared for 11 Years," *Daily Camera*.

25. Karen Enyeart, "Brenda Heist Found: Woman Missing Since 02 Alive," *eCanadanow*, May 2, 2013.

26. Enyeart, "Brenda Heist Found: Woman Missing Since 02 Alive," *eCanadanow*.

27. Enyeart, "Brenda Heist Found: Woman Missing Since 02 Alive," *eCanadanow*.

28. Enyeart, "Brenda Heist Found: Woman Missing Since 02 Alive," *eCanadanow*.

29. Enyeart, "Brenda Heist Found: Woman Missing Since 02 Alive," *eCanadanow*.

30. Pettem, *Cold Case Research*, 132.

31. Pettem, *Cold Case Research*, 134–139.

32. Megan Barreto, "Hurricane Katrina: 9 Years Later," *Aol.com Editors*, August 29, 2014.

33. Kenna Quinet, "The Missing Missing: Toward a Quantification of Serial Murder Victimization in the United States," *Homicide Studies,* Vol. 11, No. 4, (November 2007): 1.

34. Kevin A. McGregor, *Flight of Gold: Two Pilots' True Adventure Discovering Alaska's Legendary Gold Wreck* (In-depth editions, 2013), 15–26.

35. McGregor, *Flight of Gold,* 160.

36. McGregor, *Flight of Gold,* 19.

37. McGregor, Kevin A., meeting with author, August 15, 2013.

38. McGregor, *Flight of Gold,* 175.

39. Valerie van Heest, email message to author, March 1, 2016.

40. McGregor, *Flight of Gold,* 274–276.

41. Odile M. Loreille, et al., "Integrated DNA and Fingerprint Analyses in the Identification of 60-Year-Old Mummified Human Remains Discovered in an Alaskan Glacier," *Journal of Forensic Sciences,* 2010.

42. Loreille, et al., "Integrated DNA and Fingerprint Analyses in the Identification of 60-Year-Old Mummified Human Remains Discovered in an Alaskan Glacier," *Journal of Forensic Sciences.*

43. Loreille, et al., "Integrated DNA and Fingerprint Analyses in the Identification of 60-Year-Old Mummified Human Remains Discovered in an Alaskan Glacier," *Journal of Forensic Sciences.*

44. Where is Gloria Jean? Facebook group, accessed May 14, 2016, https://www.facebook.com/search/top/?q=%20Where%20is%20Gloria%20Jean.

45. Stephanie LaPoint, email message to author, November 9, 2015.

46. Stephanie LaPoint, email message to author, November 9, 2015.

47. Stephanie LaPoint, email message to author, November 9, 2015.

48. NamUs MP #543, Gloria Baird, accessed May 12, 2016, https://www.findthemissing.org/en/cases/543/4/.

49. Stephanie LaPoint, email message to author, January 5, 2016.

50. Robert Gates, email message to author, November 13, 2013.

51. Robert Gates, email message to author, November 13, 2013.

52. Robert Gates, email message to author, November 13, 2013.

53. "Mother's Compensation Act application," *Colorado State Archives,* May 21, 1917.

54. Western Newspaper Union News Service, "Aid for 148 Families," *Kiowa County Press,* March 24, 1916.

55. "Obituaries, Mrs. Delphia Gates," *The Longmont (Colo.) Ledger,* December 8, 1960.

56. Robert Gates, email message to author, November 13, 2013.

57. Associated Press, "Larimer County Probing Mystery of Skeleton Discovered in Canon," *Greeley Tribune,* February 12, 1938.

58. NamUs MP #24464, accessed May 12, 2016, https://www.findthemissing.org/en/cases/24464/0/.

CHAPTER 3

1. National Center for Missing & Exploited Children®, accessed April 20, 2016, http://www.missingkids.org/home.

2. Lena Masri, "The Missing, Searching for New York's Lost," *NYCity News Service, CityLimits.org*, 2014, accessed April 20, 2016, http://themissingny.nycitynews-service.com/part-one/runaways/#lgbt.

3. National Center for Missing & Exploited Children®, "Key Facts," accessed April 20, 2016, http://www.missingkids.org/keyfacts.

4. Masri, "The Missing, Searching for New York's Lost," *NYCity News Service, CityLimits.org*, 2014.

5. Masri, "The Missing, Searching for New York's Lost," *NYCity News Service, CityLimits.org*, 2014.

6. National Center for Missing & Exploited Children®, "Key Facts."

7. National Center for Missing & Exploited Children®, "FAQ: Child Sexual Exploitation," accessed April 21, 2016, http://www.missingkids.com/Exploitation/FAQ.

8. National Center for Missing & Exploited Children®, "FAQ: Child Sexual Exploitation."

9. Katharine Q. Seelye, "In Heroin Crisis, White Families Seek Gentler War on Drugs," *New York Times*, October 30, 2015.

10. National Runaway Safeline, accessed April 22, 2016, http://www.1800runaway.org/youth-teens/.

11. Kenna Quinet, "The Missing Missing: Toward a Quantification of Serial Murder Victimization in the United States," *Homicide Studies,* Vol. 11, No. 4 (November 2007): 1.

12. Silvia Pettem, *Cold Case Research: Resources for Unidentified, Missing, and Cold Homicide Cases* (Boca Raton: CRC Press, Taylor & Francis Group, 2013), 113.

13. Pettem, *Cold Case Research*, 113.

14. Find a Grave, Hart Island Cemetery, accessed April 22, 2016, http://www.findagrave.com/cgi-bin/fg.cgi?page=cr&CRid=65710&CScn=Hart&CScntry=4&CSst=36&CScnty=1980&.

15. National Center for Missing & Exploited Children®, "Key Facts."

16. National Center for Missing & Exploited Children®, "Key Facts."

17. Silvia Pettem, *Someone's Daughter: In Search of Justice for Jane Doe* (Lanham, MD: Taylor Trade, 2009), 96–99.

18. Dorothy Holmes Brown, email message to author, August 13, 2013.

19. Dorothy Holmes Brown, email message to author, August 13, 2013.

20. NamUs MP-5584, accessed May 12, 2016, https://www.findthemissing.org/en/cases/5584/0/.

21. Dorothy Holmes Brown, email message to author, August 13, 2013.

22. Greg Botelho, et al., "Ohio Kidnapping Case: Amanda Berry's Baby Delivered by Another Captive," *CNN.com*, May 9, 2013, accessed May 12, 2016, http://www.cnn.com/2013/05/08/us/ohio-missing-women-found/.

23. CNN Library, "Elizabeth Smart Fast Facts," accessed April 22, 2016, http://www.cnn.com/2013/04/14/us/elizabeth-smart-fast-facts/.

24. CNN Library, "Elizabeth Smart Fast Facts."

25. CNN Library, "Elizabeth Smart Fast Facts"; and uslegal.com, "Protect Act of 2003 Law & Legal Definition," accessed May 12, 2016, http://definitions.uslegal.com/p/protect-act-of-2003/.

26. National Center for Missing & Exploited Children®, "Amber Alert Program," accessed April 22, 2016, http://www.missingkids.com/CriticallyMissing.

27. Elizabeth Smart, et al., *You're Not Alone: The Journey From Abduction to Empowerment* (Washington, D.C.: US Department of Justice, 2008), 29.

28. Elizabeth Smart Foundation, accessed April 22, 2016, http://elizabethsmartfoundation.org/.

29. Richard C. Paddock, et al., "Suspect's Tip Leads to Body of Polly Klaas," *Los Angeles Times*, December 5, 1993.

30. National Center for Missing & Exploited Children®, "Key Facts."

31. Pettem, *Cold Case Research*, 3–8.

32. Pettem, *Cold Case Research*, 3–8.

33. Pettem, *Cold Case Research*, 3–8.

34. Pettem, *Cold Case Research*, 3–8.

35. Pettem, *Cold Case Research*, 3–8.

36. Paul and Ramona Blee, interview with author, February 4, 2016; and Scott Franz, "Suspect in Marie Blee Cold Case Arrested on Suspicion of Kidnapping a Different Routt County Teenager More Than 30 Years Ago," *Steamboat Today*, June 11, 2015.

37. Paul and Ramona Blee, interview with author, February 4, 2016.

38. Paul and Ramona Blee, interview with author, February 4, 2016.

39. Kirk Mitchell, "High School Student Marie Blee Vanishes From Party in Craig, Colorado," *Denver Post*, November 15, 2009; and Matt Stensland, "Unclear Whether Kidnapping Arrest Related to Marie Blee Cold Case," *Steamboat Today*, June 5, 2015.

40. Scott Franz, "Monty Dean Doolin Booked Into the Routt County Jail on 1st Degree Kidnapping Charge," *Steamboat Today*, June 12, 2015; and Scott Franz, "Suspect in Marie Blee Cold Case Arrested on Suspicion of Kidnapping a Different Routt County Teenager More Than 30 Years Ago," June 11, 2015.

41. Paul and Ramona Blee, interview with author, February 4, 2016.

42. Mitchell, "High School Student Marie Blee Vanishes From Party in Craig, Colorado."

43. Paul and Ramona Blee, "Anniversary of Disappearance Brings Back Memories, Questions," *Craig Daily Press*, November 24, 2003.

44. Paul Blee and Ramona Blee, interview with author, February 4, 2016.

45. Paul and Ramona Blee, interview with author, February 4, 2016.

46. Paul and Ramona Blee, interview with author, February 4, 2016.

47. Paul and Ramona Blee, interview with author, February 4, 2016.

48. National Center for Missing & Exploited Children®, "Critically Missing Children," accessed April 22, 2016, http://www.missingkids.com/CriticallyMissing; and National Center for Missing & Exploited Children®, "Key Facts."

49. National Center for Missing & Exploited Children®, "Critically Missing Children."

50. achildismissing.org, "Suzanne's Law," accessed May 12, 2016, https://www.achildismissing.org/suzanne.asp.

51. National Center for Missing & Exploited Children®, "Critically Missing Children."

52. National Center for Missing & Exploited Children®, *2014 Annual Report* (Alexandria: NCMEC, 2014), 2.

53. National Center for Missing & Exploited Children®, "If Your Child is Missing," accessed April 22, 2016, http://www.missingkids.org/MissingChild.

54. National Center for Missing & Exploited Children®, "A Letter From NCMEC's Founders," accessed May 13, 2016, http://blog.missingkids.com/post/135461453325/a-letter-from-ncmecs-founders.

55. National Center for Missing & Exploited Children®, "Project Alert," accessed May 13, 2016, http://www.missingkids.org/ProjectALERT.

56. National Center for Missing & Exploited Children®, "Long Term Missing Cases," accessed May 13, 2016, http://www.missingkids.org/LongTermMissing.

57. Carol Schweitzer, email message to author, January 17, 2016.

58. Carol Schweitzer, email message to author, January 24, 2016.

59. Carol Schweitzer, email message to author, January 24, 2016.

60. Carol Schweitzer, email message to author, January 24, 2016.

61. Carol Schweitzer, email message to author, January 17, 2016.

62. Carol Schweitzer, email message to author, January 24, 2016.

63. Carol Schweitzer, email message to author, January 24, 2016.

64. Carol Schweitzer, email message to author, January 24, 2016.

65. Thadeus Greenson, "The Persistence of a Mother: The Huntzinger Family's Fight to Find Curtis, and the Toll It Took," *Eureka Times-Standard,* May 10, 2009.

66. Greenson, "The Persistence of a Mother."

67. Greenson, "The Persistence of a Mother."

68. Carol Schweitzer, email message to author, January 24, 2016.

69. Sean Garmire, "Missing Teen's Remains Found After 18 Years," *Eureka Times-Standard*, December 10, 2008; and Sean Garmire, "A Momentous Find for a Metal Detector," *Eureka Times-Standard*, December 27, 2008.

70. "A Timeline of the Curtis Huntzinger Case," *Eureka Times-Standard*, May 11, 2009.

71. Carol Schweitzer, email message to author, January 24, 2016.

CHAPTER 4

1. CSO Beth Buchholtz, interview with author, June 3, 2015.

2. CSO Beth Buchholtz, interview with author, June 3, 2015.

3. CSO Beth Buchholtz, interview with author, June 3, 2015.

4. CSO Beth Buchholtz, interview with author, June 3, 2015.

5. Kevin Simpson, "DNA Match Finally Puts Name to Boy's Remains—but Mystery Persists," *Denver Post*, June 22, 2014.

6. CSO Beth Buchholtz, interview with author, June 3, 2015.

7. CSO Beth Buchholtz, interview with author, June 3, 2015.

8. CSO Beth Buchholtz, interview with author, June 3, 2015.

9. CSO Beth Buchholtz, email message to author, August 25, 2015.

10. CSO Beth Buchholtz, interview with author, June 3, 2015.

11. CSO Beth Buchholtz, interview with author, June 3, 2015.

12. NamUs UP #12154, accessed May 13, 2016, https://identifyus.org/en/cases/12154.

13. National Center for Missing & Exploited Children®, "Project Alert®," accessed May 13, 2016, http://www.missingkids.org/ProjectALERT.

14. CSO Beth Buchholtz, email message to author, January 26, 2016.

15. CSO Beth Buchholtz, email message to author, January 26, 2016.

16. CSO Beth Buchholtz, email message to author, January 26, 2016.

17. CSO Beth Buccholtz, email message to author, February 1, 2016.

18. CSO Beth Buccholtz, email message to author, February 1, 2016.

19. NamUs UP #201, accessed April 22, 2016, https://identifyus.org/en/cases/201.

20. CSO Beth Buchholtz, email message to author, January 26, 2016.

21. Detective Stuart Somershoe, email message to author, June 25, 2015.

22. Detective Stuart Somershoe, email message to author, June 25, 2015.

23. Detective Stuart Somershoe, email message to author, June 25, 2015.

24. Detective Stuart Somershoe, email message to author, June 25, 2015.

25. Detective Stuart Somershoe, email message to author, June 25, 2015.

26. Detective Stuart Somershoe, email message to author, June 25, 2015.

27. Detective Stuart Somershoe, email message to author, June 25, 2015.

28. Detective Stuart Somershoe, email message to author, June 25, 2015.

29. Detective Stuart Somershoe, email message to author, June 25, 2015.

30. Detective Stuart Somershoe, email message to author, June 25, 2015.

31. Detective Stuart Somershoe, email message to author, June 25, 2015.

32. Detective Stuart Somershoe, email message to author, June 25, 2015.

33. Detective Stuart Somershoe, email message to author, June 25, 2015.

34. Detective Stuart Somershoe, email message to author, June 25, 2015.

35. Detective Stuart Somershoe, email message to author, June 25, 2015.

36. Detective Stuart Somershoe, email message to author, June 25, 2015.

37. Detective Stuart Somershoe, email message to author, June 25, 2015.

38. Detective Stuart Somershoe, email message to author, June 25, 2015.

39. Detective Stuart Somershoe, email message to author, June 25, 2015.

40. Detective Stuart Somershoe, email message to author, June 25, 2015.

41. Detective Stuart Somershoe, email message to author, June 25, 2015.

42. Detective Stuart Somershoe, email message to author, June 25, 2015.

43. Paty Rodriguez, conversation with author, October 23, 2015.

44. Detective Stuart Somershoe, email message to author, June 25, 2015.

45. Author's visit to the Heritage Sunwest Cemetery, in El Mirage, Arizona, October 23, 2015.

46. Trooper Brian F. Gross, conversation with author, August 19, 2015.

47. Trooper Brian F. Gross, email message to author, January 4, 2016.

48. Trooper Brian F. Gross, email message to author, January 4, 2016.

49. "Deaths Mystery: Court Orders Burial of Infant, Teenager," *Greensburg Tribune*, September 26, 1967.

50. Pennsylvania Missing Persons, accessed April 22, 2016, http://pennsylvania-missing.com/salemtwpjane91967.html.

51. "Body Found on Dump: Police Seek Identity of Dead Teenage Girl," *Tribune-Review*, September 20, 1967.

52. "Search Continues for Baby's Killer," *Tribune-Review*, August 28, 1967.

53. Westmoreland Manor, accessed April 22, 2016, http://westmorelandweb400.us/cty/manor/ourhistory.htm.

54. Rich Cholodofsky, "Police Want to Exhume Bodies of Infant, Teen in Pauper's Cemetery," *TribLive News*, September 28, 2015.

55. "Motion for Exhumation and Examination of Unidentified Human Remains," (In the Court of Common Pleas of Westmoreland County, Pennsylvania, Criminal Division, 440 MISC 2015), October 27, 2015.

56. Carol Schweitzer, email message to author, January 15, 2016.

57. "Motion for Exhumation and Examination of Unidentified Human Remains," October 27, 2015.

58. "Motion for Exhumation and Examination of Unidentified Human Remains," October 27, 2015.

59. "Motion for Exhumation and Examination of Unidentified Human Remains," October 27, 2015.

60. Cholodofsky, "Police Want to Exhume Bodies of Infant, Teen in Pauper's Cemetery," September 28, 2015.

61. NamUs UP #13512 (no longer accessible to the public).

62. Trooper Brian F. Gross, email message to author, January 4, 2016.

63. "2 Bodies Exhumed from Westmoreland County Pauper's Cemetery," *Pittsburg News 2*, October 30, 2015.

64. Trooper Brian F. Gross, email message to author, January 4, 2016.

65. Trooper Brian F. Gross, email message to author, January 4, 2016.

66. "Family Provides 'Strong Lead' to ID Girl Unearthed From Hempfield Grave," *TribLive News*, October 30, 2015.

67. Trooper Brian F. Gross, email message to author, January 4, 2016.

68. "Family Provides 'Strong Lead' to ID Girl Unearthed From Hempfield Grave," October 30, 2015.

69. "Family Believes Sketch of Exhumed Girl Killed Decades Ago is Missing Sister," *News wpxi.com*, December 8, 2015; and "Bodies of Baby, Teen Exhumed From Pauper's Grave in Hempfield Township, *WTAE.com*, December 9, 2015.

70. "Homewood Girl is Missing, *Pittsburgh Press*, October 3, 1967.

71. Trooper Brian F. Gross, email message to author, December 11, 2015.

72. "Composite Sketch Released of Remains of Unidentified Teenager," *KDKA CBS Pittsburgh*, December 8, 2015.

73. "Family Provides 'Strong Lead' to ID Girl Unearthed From Hempfield Grave," *TribLive News*, October 30, 2015.

74. Kristine Guerra, "A Girl Was Found Dead in a Landfill 49 Years Ago. She Has Finally Been Identified," *Washington Post*, August 6, 2016.

CHAPTER 5

1. David Egerton, email message to author, September 30, 2015.

2. David Egerton, email message to author, September 30, 2015.

3. David Egerton, email message to author, September 30, 2015.

4. David Egerton, email message to author, September 30, 2015.

5. David Egerton, email message to author, September 30, 2015.

6. David Egerton, email message to author, September 30, 2015.

7. David Egerton, email message to author, September 30, 2015.

8. David Egerton, email message to author, September 30, 2015.

9. David Egerton, email message to author, September 30, 2015.

10. David Egerton, email message to author, September 30, 2015.

11. David Egerton, email message to author, September 30, 2015.

12. David Egerton, email message to author, September 30, 2015.

13. David Egerton, email message to author, September 30, 2015.

14. David Egerton, email message to author, September 30, 2015.

15. David Egerton, email message to author, September 30, 2015.

16. Janet Franson, email message to author, May 19, 2015.

17. Lost and Missing in Indian Country Facebook page, accessed August 18, 2016, https://www.facebook.com/LostandMissinginIndianCountry/.

18. Lost and Missing in Indian Country website, accessed April 22, 2016, http://lostandmissininindiancountry.com/about.html.

19. Wyoming LostNMissing Facebook page, accessed April 22, 2016, https://www.facebook.com/wyominglostnmissing/?fref=ts.

20. Lost and Missing in Indian Country website.

21. Janet Franson, email message to author, February 7, 2016.

22. Janet Franson, email message to author, May 19, 2015.

23. Janet Franson, email message to author, February 7, 2016.

24. Janet Franson, email message to author, February 7, 2016.

25. Lost and Missing in Indian Country Facebook page.

26. Reverend Barbara M. Rocha, accessed April 22, 2016, http://www.theangelrev. com/Maheo_o_Reiki.htm.

27. Janet Franson, email message to author, February 7, 2016.

28. Unidentified Persons Jewelry Facebook page, accessed April 22, 2016, https:// www.facebook.com/unidentifiedpersonsjewelry/.

29. Janet Franson, email message to author, May 25, 2015.

30. Jody Ewing, email message to author, October 7, 2015.

31. Iowa Cold Cases website, accessed August 19, 2016, https://iowacoldcases. org/.

32. Jody Ewing, email message to author, October 7, 2015.

33. Jody Ewing, email message to author, October 7, 2015.

34. Iowa Cold Cases website.

35. Mike Kilen, "Woman Crusades to Publicize Iowa's Unsolved Murders," *The Des Moines Register*, July 27, 2015.

36. Iowa Cold Cases, Nissen, accessed April 22, 2016, https://iowacoldcases.org/ case-summaries/wilma-june-nissen/.

37. Jody Ewing, email message to author, October 7, 2015.

38. Iowa Cold Cases, Missing Persons, accessed April 22, 2016, https://iowacold-cases.org/missing-persons/.

39. Iowa Cold Cases, Demaris, accessed April 22, 2016, https://iowacoldcases.org/ case-summaries/lillian-demaris/.

40. Iowa Cold Cases, Huisentruit, accessed April 22, 2016, https://iowacoldcases. org/case-summaries/jodi-huisentruit/.

41. Iowa Cold Cases, Solved, accessed April 22, 2016, https://iowacoldcases.org/ solved/.

42. Iowa Cold Cases, Solved, accessed April 22, 2016, https://iowacoldcases.org/ solved/.

43. Iowa Department of Public Safety, Missing Person Information Clearinghouse, accessed April 22, 2016, http://www.iowaonline.state.ia.us/mpic/.

44. Jeff Reinitz, "Now-abandoned State Cold Case Unit Solved Crimes," *Waterloo-Cedar Falls Courier*, August 1, 2015.

45. Iowa Cold Cases website.

46. Iowa Cold Cases Facebook page, accessed April 22, 2016, https://www.face-book.com/iowacoldcases/.

47. Kilen, "Woman Crusades to Publicize Iowa's Unsolved Murders."

48. Silvia Pettem, *Cold Case Research: Resources for Unidentified, Missing, and Cold Homicide Cases* (Boca Raton: CRC Press, Taylor & Francis Group, 2013), 206–208.

49. Texas EquuSearch, accessed April 22, 2016, http://www.texasequusearch.org/.

50. "More Questions than Answers in ND Man's Death," *KOTA Territory News*, August 13, 2015.

51. Colorado Forensic Canines website, accessed April 22, 2016, http://www. findthelost.org/.

52. Author's observations, June 29, 2012, Walden, Colorado.

53. Author's observations, June 29, 2012, Walden, Colorado.

54. Bonnie Guzman, email message to author, December 29, 2015.

55. Author's observations, June 29, 2012, Walden, Colorado.

56. Bonnie Guzman, email message to author, December 29, 2015.

57. Author's observations, June 29, 2012, Walden, Colorado.

58. "Search and Rescue Dogs—Canine Heroes," *Veterinary News Network*, December 22, 2015.

59. Bonnie Guzman, email message to author, February 3, 2016.

60. "More Questions than Answers in ND Man's Death."

61. Bonnie Guzman, email message to author, February 3, 2016.

CHAPTER 6

1. Celeste Shaw, "Letter to Chief of Police, Pete Carey, Colorado Springs Police Department," August 27, 2013.

2. Celeste Shaw, interview with author, May 29, 2015.

3. Celeste Shaw, interview with author, May 29, 2015.

4. Celeste Shaw, interview with author, May 29, 2015.

5. Celeste Shaw, interview with author, May 29, 2015.

6. Celeste Shaw, interview with author, May 29, 2015.

7. Celeste Shaw, interview with author, June 29, 2015.

8. Celeste Shaw, interview with author, June 29, 2015.

9. Silvia Pettem, *Cold Case Research: Resources for Unidentified, Missing, and Cold Homicide Cases* (Boca Raton: CRC Press, Taylor & Francis Group, 2013), 222.

10. Celeste Shaw, interview with author, May 29, 2015.

11. Celeste Shaw, interview with author, June 29, 2015.

12. Celeste Shaw, interview with author, June 29, 2015.

13. Celeste Shaw, interview with author, June 29, 2015.

14. The Doe Network, Unidentified Persons, accessed April 22, 2016, http://www.doenetwork.org/unidentified.php.

15. Celeste Shaw, interview with author, June 29, 2015.

16. Colorado Bureau of Investigation Cold Case Files, accessed April 22, 2016, https://www.colorado.gov/apps/coldcase/index.html.

17. Celeste Shaw, interview with author, June 29, 2015.

18. Celeste Shaw, interview with author, June 29, 2015.

19. "Presumption of Death of a Missing Person," Social Security Administration, accessed April 22, 2016, https://secure.ssa.gov/poms.nsf/lnx/0200304050.

20. Celeste Shaw, interview with author, June 29, 2015.

21. Celeste Shaw, interview with author, June 29, 2015.

22. Celeste Shaw, interview with author, June 29, 2015.

23. Celeste Shaw, interview with author, June 29, 2015.

24. Christine Pelisek, "Lost and Found in Tijuana: Behind an Amazing American Rescue," *The Daily Beast*, September 26, 2013.

25. Celeste Shaw, interview with author, June 29, 2015.

26. Celeste Shaw, interview with author, June 29, 2015.

27. Celeste Shaw, interview with author, June 29, 2015.

28. Celeste Shaw, interview with author, June 29, 2015.

29. Celeste Shaw, interview with author, June 29, 2015.

30. Celeste Shaw, interview with author, June 29, 2015.

31. Celeste Shaw, interview with author, June 29, 2015.

32. Celeste Shaw, interview with author, May 29, 2015.

CHAPTER 7

1. Beth Pearsall and Daniel Weiss, "Solving Missing Persons Cases," *National Institute of Justice Journal* 264, (November 2009): 6.

2. George Kirchhoff, interview with author, August 23, 2013.

3. George Kirchhoff, interview with author, August 23, 2013.

4. George Kirchhoff, interview with author, August 23, 2013.

5. Detective Ron Lopez, interview with author, August 23, 2013.

6. George Kirchhoff, interview with author, August 23, 2013.

7. George Kirchhoff, interview with author, August 23, 2013.

8. George Kirchhoff, interview with author, August 23, 2013.

9. George Kirchhoff, interview with author, August 23, 2013.

10. George Kirchhoff, interview with author, August 23, 2013.

11. George Kirchhoff, interview with author, August 23, 2013.

12. Detective Ron Lopez, email message to author, February 2, 2016.

13. Find A Grave, accessed April 22, 2016, http://www.findagrave.com/cgi-bin/fg.cgi?page=gr&GSln=Kirchhoff&GSiman=1&GScid=2260132&GRid=109673792&.

14. Detective Ron Lopez, email message to author, February 2, 2016.

15. Detective Ron Lopez, email message to author, February 2, 2016.

16. Detective Ron Lopez, email message to author, February 2, 2016.

17. Detective Ron Lopez, email message to author, February 2, 2016.

18. Detective Ron Lopez, email message to author, February 2, 2016.

19. Detective Ron Lopez, email message to author, February 2, 2016.

20. Detective Ron Lopez, email message to author, January 9, 2016.

21. Detective Ron Lopez, email message to author, January 9, 2016.

22. Detective Ron Lopez, interview with author, August 23, 2013.

23. Detective Ron Lopez, email message to author, February 2, 2016.

24. George Kirchhoff, "Letter to the Colorado Springs Police Department, Chief of Police," April 25, 2013.

25. George Kirchhoff, interview with author, August 23, 2013.

26. Melissa Gregory, interview with author, January 21, 2016.

27. Melissa Gregory, interview with author, January 21, 2016.

28. Melissa Gregory, interview with author, January 21, 2016.

29. Melissa Gregory, interview with author, January 21, 2016.

30. Melissa Gregory, interview with author, January 21, 2016.

31. Melissa Gregory, interview with author, January 21, 2016.

32. Melissa Gregory, interview with author, January 21, 2016.

33. Melissa Gregory, interview with author, January 21, 2016.

34. Melissa Gregory, interview with author, January 21, 2016.

35. NamUs, accessed April 22, 2016, http://www.namus.gov/.

36. NamUs, accessed April 22, 2016, http://www.namus.gov/.

37. Welcome to NamUs Missing Persons page, accessed April 22, 2016, https://www.findthemissing.org/en.

38. NamUs, accessed April 22, 2016, http://www.namus.gov/.

39. NamUs, FAQ page, accessed April 22, 2016, https://www.findthemissing.org/en/homes/faq.

40. Colorado Bureau of Investigation, Cold Case Files, accessed August 22, 2016, https://www.colorado.gov/apps/coldcase/index.html.

41. Welcome to NamUs Unidentified Persons page, accessed April 22, 2016, https://identifyus.org/en.

42. Silvia Pettem, *Cold Case Research: Resources for the Unidentified, Missing, and Cold Homicide Cases* (Boca Raton: CRC Press, Taylor & Francis Group, 2013), 85.

43. Pettem, *Cold Case Research*, 85.

44. Pettem, *Cold Case Research*, 85.

45. Silvia Pettem, *Cold Case Research*, 85.

46. Silvia Pettem, *Cold Case Research*, 85.

47. Find A Grave, accessed April 22, 2016, http://www.findagrave.com/cgi-bin/fg.cgi?page=gr&GRid=48081381.

CHAPTER 8

1. Lindsey Bever, "How a Man Solved the 30-year Mystery of His Own Disappearance," *The Washington Post*, February 12, 2016.

2. Lindsey Bever, "How a Man Solved the 30-year Mystery of His Own Disappearance."

3. R. H. Walton, email message to author, January 12, 2016.

4. Silvia Pettem, *Cold Case Research: Resources for the Unidentified, Missing, and Cold Homicide Cases* (Boca Raton: CRC Press, Taylor & Francis Group, 2013), 217.

5. Katie Rogers, "Grateful Doe is Identified 20 Years After Road Trip Death," *New York Times*, December 11, 2015.

6. Rogers, "Grateful Doe is Identified 20 Years After Road Trip Death."

7. Rogers, "Grateful Doe is Identified 20 Years After Road Trip Death."

8. Rogers, "Grateful Doe is Identified 20 Years After Road Trip Death."

9. University of North Texas Health Science Center, Forensic Services Unit, Frequently Asked Questions, accessed April 22, 2016, http://www.untfsu.com/NamUs/FAQ_DNA.html.

10. Missing in Michigan website, accessed April 22, 2016, http://www.missingin-michigan.com/.

11. Sergeant Sarah Krebs, email message to author, November 4, 2015.

12. Missing in Michigan website, accessed April 22, 2016, http://www.missingin-michigan.com/.

13. Sergeant Sarah Krebs, email message to author, November 4, 2015.

14. Sergeant Sarah Krebs, email message to author, November 4, 2015.

15. Missing in Michigan Facebook group, accessed April 22, 2016, https://www.facebook.com/groups/MichigansMissing/#_=_.

16. New York City Office of Chief Medical Examiner website, accessed April 22, 2016, http://www.nyc.gov/html/ocme/html/mpi/mpi_home.shtml.

17. Amy Taxin, "Authorities Ask Family of Missing Persons for DNA, Records," *Associated Press*, September 29, 2015.

18. New York City Office of Chief Medical Examiner website.

19. Taxin, "Authorities Ask Family of Missing Persons for DNA, Records."

20. Orange County Sheriff's Department Coroner Division website, "Identify the Missing, Orange County 2015 Flyer," accessed April 22, 2016, http://ocsd.org/divisions/fieldops/coroner/ud.

21. Orange County Sheriff's Department Coroner Division website.

22. Missing in Arizona Facebook page, accessed May 14, 2016, https://www.facebook.com/AZmissing/?fref=photo.

23. Author's observation, October 24, 2015.

24. Detective Stuart Somershoe, email message to author, November 1, 2015.

25. NamUs MP #30248, Darian Nevayaktewa, accessed April 22, 2016, https://www.findthemissing.org/en/cases/30248/24.

26. Elmo Nevayaktewa, conversation with author, October 24, 2015.

27. Detective Stuart Somershoe, email message to author, November 1, 2015.

28. NamUs MP #30248, Darian Nevayaktewa, accessed April 22, 2016, https://www.findthemissing.org/en/cases/30248/24.

29. Detective Stuart Somershoe, email message to author, November 1, 2015.

30. Author's observation, October 24, 2015.

31. Detective Stuart Somershoe, email message to author, November 1, 2015.

32. Melissa Gregory, email message to author, February 22, 2016.

33. Missouri Missing website, accessed April 22, 2016, http://www.missourimiss-ing.org/index.html.

34. Families of Homicide Victims and Missing Persons website, accessed April 22, 2016, http://www.unresolvedhomicides.org/about-us/.

35. National Center for Missing and Exploited Children®, Team HOPE website, accessed April 22, 2016, http://www.missingkids.com/teamhope.

36. National Center for Missing and Exploited Children®, Team HOPE website.

37. Robert G. Lowery, Jr. and Robert Hoever, "Family Dynamics and Survivor Recovery: Understanding the Relationships," *Long-term Missing Child Guide for Law Enforcement: Strategies for Finding Long-term Missing Children* (National Center for Missing and Exploited Children® (2016): 195.

38. Pettem, *Cold Case Research*, 251–256.

39. The Statistics Portal, accessed April 22, 2016, http://www.statista.com/topics/751/facebook/.

40. Pew Research Center, accessed April 22, 2016, http://www.pewinternet.org/2015/08/19/the-demographics-of-social-media-users/.

41. Help ID Me, Facebook page, accessed April 22, 2016, https://www.facebook.com/HelpIDMe/.

42. Carol Schweitzer, email message to author, January 24, 2016.

43. Angie Yarnell Still Missing and Loved Facebook page, accessed May 14, 2016, https://www.facebook.com/search/top/?q=Angie%20Yarnell%20Still%20Missing%20and%20Loved.

44. "Where is Gloria Jean?" Facebook group, accessed May 14, 2016, https://www.facebook.com/search/top/?q=%20Where%20is%20Gloria%20Jean.

45. Reddit website, accessed may 14, 2016, https://www.reddit.com/.

46. Websleuths, Missing Forum, accessed April 22, 2016, http://www.websleuths.com/forums/forumdisplay.php?16-MISSING.

47. Pettem, *Cold Case Research*, 259.

48. Pettem, *Cold Case Research*, 258.

CHAPTER 9

1. The Doe Network, accessed April 22, 2016, http://www.doenetwork.org/index.php.

2. Silvia Pettem, *Someone's Daughter: In Search of Justice for Jane Doe* (Lanham, Maryland: Taylor Trade, 2009), 111.

3. Pettem, *Someone's Daughter*, 174–175.

4. Pettem, *Someone's Daughter*, 174–175.

5. Pettem, *Someone's Daughter*, 174–175.

6. Veromi, accessed April 22, 2016, http://www.veromi.net/.

7. Silvia Pettem, "Out of the Past: A Fresh Look at Cold Cases," *Evidence Technology Magazine*, Vol. 8, No. 2 (March–April 2010): 24–27.

8. Family Search, Social Security Death Index, accessed April 22, 2016, https://familysearch.org/search/collection/1202535.

9. Pettem, *Someone's Daughter*, 175.

10. Silvia Pettem, *Cold Case Research: Resources for Unidentified, Missing, and Cold Homicide Cases* (Boca Raton: CRC Press, Taylor & Francis Group, 2013), 186.

11. FBI Records: Freedom of Information Act/Privacy Act, accessed April 22, 2016, http://www.fbi.gov/foia/requesting-fbi-records.

12. National Archives: Research Our Records, accessed April 22, 2016, http://www.archives.gov/research/.

13. National Archives: Research Our Records, accessed April 22, 2016, http://www.archives.gov/research/.

14. Silvia Pettem, *Cold Case* Research, 137.

15. Silvia Pettem, *Cold Case Research*, 138.

16. Silvia Pettem, *Cold Case Research*, 138.

17. Ballotpedia, Colorado Open Records Act, accessed April 22, 2016, http://sunshinereview.org/index.php/Colorado_Open_Records_Act.

18. Corrections Records, Colorado State Archives, accessed May 14, 2016, https://www.colorado.gov/pacific/archives/corrections-records.

19. Maricopa County Recorder, accessed April 22, 2016, http://recorder.maricopa.gov/recdocdata/.

20. Pettem, *Someone's Daughter*, 133.

CHAPTER 10

1. "Spiritualism," *The Encyclopedia Britannica, a Dictionary of Arts, Sciences, and General Literature,* Vol. XXII (New York: Henry G. Allen and Company, 1888), 404–405.

2. Merriam-Webster website, accessed May 14, 2016, http://www.merriam-webster.com/dictionary/psychic.

3. Detective Stuart Somershoe, email message to author, March 26, 2016.

4. Detective Stuart Somershoe, email message to author, March 26, 2016.

5. Joseph K. Reynolds, interview with author, March 15, 2016.

6. Social Security Administration, "Presumption of Death of a Missing Person," accessed April 22, 2016, https://secure.ssa.gov/poms.nsf/lnx/0200304050.

7. Joseph K. Reynolds, interview with author, March 15, 2016.

8. Joseph K. Reynolds, interview with author, March 15, 2016.

9. Joseph K. Reynolds, interview with author, March 15, 2016.

10. Straight Dope Science Advisory Board, "What Happens When Someone 'Legally Dead' Shows Up Alive?" *The Straight Dope*, June 13, 2006.

11. Straight Dope Science Advisory Board, "What Happens When Someone 'Legally Dead' Shows Up Alive?" *The Straight Dope*, June 13, 2006.

12. Tom Asimou and Kaysey Fung, "Vanished: When Loved Ones are Presumed Dead," *The Arizona Republic*, March 13, 2015.

13. Silvia Pettem, *Cold Case Research: Resources for Unidentified, Missing, and Cold Homicide Cases* (Boca Raton: CRC Press, Taylor & Francis Group, 2013), 127.

14. Thadeus Greenson, "Curtis Huntziner's Mother Wins Wrongful Death Lawsuit," *The Times-Standard*, September 29, 2009.

15. Wesierski & Zurek, "Who Can Recover in a Wrongful Death Action?" October 18, 2012, accessed April 23, 2016, http://www.wzllp.com/who-can-recover-in-a-wrongful-death-action/.

16. FindLaw, "Wrongful Death Claims: Time Limits and the 'Discovery' Rule," 2016, accessed April 23, 2016, http://injury.findlaw.com/torts-and-personal-injuries/wrongful-death-claims-time-limits-and-the-discovery-rule.html.

17. FindLaw, "Wrongful Death Claims: Time Limits and the 'Discovery' Rule," 2016, accessed April 23, 2016.

18. CBS News, "Lead Attorney Johnnie Cochran—The O.J. Simpson Murder Trial 20 Years Later," accessed May 14, 2016, http://www.cbsnews.com/pictures/the-o-j-simpson-trial-where-are-they-now/26/.

19. CNN.com, "Jury Unanimous: Simpson is Liable," February 4, 1997, accessed April 23, 2016, http://www.cnn.com/US/9702/04/simpson.verdict1/.

20. CNN.com, "Jury Unanimous: Simpson is Liable," February 4, 1997.

21. Dana Bartholomew, "Lovelock, Nevada—Home to the Barren, Desert Prison Where O.J. Simpson Lives," *Los Angeles Daily News*, June 11, 2014.

CHAPTER 11

1. Larry Seward, "Missing Girl Mystery Solved in Minnesota," *KHOU 11 News*, July 15, 2015.

2. Seward, "Missing Girl Mystery Solved in Minnesota."

3. Sergeant Teresa Jeremiah, email message to author, July 21, 2015.

4. RoadsideAmerica.com, accessed May 15, 2016, http://www.roadsideamerica.com/story/35952.

5. Deputy Sheriff Jerry Kabe, "Interview of Robert Leroy Nelson," Faribault County Sheriff's Office, Blue Earth Jane Doe case file, July 17, 1989.

6. "Who Was She?" *Blue Earth Post*, June 5, 1980.

7. "Who Was She?" *Blue Earth Post*, June 5, 1980.

8. M.B. McGee, M.D., "Autopsy report, ME80-491," Faribault County Sheriff's Office, Blue Earth Jane Doe case file, June 2, 1980.

9. M.B. McGee, M.D., "Autopsy report, ME80-491," Faribault County Sheriff's Office, Blue Earth Jane Doe case file, June 2, 1980.

10. Jim Parseas, "Case of Woman Without a Name Leaves Police Without a Suspect," *Minneapolis Tribune*, July 15, 1980.

11. Investigator Jerry Kabe, telephone conversation with author, July 8, 2015.

12. Parseas, "Case of Woman Without a Name Leaves Police Without a Suspect," July 15, 1980.

13. Investigator Jerry Kabe, telephone conversation with author, July 8, 2015.

14. Chuck Hunt, "A 35-year Investigation Now Over," *Faribault County Register*, March 22, 2015.

15. "Missing Person, Victim: Michelle Yvette Busha," Faribault County Sheriff's Office, Blue Earth Jane Doe case file, undated (after Busha's identification).

16. Phil Lerman, telephone conversation with author, June 25, 2015.

17. Sarah Day, "Identity of Jane Doe Still a Mystery," *Fairmont Sentinel*, June 6, 2008.

18. Anonymous letter, Faribault County Sheriff's Office, Blue Earth Jane Doe case file, 1980.

19. Special Agent Robert Berg, Minnesota Bureau of Criminal Apprehension (MNBCA), "Report of Robert Leroy Nelson," Faribault County Sheriff's Office, Blue Earth Jane Doe case file, March 31, 1988.

20. Special Agent Robert Berg, MNBCA, "Report of Robert Leroy Nelson," March 31, 1988.

21. Special Agent Robert Berg, MNBCA, "Report of Robert Leroy Nelson," March 31, 1988.

22. Special Agent Robert Berg, MNBCA, "Report of Robert Leroy Nelson," March 31, 1988.

23. Special Agent Robert Berg, Minnesota Bureau of Criminal Apprehension, "Report of Robert Leroy Nelson," Faribault County Sheriff's Office, Blue Earth Jane Doe case file, April 15, 1988.

24. Faribault County Attorney, "Press Release," Faribault County Sheriff's Office, Blue Earth Jane Doe case file, May 27, 1988.

25. Bailey Blethen to Arvid Wendland Memorandum, "State of Minnesota v. Robert Leroy Nelson," Faribault County Sheriff's Office, Blue Earth Jane Doe case file, August 19,1988.

26. Investigator Jerry Kabe, telephone conversation with author, July 8, 2015.

27. Deputy Sheriff Jerry Kabe, "Interview of Robert Leroy Nelson," July 17, 1989.

28. Deputy Sheriff Jerry Kabe, "Interview of Robert Leroy Nelson," July 17, 1989.

29. Deputy Sheriff Jerry Kabe, "Interview of Robert Leroy Nelson," July 17, 1989.

30. Deputy Sheriff Jerry Kabe, "Interview of Robert Leroy Nelson," July 17, 1989.

31. Faribault County Attorney's Office and the Faribault County Sheriff's Office, "Joint Press release," Faribault County Sheriff's Office, Blue Earth Jane Doe case file, August 25, 1989.

32. State of Minnesota, County of Faribault, District Court, "Sentence of Robert Leroy Nelson," Faribault County Sheriff's Office, Blue Earth Jane Doe case file, August 25, 1989.

33. Texas Department of Criminal Justice, Offender Information Details, accessed April 23, 2016, https://offender.tdcj.texas.gov/OffenderSearch/offenderDetail.action?sid=04082389.

34. Investigator Jerry Kabe, telephone conversation with author, July 8, 2015.

35. Richard Saferstein, *Criminalistics: An Introduction to Forensic Science* (Upper Saddle River: Pearson Prentice Hall, 2004), 384.

36. Saferstein, *Criminalistics*, 372.

37. Phil Lerman, "Lessons From 'America's Most Wanted': Never Give Up," *CNN*, May 9, 2013.

38. Deb Anderson, telephone interview with author, October 22, 2014.

39. Deb Anderson, telephone interview with author, October 22, 2014.

40. Ruben Rosario, "Victim Deserves a Name, Doe Group Says," *Pioneer Press, TwinCities.com*, September 15, 2003.

41. Deb Anderson, telephone interview with author, October 22, 2014.

42. Deb Anderson, telephone interview with author, October 22, 2014.

43. Minnesota Bureau of Criminal Apprehension, "Evidence Receipt," Faribault County Sheriff's Office, Blue Earth Jane Doe case file, June 2, 1980.

44. Minnesota Bureau of Criminal Apprehension, "ACISS Investigative Supplement 1980000335/1," Faribault County Sheriff's Office, Blue Earth Jane Doe case file, June 27, 2014.

45. Faribault County Sheriff's Office, Blue Earth Jane Doe case file, "Sheriff Memorandum to Investigator Tom Dybvik," May 25, 2004.

46. Rosario, "Victim Deserves a Name, Doe Group Says."

47. Sarah Day, "Jane Doe Finds an Advocate," *Fairmont Sentinel*, January 19, 2008.

48. Sergeant Teresa Jeremiah, email message to author, July 21, 2015.

49. Sergeant Teresa Jeremiah, email message to author, July 21, 2015.

50. Sergeant Teresa Jeremiah, email message to author, July 21, 2015.

51. Minnesota Department of Public Safety, "DPS News Conference: DNA Leads BCA to Victim's Identity in 1980 Homicide," March 17, 2015, accessed April 23, 2016, https://www.youtube.com/watch?v=O8Tw4FGOJJg.

52. Minnesota Bureau of Criminal Apprehension, "ACISS Investigative Supplement 1980000335/1," June 27, 2014 (updated September 24, 2014).

53. Sheriff Roger Fletcher, telephone conversation with author, July 8, 2015.

54. Jill Oliveira, email message to author, October 9, 2015.

55. Minnesota Bureau of Criminal Apprehension, ACISS Investigative Supplement 1980000335/4, Faribault County Sheriff's Office, Blue Earth Jane Doe case file, March 16, 2015.

56. Minnesota Bureau of Criminal Apprehension, ACISS Investigative Supplement 1980000335/4, March 16, 2015.

57. State of Minnesota, County of Faribault, District Court, Fifth Judicial District, "Petition for Exhumation," Faribault County Sheriff's Office, Blue Earth Jane Doe case file, July 30, 2014.

58. Minnesota Bureau of Criminal Apprehension, ACISS Investigative Supplement 1980000335/4, March 16, 2015.

59. Minnesota Bureau of Criminal Apprehension, ACISS Investigative Supplement 1980000335/4, March 16, 2015.

60. Minnesota Bureau of Criminal Apprehension, ACISS Investigative Supplement 1980000335/4, March 16, 2015. (According to the death certificate, Michelle was born in Muscogee, Oklahoma, on November 2, 1961.)

61. Minnesota Department of Public Safety, "DPS News Conference: DNA Leads BCA to Victim's Identity in 1980 Homicide," March 17, 2015, accessed April 23, 2016, https://www.youtube.com/watch?v=O8Tw4FGOJJg.

CHAPTER 12

1. Lake County Library, Evergreen Cemetery Records, accessed April 23, 2016, http://www.lakecountypubliclibrary.org/Cemetery%20Records.htm.

2. Author's observation, July 11, 2016.

3. John Piearson, interview with author, August 14, 2011.

4. "Decomposed Body Found in Ditch on Independence Pass," *Herald Democrat*, June 22, 1970.

5. *Herald Democrat* article of July 17, 1970 referenced in Marcia Martinek, "Can This John Doe be Identified?" *Herald Democrat*, March 23, 2016, accessed April 23, 2016, http://www.leadvilleherald.com/free_content/article_4259a4f6-f140-11e5-aca1-d3c184426a84.html.

6. "Decomposed Body Found in Ditch on Independence Pass," *Herald Democrat*, June 22, 1970.

7. "Man's Body Found," *Associated Press*, undated (circa June 22, 1970).

8. "Decomposed Body Found in Ditch on Independence Pass," *Herald Democrat*, June 22, 1970.

9. NamUs UP #10738, accessed April 23, 2016, https://identifyus.org/en/cases/10738.

10. Marcia Martinek, "Can This John Doe be Identified?" *Herald Democrat*, March 23, 2016, accessed April 23, 2016, http://www.leadvilleherald.com/free_content/article_4259a4f6-f140-11e5-aca1-d3c184426a84.html.

11. "Body of Small Girl Found: Unidentified Body Found on Desert," *Prescott Evening Courier*, August 1, 1960.

12. "Prescottonians Do Care! Open Hearts to Dead Girl," *Prescott Evening Courier*, August 10, 1960.

13. "Prescottonians Do Care! Open Hearts to Dead Girl," August 10, 1960.

14. "Prescottonians Do Care! Open Hearts to Dead Girl," August 10, 1960.

15. Ken Shake, "Clue to 'Little Miss Nobody' Still Sought," *Prescott Evening Courier,* November 4, 1960.

16. "Unidentified Female Child," Certificate of Autopsy or Inquest, Arizona State Department of Health, approximate date of death July 15, 1960, signed October 14, 1960.

17. NamUs UP #10741, accessed April 23, 2016, https://identifyus.org/en/cases/10741.

18. History Flight, Inc., accessed April 23, 2016, http://historyflight.com/nw/.

19. History Flight, Inc., "History Flight Recovers Dozens of Tarawa Marines From Burial Site Lost in 1943," *History Flight Press Release*, June 27, 2015.

20. Clay Bonnyman Evans, email message to author, April 6, 2016.

21. Clay Bonnyman Evans, email message to author, April 6, 2016.

22. Michael E. Miller, "Golden Ending: How One Man Discovered his War Hero Grandfather's Long-lost Grave," *The Washington Post*, July 2, 2015.

23. History Flight, Inc., "History Flight Recovers Dozens of Tarawa Marines From Burial Site Lost in 1943," *History Flight Press Release*, June 27, 2015.

24. Clay Bonnyman Evans, email message to author, April 6, 2016.

25. Clay Bonnyman Evans, email message to author, April 6, 2016.

26. Abijah P. Marvin, *History of Worcester in the War of the Rebellion* (Worcester: "The Author," 1870), 453.

27. Abijah P. Marvin, *History of Worcester in the War of the Rebellion*, 1870.

28. Nick Miller, "I Once Was Lost But Now Am Found, Anzac's Grave Finally Named," *The Sidney Morning Herald*, April 27, 2015.

29. Miller, "I Once Was Lost But Now Am Found, Anzac's Grave Finally Named," 2015.

30. Miller, "I Once Was Lost But Now Am Found, Anzac's Grave Finally Named," 2015.

31. Larry Hendricks, "Helping the Lost," *Arizona Daily Sun*, March 18, 2015.

32. Hendricks, "Helping the Lost," March 18, 2015.

33. Hendricks, "Helping the Lost," March 18, 2015.

34. Hendricks, "Helping the Lost," March 18, 2015.

35. Alexa Talamo, "Database Reveals Parish-wide Counts of Unidentified," *Shreveport Times*, January 4, 2016.

36. Carol Ann Project, accessed April 23. 2016, Carol Ann Project Facebook page, https://www.facebook.com/CarolAnnProject/timeline.

Bibliography

INTERVIEWEES

Anderson, Deb
Blee, Paul and Ramona
Bloemendaal, Sheriff Blythe
Brown, Dorothy Holmes
Buchholtz, CSO Beth
Egerton, David
Evans, Clay Bonnyman
Ewing, Jody
Fletcher, Sheriff Roger
Franson, Janet
Gates, Robert
Gregory, Melissa
Gross, Trooper Brian F.
Guzman, Bonnie
Halpern, Roland
Hoogendoorn, Gina
Jeremiah, Sergeant Teresa
Johanneck, Lesha
Kabe, Chief Investigator Jerry
Kirchhoff, George
Krebs, Sergeant Sarah
LaPoint, Stephanie
Lavigne, Micki
Lerman, Phil
Lopez, Detective Ron Lopez
McGregor, Kevin A.
Moore, Investigator Cheryl

Piearson, John
Ralston, Gene
Reynolds, Joseph K.
Schweitzer, Carol
Shaw, Celeste
Somershoe, Detective Stuart
Walton, R.H.

BOOKS

The Encyclopedia Britannica, a Dictionary of Arts, Sciences, and General Literature, Vol. XXII. Henry G. Allen and Company, 1888.

Marvin, Abijah P. *History of Worcester in the War of the Rebellion.* Worcester: "The Author," 1870.

McGregor, Kevin A. *Flight of Gold: Two Pilots' True Adventure Discovering Alaska's Legendary Gold Wreck.* In-depth editions, 2013.

Pettem, Silvia. *Cold Case Research: Resources for Unidentified, Missing, and Cold Homicide Cases.* Boca Raton: CRC Press, Taylor & Francis Group, 2013.

Pettem, Silvia. *Someone's Daughter: In Search of Justice for Jane Doe.* Lanham: Taylor Trade, 2009.

Saferstein, Richard. *Criminalistics: An Introduction to Forensic Science.* Upper Saddle River: Pearson Prentice Hall, 2004.

Smart, Elizabeth, et al. *You're Not Alone: The Journey From Abduction to Empowerment.* Washington, D.C.: US Department of Justice, 2008.

NEWSPAPER ARTICLES AND TELEVISION BROADCASTS

Asimou, Tom and Kaysey Fung. "Vanished: When Loved Ones are Presumed Dead." *The Arizona Republic*, March 13, 2015.

Barreto, Megan. "Hurricane Katrina: 9 Years Later." *Aol.com Editors*, August 29, 2014.

Bartholomew, Dana. "Lovelock, Nevada—Home to the Barren, Desert Prison Where O.J. Simpson Lives." *Los Angeles Daily News*, June 11, 2014.

Blee, Paul and Ramona Blee. "Anniversary of Disappearance Brings Back Memories, Questions." *Craig Daily Press*, November 24, 2003.

Botelho, Greg, et al. "Ohio Kidnapping Case: Amanda Berry's Baby Delivered by Another Captive." *CNN.com*, May 9, 2013.

Butz, Dolly A. "Looking for Buried Answers." *Sioux City Journal*, September 16, 2007.

Butz, Dolly A. "Saying a Final Goodbye." *Sioux City Journal*, June 4, 2006.

Cholodofsky, Rich. "Police Want to Exhume Bodies of Infant, Teen in Pauper's Cemetery." *TribLive News*, September 28, 2015.

Day, Sarah. "Identity of Jane Doe Still a Mystery." *Fairmont Sentinel*, June 6, 2008.

Day, Sarah. "Jane Doe Finds an Advocate." *Fairmont Sentinel*, January 19, 2008.

Enyeart, Karen. "Brenda Heist Found: Woman Missing Since 02 Alive." *eCanadanow*, May 2, 2013.

Franz, Scott. "Monty Dean Doolin Booked Into the Routt County Jail on 1st Degree Kidnapping Charge." *Steamboat Today*, June 12, 2015.

Franz, Scott. "Suspect in Marie Blee Cold Case Arrested on Suspicion of Kidnapping a Different Routt County Teenager More Than 30 Years Ago." *Steamboat Today*, June 11, 2015.

Garmire, Sean. "A Momentous Find for a Metal Detector." *Eureka Times-Standard*, December 27, 2008.

Garmire, Sean. "Missing Teen's Remains Found After 18 Years." *Eureka Times-Standard*, December 10, 2008.

Greenson, Thadeus. "Curtis Huntziner's Mother Wins Wrongful Death Lawsuit." *The Times-Standard*, September 29, 2009.

Greenson, Thadeus. "The Persistence of a Mother: The Huntzinger Family's Fight to Find Curtis, and the Toll It Took." *Eureka Times-Standard*, May 10, 2009.

Guerra, Kristine, "A Girl Was Found Dead in a Landfill 49 Years Ago. She Has Finally Been Identified." *Washington Post*, August 6, 2016.

Hendricks, Larry. "Helping the Lost." *Arizona Daily Sun*, March 18, 2015.

History Flight, Inc. "History Flight Recovers Dozens of Tarawa Marines From Burial Site Lost in 1943." *History Flight Press Release*, June 27, 2015.

Hunt, Chuck. "A 35-year Investigation Now Over." *Faribault County Register*, March 22, 2015.

Kilen, Mike. "Woman Crusades to Publicize Iowa's Unsolved Murders." *The Des Moines Register*, July 27, 2015.

Langbein, Sarah. "16 Years Later 'Jane Doe' Has a Name." *Rocky Mountain News*, January 25, 2006.

Lerman, Phil. "Lessons From 'America's Most Wanted': Never Give Up." *CNN*, May 9, 2013.

Lindsey Bever. "How a Man Solved the 30-year Mystery of His Own Disappearance." *The Washington Post*, February 12, 2016.

Martinek, Marcia. "Can this John Doe Be Identified?" *Herald Democrat*, March 23, 2016, accessed April 23, 2016, http://www.leadvilleherald.com/free_content/article_4259a4f6-f140-11e5-aca1-d3c184426a84.html

Matas, Kimberly. "Missing 30 Years, Victim Was Right Here." *Arizona Daily Star*, April 14, 2012.

Miller, Michael E. "Golden Ending: How One Man Discovered His War Hero Grandfather's Long-lost Grave." *The Washington Post*, July 2, 2015.

Miller, Nick. "I Once Was Lost But Now Am Found, Anzac's Grave Finally Named." *The Sidney Morning Herald*, April 27, 2015.

Miller, Vanessa. "Family in Boulder for 'Jane Doe' Memorial, 56 Years after Her Murder." *Daily Camera*, May 20, 2010.

Mitchell, Kirk. "High School Student Marie Blee Vanishes From Party in Craig, Colorado." *Denver Post*, November 15, 2009.

Paddock, Richard C., et al. "Suspect's Tip Leads to Body of Polly Klaas." *Los Angeles Times*, December 5, 1993.

Parseas, Jim. "Case of Woman Without a Name Leaves Police Without a Suspect." *Minneapolis Tribune*, July 15, 1980.

Pelisek, Christine. "Lost and Found in Tijuana: Behind an Amazing American Rescue." *The Daily Beast*, September 26, 2013.

Pettem, Silvia. "Ellenor Hacker Took Out the Trash and Disappeared for 11 Years." *Daily Camera*, September 13, 2009.

Reinitz, Jeff. "Now-abandoned State Cold Case Unit Solved Crimes." *Waterloo-Cedar Falls Courier*, August 1, 2015.

Rogers, Katie. "Grateful Doe Is Identified 20 Years After Road Trip Death." *New York Times*, December 11, 2015.

Rosario, Ruben. "Victim Deserves a Name, Doe Group Says." *Pioneer Press, TwinCities.com*, September 15, 2003.

Seelye, Katharine Q. "In Heroin Crisis, White Families Seek Gentler War on Drugs." *New York Times*, October 30, 2015.

Seward, Larry. "Missing Girl Mystery Solved in Minnesota." *KHOU 11 News*, July 15, 2015.

Shake, Ken. "Clue to 'Little Miss Nobody' Still Sought." *Prescott Evening Courier*, November 4, 1960.

Simpson, Kevin. "DNA Match Finally Puts Name to Boy's Remains—but Mystery Persists." *Denver Post*, June 22, 2014.

Staff. "2 Bodies Exhumed from Westmoreland County Pauper's Cemetery." *Pittsburg News 2*, October 30, 2015.

Staff. "A Timeline of the Curtis Huntzinger Case." *Eureka Times-Standard*, May 11, 2009.

Staff. "Bodies of Baby, Teen Exhumed From Pauper's Grave in Hempfield Township." *WTAE.com*, December 9, 2015.

Staff. "Body Found on Dump: Police Seek Identity of Dead Teenage Girl." *Tribune-Review*, September 20, 1967.

Staff. "Homewood Girl Is Missing." *Pittsburgh Press*, October 3, 1967.

Staff. "Deaths Mystery: Court Orders Burial of Infant, Teenager." *Greensburg Tribune*, September 26, 1967.

Staff. "Decomposed Body Found in Ditch on Independence Pass." *Leadville Herald*, June 22, 1970.

Staff. "Family Believes Sketch of Exhumed Girl Killed Decades Ago Is Missing Sister." *News wpxi.com*, December 8, 2015.

Staff. "Family Provides 'Strong Lead' to ID Girl Unearthed From Hempfield Grave." *TribLive News*, October 30, 2015.

Staff. "Larimer County Probing Mystery of Skeleton Discovered in Canon." *Greeley Tribune,* February 12, 1938.

Staff. "More Questions than Answers in ND Man's Death." *KOTA Territory News*, August 13, 2015.

Staff. "Obituaries, Mrs. Delphia Gates." *The Longmont (Colo.) Ledger*, December 8, 1960.

Staff. "Body of Small Girl Found: Unidentified Body Found on Desert." *Prescott Evening Courier*, August 1, 1960.

Staff. "Prescottonians Do Care! Open Hearts to Dead Girl." *Prescott Evening Courier,* August 10, 1960.

Staff. "Project Lifesaver Helps Law Enforcement Agencies Track Down At-risk Missing Persons." *KSBY TV*, October 28, 2015.

Staff. "Search and Rescue Dogs—Canine Heroes." *Veterinary News Network*, December 22, 2015.

Staff. "Search Continues for Baby's Killer." *Tribune-Review*, August 28, 1967.

Staff. "Who Was She?" *Blue Earth Post*, June 5, 1980.

Staff. "Man's Body Found." *Associated Press*, undated (circa June 22, 1970).

Staff. "Decomposed Body Found in Ditch on Independence Pass." *Herald Democrat*, June 22, 1970.

Stensland, Matt. "Unclear Whether Kidnapping Arrest Related to Marie Blee Cold Case." *Steamboat Today*, June 5, 2015.

Straight Dope Science Advisory Board. "What Happens When Someone 'Legally Dead' Shows Up Alive?" *The Straight Dope*, June 13, 2006.

Talamo, Alexa. "Database Reveals Parish-wide Counts of Unidentified." *Shreveport Times*, January 4, 2016.

Taxin, Amy. "Authorities Ask Family of Missing Persons for DNA, Records." *Associated Press*, September 29, 2015.

Western Newspaper Union News Service. "Aid for 148 Families." *Kiowa County Press*, March 24, 1916.

MAGAZINE AND JOURNAL ARTICLES

Loreille, Odile M., et al. "Integrated DNA and Fingerprint Analyses in the Identification of 60-Year-Old Mummified Human Remains Discovered in an Alaskan Glacier." *Journal of Forensic Sciences* (2010): 1

Lowery, Robert G., Jr, and Robert Hoever. "Family Dynamics and Survivor Recovery: Understanding the Relationships." *Long-term Missing Child Guide for Law Enforcement: Strategies for Finding Long-term Missing Children* (2016): 195.

Masri, Lena. "The Missing, Searching for New York's Lost." *NYCity News Service, CityLimits.org* (2014): 1.

Pearsall, Beth and Daniel Weiss. "Solving Missing Persons Cases." *National Institute of Justice Journal* 264, (November 2009): 6.

Pettem, Silvia. "Out of the Past: A Fresh Look at Cold Cases." *Evidence Technology Magazine*, Vol. 8, No. 2, (March–April 2010): 24–27.

Quinet, Kenna, "The Missing Missing: Toward a Quantification of Serial Murder Victimization in the United States." *Homicide Studies*, Vol. 11, No. 4, (November 2007): 1.

DOCUMENTS AND REPORTS

"Mother's Compensation Act application," Colorado State Archives, May 21, 1917.

"Motion for Exhumation and Examination of Unidentified Human Remains," (In the Court of Common Pleas of Westmoreland County, Pennsylvania, Criminal Division, 440 MISC 2015), October 27, 2015.

Anonymous letter, Faribault County Sheriff's Office, Blue Earth Jane Doe case file, 1980.

Berg, Special Agent Robert, Minnesota Bureau of Criminal Apprehension, "Report of Robert Leroy Nelson," Faribault County Sheriff's Office, Blue Earth Jane Doe case file, March 31, 1988.

Blethen, Bailey to Arvid Wendland Memorandum, "State of Minnesota v. Robert Leroy Nelson," Faribault County Sheriff's Office, Blue Earth Jane Doe case file, August 19, 1988.

California Commission on Peace Officer Standards and Training, *Missing Persons Investigations Guidelines & Curriculum* (California Commission 2007, revised 2011).

Center for Public Safety and Justice, "Alzheimer's Aware: A Guide for Implementing a Law Enforcement Program to Address Alzheimer's in the Community" (University of Illinois, 2015).

Connecticut State Police Officer Standards and Training Council, "Connecticut Police Officer Standards and Training Policy for Handling Missing Persons Investigations".

Faribault County Attorney, "Press Release," Faribault County Sheriff's Office, Blue Earth Jane Doe case file, May 27, 1988.

Faribault County Attorney's Office and the Faribault County Sheriff's Office, "Joint Press release," Faribault County Sheriff's Office, Blue Earth Jane Doe case file, August 25, 1989.

Faribault County Sheriff's Office, Blue Earth Jane Doe case file, "Sheriff Memorandum to Investigator Tom Dybvik," May 25, 2004.

Kabe, Deputy Sheriff Jerry, "Interview of Robert Leroy Nelson," Faribault County Sheriff's Office, Blue Earth Jane Doe case file, July 17, 1989.

Kirchhoff, George, "Letter to the Colorado Springs Police Department, Chief of Police," April 25, 2013.

McGee, M.D., M.B., "Autopsy report, ME80-491," Faribault County Sheriff's Office, Blue Earth Jane Doe case file, June 2, 1980.

Minnesota Bureau of Criminal Apprehension, "ACISS Investigative Supplement 1980000335/1," Faribault County Sheriff's Office, Blue Earth Jane Doe case file, June 27, 2014.

Minnesota Bureau of Criminal Apprehension, "ACISS Investigative Supplement 1980000335/4, Faribault County Sheriff's Office, Blue Earth Jane Doe case file, March 16, 2015.

Minnesota Bureau of Criminal Apprehension, "Evidence Receipt," Faribault County Sheriff's Office, Blue Earth Jane Doe case file, June 2, 1980.

National Center for Missing and Exploited Children, "2014 Annual Report" (Alexandria: NCMEC, 2014).

Shaw, Celeste, "Letter to Chief of Police, Pete Carey, Colorado Springs Police Department," August 27, 2013.

State of Minnesota, County of Faribault, District Court, "Sentence of Robert Leroy Nelson," Faribault County Sheriff's Office, Blue Earth Jane Doe case file, August 25, 1989.

State of Minnesota, County of Faribault, District Court, Fifth Judicial District, "Petition for Exhumation," Faribault County Sheriff's Office, Blue Earth Jane Doe case file, July 30, 2014.

"Unidentified Female Child," Certificate of Autopsy or Inquest, Arizona State Department of Health, approximate date of death July 15, 1960, signed October 14, 1960.

WEBSITES

Angie Yarnell Still Missing and Loved Facebook page. Accessed May 14, 2016. https://www.facebook.com/search/top/?q=Angie%20Yarnell%20Still%20 Missing%20and%20Loved.

Ballotpedia. Colorado Open Records Act. Accessed April 22, 2016. http://sunshinereview.org/index.php/Colorado_Open_Records_Act.

Carol Ann Project. Carol Ann Project Facebook page. Accessed April 23, 2016. https://www.facebook.com/CarolAnnProject/timeline.

CBS News, "Lead Attorney Johnnie Cochran—The O.J. Simpson Murder Trial 20 Years Later." Accessed May 14, 2016. http://www.cbsnews.com/pictures/ the-o-j-simpson-trial-where-are-they-now/26/.

CNN Library. Elizabeth Smart Fast Facts. Accessed April 22, 2016. http://www.cnn. com/2013/04/14/us/elizabeth-smart-fast-facts/.

CNN.com. "Jury Unanimous: Simpson is Liable." Accessed April 23, 2016. http:// www.cnn.com/US/9702/04/simpson.verdict1/.

Colorado Bureau of Investigation Cold Case Files. Accessed April 22, 2016. https:// www.colorado.gov/apps/coldcase/index.html.

Colorado Forensic Canines website. Accessed April 22, 2016. http://www.findthelost. org/.

Corrections Records, Colorado State Archives. Accessed May 14, 2016. https://www. colorado.gov/pacific/archives/corrections-records.

Elizabeth Smart Foundation. Accessed April 22, 2016. http://elizabethsmartfoundation.org/.

Families of Homicide Victims and Missing Persons website. Accessed April 22, 2016. http://www.unresolvedhomicides.org/about-us/.

Family Search, Social Security Death Index. Accessed April 22, 2016. https://familysearch.org/search/collection/1202535.

FBI Records: Freedom of Information Act/Privacy Act. Accessed April 22, 2016. http://www.fbi.gov/foia/requesting-fbi-records.

Find A Grave. Accessed April 22, 2016. http://www.findagrave.com.

FindLaw. "Wrongful Death Claims: Time Limits and the 'Discovery' Rule." Accessed April 23, 2016. http://injury.findlaw.com/torts-and-personal-injuries/ wrongful-death-claims-time-limits-and-the-discovery-rule.html.

Florida Silver Alert. Accessed April 20, 2016. http://www.floridasilveralert.com/home.

Help ID Me Facebook page. Accessed April 22, 2016. https://www.facebook.com/ HelpIDMe/.

History Flight, Inc. Accessed April 23, 2016. http://historyflight.com/nw/.

Integrated Automated Fingerprint Identification System. Accessed April 20, 2016. https://www.fbi.gov/about-us/cjis/fingerprints_biometrics/iafis/iafis.

Iowa Cold Cases Facebook page. Accessed April 22, 2016. https://www.facebook.com/iowacoldcases/.

Iowa Cold Cases website. Accessed April 22, 2016. https://iowacoldcases.org/.

Iowa Department of Public Safety, Missing Person Information Clearinghouse. Accessed April 22, 2016. http://www.iowaonline.state.ia.us/mpic/.

Lake County Library. Evergreen Cemetery Records, Accessed April 23, 2016. http://www.lakecountypubliclibrary.org/Cemetery%20Records.htm.

Lost and Missing in Indian Country Facebook page. Accessed April 22, 2016. https://www.facebook.com/LostandMissinginIndianCountry/.

Lost and Missing in Indian Country website. Accessed April 22, 2016. http://lostandmissinginindiancountry.com/about.html.

Maricopa County Recorder. Accessed April 22, 2016. http://recorder.maricopa.gov/recdocdata/.

Merriam-Webster website. Accessed May 14, 2016. http://www.merriam-webster.com/dictionary/psychic.

Minnesota Department of Public Safety. "DPS News Conference: DNA Leads BCA to Victim's Identity in 1980 Homicide." Accessed April 23, 2016. https://www.youtube.com/watch?v=O8Tw4FGOJJg.

Missing in Michigan Facebook group. Accessed April 22, 2016. https://www.facebook.com/groups/MichigansMissing/#_=_.

Missing in Michigan website. Accessed April 22, 2016. http://www.missinginmichigan.com/.

Missouri Missing website. Accessed April 22, 2016. http://www.missourimissing.org/index.html.

NamUs Unidentified Persons Welcome page. Accessed April 22, 2016. https://identifyus.org/en.

NamUs, Missing Persons Welcome page. Accessed April 22, 2016. https://www.findthemissing.org/en.

National Archives: Research Our Records. Accessed April 22, 2016. http://www.archives.gov/research/.

National Center for Missing and Exploited Children. Accessed April 20, 2016. http://www.missingkids.org/home.

National Runaway Safeline. Accessed April 22, 2016. http://www.1800runaway.org/youth-teens/.

New Jersey State Police, Missing Persons & Child Exploitation Unit. Accessed April 20, 2016. http://www.state.nj.us/njsp/division/investigations/missing-persons-child-exploit.shtml.

New York City Office of Chief Medical Examiner. Accessed April 20, 2016. http://www.nyc.gov/html/ocme/html/mpi/mpi_home.shtml.

Orange County Sheriff's Department Coroner Division website. "Identify the Missing, Orange County 2015 Flyer." Accessed April 22, 2016. http://ocsd.org/divisions/fieldops/coroner/ud.

Pennsylvania Missing Persons website. Accessed April 22, 2016. http://pennsylvania-missing.com/salemtwpjane91967.html.

Pew Research Center website. Accessed April 22, 2016. http://www.pewinternet.org/2015/08/19/the-demographics-of-social-media-users/.

Project Lifesaver website. Accessed April 20, 2016. http://www.projectlifesaver.org/.

RoadsideAmerica.com. Accessed May 15, 2016. http://www.roadsideamerica.com/story/35952.

Reddit website. Accessed May 14, 2016. https://www.reddit.com/.

Reverend Barbara M. Rocha website. Accessed April 22, 2016. http://www.theangel-rev.com/Maheo_o_Reiki.htm.

Social Security Administration website. "Presumption of Death of a Missing Person." Accessed April 22, 2016. https://secure.ssa.gov/poms.nsf/lnx/0200304050.

Texas Department of Criminal Justice website. "Offender Information Details." Accessed April 23, 2016. https://offender.tdcj.texas.gov/OffenderSearch/offender-Detail.action?sid=04082389.

Texas EquuSearch website. Accessed April 22, 2016. http://www.texasequusearch.org/.

The Doe Network website. Accessed April 22, 2016. http://www.doenetwork.org/index.php.

The Statistics Portal website. Accessed April 22, 2016. http://www.statista.com/topics/751/facebook/.

Unidentified Persons Jewelry Facebook page. Accessed April 22, 2016. https://www.facebook.com/unidentifiedpersonsjewelry/.

University of North Texas Health Science Center, Forensic Services Unit website. "Frequently Asked Questions." Accessed April 22, 2016. http://www.untfsu.com/NamUs/FAQ_DNA.html.

uslegal.com, "Protect Act of 2003 Law & Legal Definition." Accessed May 12, 2016, http://definitions.uslegal.com/p/protect-act-of-2003/.

Veromi website. Accessed April 22, 2016. http://www.veromi.net/.

Websleuths website. "Missing Forum." Accessed April 22, 2016. http://www.web-sleuths.com/forums/forumdisplay.php?16-MISSING.

Wesierski & Zurek. "Who Can Recover in a Wrongful Death Action?" October 18, 2012. Accessed April 23, 2016. http://www.wzllp.com/who-can-recover -in-a-wrongful-death-action/.

Westmoreland Manor website. Accessed April 22, 2016. http://westmorelandweb400.us/cty/manor/ourhistory.htm.

Wyoming LostNMissing Facebook page. Accessed April 22, 2016. https://www.facebook.com/wyominglostnmissing/?fref=ts.

Index

Note: Page references for figures are italicized.

Abbott, Tony (Prime Minister), 193
AFDIL. *See* Armed Forces DNA
    Identification Laboratory
AFIS. *See* Automated Fingerprint
    Identification System
AIF. *See* Australian Imperial Force
AISOCC. *See* American Investigative
    Society of Cold Cases
Alaska:
    State Police, 25.
    See also medical examiners, Office
    of the Medical Examiner,
    Anchorage
Alzheimer's:
    Aware Initiative, 19, 129;
    disease, 18–19, 59
AMBER Alert Program, 36
American:
    Graves Registration Services, 189;
    Investigative Society of Cold Cases
    (AISOCC), 83, 241;
    Red Cross, 98, 125
Andersen, William (Detective), *63*
Anderson;
    Deb, xv, 11, 78, 168, 177–79, *180*,
    181–82, 185;
    Deputy Jerry, 170;

Dr. Bruce, 17;
    Special Agent Micheal, 182
Arizona:
    Child Safety and Family Services, 61;
    Department of Public Safety, 113, 129;
    Law Enforcement Academy, 58
Armed Forces DNA Identification
    Laboratory (AFDIL), 25.
    See also United States Merchant
    Marines
Aumock, Shannon Michelle, 33, 61–62,
    63, 64, *65*, *130*, 194, *195*
Australian Imperial Force (AIF), 193
Automated Fingerprint Identification
    System (AFIS), 6.
    See also, Kelly, Lisa Kay

Bacha, Coroner Ken, 67, 69
Baird, Gloria Jean, 26–27, 137
Baker, Kristen N., 190
Battle of Ball's Bluff, 191
Bay City Police Department, 179
Berg, Special Agent Robert, 173, 178
Berry, Amanda, 35
Beverly, Paula E., 101, 114, *115*, 116,
    142
BIA. *See* Bureau of Indian Affairs

Birkby, Walter, Dr., 17, 52
Birkey, Chief Deputy Jerry, 9–10, *12, 195*
Blee:
    Marie Ann, *39*, 40–42, 120;
    Paul, *39*, 40–42, 120;
    Ramona, *39*, 40–42, 120
Bloemendaal, Blythe (Sheriff), 8–11, *12*, 13, 78, 83
Blue Earth Jane Doe. *See* Busha, Michelle Yvette
Bonnyman, Alexander "Sandy" (Jr. Lieutenant), 190–91
Bossier:
    City Police Department, 194;
    Jane Doe (*See* Cole, Carol Ann).
    See also coroners, Bossier Parish Coroner's Office
Boulder:
    County Sheriff's Office, 20, 51;
    Jane Doe (*See* Howard, Dorothy Gay);
    Police Department, 21, 241.
    See also coroners, Boulder County Coroner's Office
Bowling Green Police Department, 138
Brosnahan, Kevin (Officer), 97
Brown:
    Dorothy Holmes, 34–35;
    Jerry, 105;
    Sheriff Bill, 19
Buchholtz, Beth (CSO), 51–57, 59
Bureau of Indian Affairs (BIA), 80, 128
Burney, John, 163
Busha:
    Don, 167;
    Michelle Yvette, xv, 11, 167–70, *171*, 172–79, *180*, 181–82

California:
    Commission on Peace Officer Standards and Training, 16, 18;
    Department of Justice, 126;
    State Prison, 154
Callahan, Jason, 119–21, 136

Campbell, Sheriff Scott, 176, 179
Can You Identify Me?, 129
catastrophic missing, definition of, 23
CBI. *See* Colorado Bureau of Investigation
CCC. *See* Civilian Conservation Corps
cemeteries:
    Bracken Cemetery (Bracken, Texas), 104, *106*;
    Cemetery 27 (Betio Island, Republic of Kiribati, Gilbert Islands), 189–91;
    Columbia Cemetery (Boulder, Colorado), *196*;
    Crucifix Corner Cemetery (Villers-Bretonneux, France), 193;
    Evergreen Cemetery (Leadville, Colorado), 183, *184*, 186;
    Floral Hills East Memorial Gardens (Lee's Summit, Missouri), *115*, 116;
    Golden Cemetery (Golden, Colorado), 6, *7*;
    Heritage Sunwest Cemetery (El Mirage, Arizona), 64, *65, 195*;
    Highland Memorial Park Cemetery (Knoxville, Tennessee), 190;
    Maple Grove Cemetery (Comstock Township, Michigan), 194;
    Mountain View Cemetery (Prescott, Arizona), *186*, 187;
    New York Cemetery (Hart Island, New York), 33–34;
    Riverside Cemetery (Blue Earth, Minnesota), 168, *180*;
    Riverview Cemetery (Rock Rapids, Iowa), 9, 11, *12, 195*;
    Twin Buttes Cemetery (Tempe, Arizona), 61, *63*;
    Westmoreland County Home Cemetery (Greensburg, Pennsylvania), *69*
Center for HOPE, 125
Chapman, Sergeant Bryan, 60, 62, *63*, 64
Child Identification Program:

Arizona Masonic Foundation, 129;
Nevada Lodge #4 (Colorado), 131
Children's Hospital of Pittsburgh, 70
Christ Church of the Valley, 64
Church of Jesus Christ of Latter-Day
Saints, 145
Civilian Conservation Corps (CCC), 150
Clark, Surette, 38–39, 141
Cochran, Johnnie, 165
Coconino County:
Sheriff's Office, 193.
See also medical examiners;
Coconino County Office of the
Medical Examiner
CODIS. *See* Combined DNA Index
System
Cole, Carol Ann, 193–94
Colibri Center for Human Rights, 129
Colorado:
Bureau of Investigation (CBI), 7, 95,
113, 185, 241;
Capitol Building, 42;
Department of Public Safety, Cold
Case Task Force, 42;
General Assembly, 28;
Open Records Act, 150;
Revised Statutes, 150;
State Archives, 27, 151–52
Colorado Forensics Canines, 86–87, *88*,
89, 131;
Lena, *88*, 89;
Porter, 89;
Stoner, 89
Colorado Springs Police Department,
91, 93, 103–6
Columbia Elementary School, 103
Colvan Sanitary Landfill, 66
Comal County:
Sheriff's Office, 103–5.
See also medical examiners; Comal
County Medical Examiner
Craig Police Department, 40
Combined DNA Index System
(CODIS), 7, 45, 52, 57, 62, 64,
179, 181–82

Commonwealth War Graves Office
(Australia), 193
Connecticut Police Officer Standards
and Training, 18
Consulado General de Mexico en
Phoenix, Arizona, 129
Coogan, Joseph, 136
CORA. *See* Colorado Open Records Act
coroners:
Bossier Parish Coroner's Office, 194;
Boulder County Coroner's Office,
51–52, 131;
Coroner Division, Orange County
Sheriff's Department, 125;
Jefferson County Coroner's Office, 6;
Lake County Coroner's Office, 186;
Westmoreland County Coroner's
Office, 65–69.
See also medical examiners
Cox, Investigator Wayne, 49
Curtis:
Regina Marie, 81;
Virgil, 81

Davis, Paula Beverly. *See* Beverly,
Paula E.
DCI. *See* Iowa, Division of Criminal
Investigation
Defense POW/MIA Accounting
Agency, 189–90
DeJesus, Georgina, 35
Demaris, Lillian, 84
dental records, xv, 45–46, 52, 54, 108,
110–12, 114, 125;
Aumock case, 62;
Bonnyman, used to identify, 190;
Busha case, 170–72, 178–79, 182;
Independence Pass John Doecase,
185–86;
Kirchhoff case, 104–6;
Overstreet case, 16–17;
Sara (Celeste Shaw's sister) case,
91, 94;
Thompson case, 68
Denver:

County Jail, 7;
   Probate Court, 154
Dirkmaat, Dennis, Dr., 69–70
Disaster Chaplaincy Services, 125
Discovery Investigations, 87
Doe Network, 62, 77, 79, 95, 125, 143,
   177–78
DPAA. *See* Defense POW/MIA
   Accounting Agency
Dugard, Jaycee, 35
Dyer, Katharine Farrand, 20

Egerton, David, 73, *74*, 75–78
El Paso County:
   Court, 97;
   Sheriff's Office, 105
Elizabeth Smart Foundation, 35, 37
Embrey, Twylia May, 143, 145–46
Evans, Clay Bonnyman, 189–91
Ewing, Jody, 82–86, 136
exhumations, 44–46, 55, 57;
   Blue Earth Jane Doe (Busha), 178,
      180, 181;
   Bonnyman, 189–90;
   Boulder Jane Doe (Howard), 51–52;
   Independence Pass John Doe, *184*,
      186;
   Jane Doe 1967 (Thompson) and
      infant, 67–70, 135;
   Jane Doe 92–1169 (Aumock), *63*, 64;
   Our Girl (Nissen), 11–13

Facebook, 26, 76–77, 119–20, 138, 144,
   194;
   Angie Yarnell Still Missing and
      Loved, 137;
   Carol Ann Project, 194;
   Coconino County Sheriff's Office
      Cold Cases & Missing Persons,
      136;
   defined, 136;
   Grateful Doe, 119–20;
   Help ID Me, 46, 137;
   Iowa Cold Cases, 85, 136;
   launching pages and groups, 137;

Lost and Missing in Indian Country,
      79, *80*, 81, 129, 136;
   Missing in Arizona, 126, 136;
   Missing in Colorado, 131;
   Missing in Michigan, 124, 132, 136;
   Missouri Missing, 136;
   Unidentified Persons Jewelry, 81;
   Unsolved & Missing in Texas, 136;
   Where is Gloria Jean?, 26, 137;
   Wyoming LostNMissing, 79, 136
facial reconstructions, 38, 67, 70, *71*,
   74–76, 78, 119, 178, 181;
   Manchester Method of Facial
      Reconstruction, 56;
   NCMEC Forensic Imaging Team,
      44–46;
   NCMEC forensic workshop, 55–57
familial DNA, 52, 55, 73, 104, 121,
   124–26, 131
Families of Homicide Victims and
   Missing Persons (FOHVAMP),
   42, 131–32, 241
Faribault County:
   Attorney, 174–76;
   Sheriff's Office, 170, *171*, 172–80
FBI. *See* Federal Bureau of
   Investigation
Federal Bureau of Investigation (FBI),
   46, 80, 193;
   DNA comparison by, 45, 52,
      178–79, 181–82;
   federal records maintained by, 149;
   fingerprints maintained by, 9–10,
      150;
   NCIC maintained by, 43;
   participant in Missing in Arizona
      Day event, 129;
   participant in task force, 40;
   policy for DNA comparison, 114
Feeney, Judge John E., 164
First Judicial District (Colorado), 8
Flaming Gorge Reservoir, 2, 23
Fletcher, Sheriff Roger, 170, 175–76,
   181
Flores, Cristobal James, 52–54

Florida Institute for Forensic Anthropology and Applied Science, 55–56
FOHVAMP. *See* Families of Homicide Victims and Missing Persons
FOIA. *See* Freedom of Information Act
Ford Field, 123
Fort:
  Benjamin Harrison, 26;
  McClellan, 26
Franson, Janet, 79–82, 129
Freedom of Information Act (FOIA), 149–50

Galzi, Paloma, 70, *71*
Gates:
  Delphia, *27*, 28–29;
  Herman Albert, *27*, 28;
  John William, *27*, 28–29;
  Robert, *27*, 29
genealogical resources:
  Ancestry.com, 121, 142, 145;
  FamilySearch.org, 142, 145;
  RootsWeb.com, 55, 142
George Washington Bridge, 73, 76
Georgia Bureau of Investigation, 113
Glatman:
  Harvey, 151, 154;
  Ophelia, 154
Goldman, Ron, 164–65
Google, 3, 55, 76, 95, 143–44, 153, 156, 158
Gordon, Detective Edwin, 66
Gormley, Sheriff Michael S., *171*, 179
Grateful Doe. *See* Callahan, Jason
Green, John David, 84
Gregory, Melissa, 101, 107–9, 131
Gross, Trooper Brian F., 44, 64–66, 68–70, 114, 135, 181
Grout, Lieutenant John William, 191
Guzman, Bonnie, 87–90

Hacker, Ellenor, 21–22
Hagerman, Amber, 36
Haider, Eric, 86–87, 90

Halpern:
  Joseph Laurence, 23, 27, 149–50;
  Roland, 23, 149–50
Hare Krishna, 32
Harvey M. Glatman Memorial Scholarship, 154
Hayden:
  High School, 41;
  Police Department, 40–41
Health Insurance Portability and Accountability Act (HIPPA), 154
Heist, Brenda, 22, 162–63
Herren:
  Gina (*See* Hoogendoorn, Gina);
  Linda, 2, *3*, 4–5;
  Richard DeWayne "Rick," 2, *3*, 4–5, 23
Hess, Dr. Gregory, 17
Hillman, Alyssa, 119
HIPPA. *See* Health Insurance Portability and Accountability Act
History Flight, Inc., 189–91
Hoffa, Jimmie, 163
Holland, Undersheriff Stephen, *88*
Holloway, Natalee, 163
Holmes, Frederick "Freddie," 34–35
Hoogendoorn, Gina, xv, 2–5, 87
Hopi Indian Reservation, 128
Howard, Dorothy Gay, 1, 20, 177, 194, *196*
Huisentruit, Jodi Sue, 84
Hull, Trooper Richard, 170, 173
Humboldt County District Attorney's Office, 49
Huntzinger:
  Curtis, 48–49, 163–64;
  Nancy, 49, 163–64
Hurricane Katrina, 23, 47
Hyde, Sergeant 1st Class Gordon, *96*

IAFIS. *See* Integrated Automated Fingerprint Identification System
INA. *See* Iowa Newspaper Association
Independence Pass John Doe, *184*, 185–86

Innocence Lost Initiative, 47
Integrated Automated Fingerprint
    Identification System (IAFIS), 9,
    13.
    See also Nissen, Wilma June
Internet research:
    new era for cold cases, 51, 142–43,
    147, 177;
    newspapers, finding information in,
    155;
    use in missing person cases, 76, 81,
    84, 114, 193
Interpol, 46
Iowa:
    Cold Cases, Inc., 82–85;
    Division of Criminal Investigation
    (DCI), 9, 12, 84–85, 113;
    Newspaper Association (INA), 85

Jackson County Sheriff's Department, *88*
Jane Doe 1967, *71*.
    See *also* Thompson, Teala Patricia
Jane Doe 1989. *See* Kelly, Lisa Kay
Jane Doe 92–1169. *See* Aumock,
    Shannon Michelle
Jeannette Sewage Plant, 66
Jefferson County:
    District Attorney's Office, 8;
    Sheriff's Office, 6, 8.
    See also coroners; Jefferson County
    Coroner's Office
Jeremiah, Sergeant Teresa, 179
Johanneck, Lesha, 119–20
Jolly Green Giant, 169
Jones, Agent Chuck, 193

K–9 testing agencies:
    Law Enforcement Training
    Specialists, 89;
    North American Police Work Dog
    Association, 89
Kabe:
    Chief Investigator Jerry, 170, 172,
    175–76, 181;

Deputy Sheriff Gerald (*See* Kabe,
    Jerry (Chief Investigator))
Karl, Captain Vergil, 170, 173
Kelly, Lisa Kay, 5–6, *7*, 8, 183
Kirchhoff:
    George, 102–6, 109;
    Paul Daniel, 18, 102–5, *106*
Kirkland, Athol Goodwin (Corporal), 193
Klass, Polly, 35, 37.
    See also Polly Klass Foundation
Knight, Michelle, 35
Knutson, Catherine, 182
Koster, Mark Edgar, 84
Krebs, Sergeant Sarah, 123–24
Kroner, Ashley, 79–80, 136

Lakeland Police Department, 79
Lamborn, US Congressman Doug, 98
LaPoint, Stephanie, 26–27
Latulip, Edgar, 117
Lavigne, Micki, 143
Lerman:
    Jackie, 172, 177–78;
    Phil, 172, 177–78
Lewinsky, Monica, 176
Lewis Brothers Circus, 150
libraries:
    Blue Earth Community Library, 156;
    Denver Public Library, 132;
    Lake County Public Library, 185
Linn, John, 4
Little:
    Jane Doe (*See* Clark, Surette);
    Miss Nobody, *186*, 187–88
Lititz Borough Police Department, 22
Longmont Police Department, 51–55
Lopez, Detective Ron, 91, 95, 97,
    104–6, 109
Los Angeles Police Department, 10, 58
Loughran, District Attorney Joseph M.,
    66
Lovelock Correctional Center, 165
Lucas, Henry Lee, 172
Lyall, Suzanne, 43

Lyon County Sheriff's Department, 8–11, *12*, 13, *195*

Mack, Lieutenant Shannon, 194
maliciously missing, definition of, 20
Maricopa County:
  Attorney's Office, 60;
  Public Health Department, Office of Vital Registration, 129;
  Recorder, 152;
  Sheriff's Office, 126, 129.
  See also medical examiners; Maricopa County Office of the Medical Examiner
Marion, Daniel, Jr. (PhD), 131
Marsh, Cynthia, 131
Matagorda County Sheriff's Office, 167, 169, 172, 179, 182
Matthews, J. Todd, 101, *108*
Mauer, Ben, 33–34
McDowell, Marion Joan, 34
McGee, Dr. Michael B., 171–72
McGregor, Kevin A., 24–25
McLaughlin, John S., 150
McWilliams, Megan, 79–80, 136
Medicaid, 98
medical examiners:
  Coconino County Office of the Medical Examiner, 129;
  Comal County Medical Examiner, 103–5;
  Maricopa County Office of the Medical Examiner, 95, 126, 129, *130*;
  Montgomery County Medical Examiner, 114;
  New York City Office of Chief Medical Examiner, 15, 77–78, 125;
  Office of the Medical Examiner, Anchorage, 25;
  Olmsted County Medical Examiner, 181;
  Pima County Office of Medical Examiner, 17, 130;

Ramsey County Medical Examiner's Office, 171–72, 178, 182;
  Southern Minnesota Regional Medical Examiner's Office, 181;
  Travis County Medical Examiner, 104.
  See also coroners
mental illness, 17–18, 76, 93, 98–99, 102–3, 117, 128, 172
Mercyhurst College, 67, 69
Merwin, Kelley, *63*
Mesa County:
  Meth Task Force, 42;
  Sheriff's Office, 42
microfilm scanner, 153, 155–56, *157*, 158, 185
Miller:
  Laura, 86;
  Tim, 86
Millican, Marc, 24–25
Minnesota:
  Bureau of Criminal Apprehension (MNBCA), 170–71, 173–74, 178–82;
  State Patrol, *171*
Missal, Stephen J., 130
missing day events:
  Identify the Missing (Michigan), 124;
  Identify the Missing (Orange County, California), 125;
  Missing in Arizona, 126, *127–28*, 129, *130*, 131, 160;
  Missing in Colorado, 57, 131;
  Missing in Michigan, 123–24, 126;
  New York City Missing Persons, 125
missing, definition of, 24, 33
Missouri Missing (support group), 132, 136–37
MNBCA. *See* Minnesota Bureau of Criminal Apprehension
Moffat County:
  Fairgrounds, 40;
  Sheriff's Office, 40–41

Monroe County Sheriff's Office, 22
Monterey County Sheriff's Office, 136
Montgomery County. *See* medical
    examiners, Montgomery County
    Medical Examiner
Moonies, 32
Moore, Investigator Cheryl, 6–8
Morton, Howard, 42
Moser, Agent Dan, 10
Mother's Compensation Act, 27–28
Mullins, Joe, 55
music:
    Amazing Grace, 64, 192, 195;
    The Vacant Chair, 191–92
musicians:
    Eagles, 169;
    Grateful Dead, 120, 169;
    Jennings, Waylon, 169
Myster, Susan, 181

NamUs System (NamUs), xv, 13, 79,
    101–2, 122, 125, 127–28, 130–31;
    families, use by, 109–14, 117,
    120–21, 142, 146, 161;
    logo, *108*;
    NCMEC, use by, 45–46;
    police, use by, 55, 57, 62, 64, 68, 71;
    regional administrators, use by, 107,
    108, 109.
    See also Baird, Gloria Jean;
    Beverly, Paula E.; Sara (Celeste
    Shaw's sister); Cole, Carol Ann;
    Flores, Cristobal James; Gates,
    John William; Halpern, Joseph
    Laurence; Holmes, Frederick
    "Freddie" ; Kirchhoff, Paul
    Daniel; Little Miss Nobody;
    Nevayaktewa, Darian; Ulrich,
    Rosemary "Ro"
Nance:
    Jerry, 48;
    Mike, 105
National:
    Archives, 149;
    Coalition for the Homeless, 32;

Crime Information Center (NCIC), 43,
    45–46, 61–62, 64, 71, 105, 111;
Institute of Justice (NIJ), xiii, 101,
    104, 108, 111, 189;
Maritime Center, 25;
Missing and Unidentified Persons
    System (*See* NamUs System
    (NamUs));
Runaway Safeline, 33, 130–31.
See National Center for Missing &
    Exploited Children® (NCMEC)
National Center for Missing &
    Exploited Children® (NCMEC),
    31, 43–49, 107, 161;
    Aumock case, 62;
    Biometrics Team, 44–45;
    Blee case, 39;
    Blue Earth (Busha) case, 181;
    Family Advocacy Division, 133;
    Flores case, 52;
    Forensic Imaging Team, 44, 46, 57;
    Forensic Services Unit, 45–49;
    Grateful Doe (Callahan) case, 119;
    Holmes case, 35;
    Huntzinger case, 49;
    Jane Doe 1977 (Thompson) case,
    67–68, 70, *71*;
    Little Jane Doe (Clark) case, 38;
    missing day events, participation in,
    125, 130–31;
    Project ALERT®, 44–45, 55, 79;
    statistics, 32, 34, 37, 43;
    Team Hope, 124, 130, 133–34.
    See also Facebook; Help ID Me
Naval Criminal Investigative Service
    (NCIS), 46
NCIC. *See* National Crime Information
    Center
NCIS. *See* Naval Criminal Investigative
    Service
NCMEC. *See* National Center for
    Missing & Exploited Children®
Nelson, Trooper Robert Leroy, 173–74
Nevayaktewa, Darian, 128–29
New Jersey State Police, 15

New York City:
   Administration for Children's
      Services, 125;
   Department of Health and Mental
      Hygiene, 125;
   Human Resources Administration/
      Department of Social Services,
      125;
   Mayor's Community Affairs Unit,
      125;
   Mayor's Office for International
      Affairs, 125;
   Office of Emergency Management,
      125;
   Police Department, 125.
   See also medical examiners; New
      York City Office of Chief
      Medical Examiner
New York State Division of Criminal
   Justice Services, 32
NewsBank, America's News, 155–158
Newton, John, 192
NIJ. *See* National Institute of Justice
Nissen, Wilma June, 8–11, *12*, 13, 83,
   194, *195*
Noah, Mark, 190
no-body homicides, definition of, 60.
   See also Clark, Surette
North Junior High School, 103
Northern Colorado Crime Stoppers,
   Inc., 131
Northwest Airlines, 24

Oklahoma City Police Department, 81
Oliveira, Public Information Officer Jill,
   181
Olmsted County. *See* medical
   examiners, Olmsted County
   Medical Examiner
Open Records Requests, 153–54
Orange County Sheriff's Department,
   125–26
Ouija Board, 159
Our Girl. *See* Nissen, Wilma June
Overstreet, Jeanne, 16–17, 19, 121

Palmer High School, 103
Parker, Dr. Charles Franklin, 187–88
Parson's School of Design, 73, *74*, 75–76
Peck, District Attorney John, 68
Pennsylvania:
   Coroner's Act, 68;
   State Police, 64–65, 68, 113, 135
Peterson, Delphia Carrie. *See* Gates,
   Delphia
Pew Research Center, 136
Phelps, Jeanie, 193
Phillips, Detective Doug, 106
Phoenix Police Department, xiii, 38,
   57–64, 126–27, 160, *195*
Piakis, John, Dr., 62
Piearson, John, *184*, 185–86
Pima County. *See* medical examiners,
   Pima County Office of Medical
   Examiner
Pittsburgh Police Department, 70
Point Reyes National Seashore, 135
Polly Klass Foundation, 35
POW/MIA Accounting Agency, 189
presidents:
   Bush, US President George W., 36;
   Carter, US President Jimmy, 169;
   Clinton, US President Bill, 176
presumption of death, 96, 161–62
Priest Lake, 23
Project Lifesaver International, 19
PROTECT Act of 2003, 36, 43

Ramsey County. *See* medical examiners,
   Ramsey County Medical
   Examiner's Office
Ralston & Associates, 86–87
Ralston:
   and Associates, 86–87;
   Gene, 3–5, 86–87;
   Sandy, 3–5, 86
Raveill, Jay, *115*
Reid, Billy Edwin, 7–8
Reynolds, Joseph K., 162
Robert F. Kennedy Memorial Stadium,
   120

Rocky Mountain National Park, 23, 150
Rodriguez:
    Ashley, 47;
    Paty, 64
Root, George, 191
Routt County Sheriff's Office, 40–41
Rowe:
    Chad, 193;
    Cheryl, 193
Ryan, Carol, 124

Sac City Police Department, 84
Sadar, Kim, 87–88
Sara (Celeste Shaw's sister), 91, *92*,
    93–99
Schewe, Gilbert, 170
Schofield, Detective John, 22
Schweitzer, Carol, 46–49, 137
Sculco, Judge L. Alexander, 66
sex-trafficking victims, 32–33
Shaw, Celeste, xv, 91, *92*, 93–99, 146,
    161
Silver Alerts, 18
Simpson:
    Nicole Brown, 164;
    O.J., 164–65, 176
Smart:
    Ed, 36, *37*;
    Elizabeth, 35–36, *37*;
    Mary Katherine, 36.
    See also Elizabeth Smart
    Foundation
Smithsonian Institute, 181
social media and forums:
    Reddit, 137–38;
    Reunion.com, 145;
    RootsWeb.com, 55, 142;
    Websleuths, 137, 138.
    See also Facebook
Social Security:
    benefits, 21, 94, 161;
    Death Index, 145–46;
    numbers, 55, 96, 146, 149;
    records, 104
Somershoe, Detective Stuart, xiii–xv,
    33, 57–62, *63*, 64, 127–29, 160

Southern Minnesota. *See* medical
    examiners, Southern Minnesota
    Regional Medical Examiner's
    Office
Spiritualism, 159
Storey, District Attorney Scott, 8
Streetlight USA, 131
Sunwest Mortuary, 64
Suzanne's Law, 43

Talbot, John Michael, 11
television shows:
    America's Most Wanted, 62, 177;
    John Walsh show, *37*;
    Mad Men, 20
Tempe Police Department, 38
Texas:
    EquSearch, 86;
    State Penitentiary, 173, 176
Thelander, Earl, 82
Thompson:
    Mary, 70–71;
    Teala Patricia, 44, 70–71, 121
thrown-away children, definition of, 33,
    47, 61–62
Tijuana, Mexico, *96*, 97–98
Tip Top Search and Rescue, 4
Township of Kalamazoo Police
    Department, 193
Travis County. *See* medical examiners,
    Travis County Medical Examiner
Tucson Police Department, 16

Ulrich, Rosemary "Ro," 18, 56, 73, *74*,
    75–78, 125
United States:
    Air Force, 24;
    Army, 26;
    Coast Guard (USCG), 46, 136;
    Marines, 189–91;
    Merchant Marines, 24–26;
    Secret Service (USSS), 46
Universities:
    Arizona State University, 126, 129;
    Boston University, 76;
    Brigham Young University, *37*;

Colorado State University, 56;
Denver University, 154;
Harvard University, 136;
La Salle University, 58;
Louisiana State University, 194;
Metropolitan State University of
Denver, Human Identification
Lab, 131;
State University of New York at
Albany, 43;
University of Nebraska-Lincoln, 107;
University of North Texas Center
for Human Identification. (*See*
University of North Texas Health
Science Center);
University of Pittsburgh, 65;
University of South Florida, 56
University of North Texas Health
Science Center, 70, 104–5, 107,
121, 130, 179
US:
Consulate, Tijuana, 93, 97;
Department of Justice, 36, 85

van Heest, Valerie, 25
van Zandt, Seaman Francis Joseph,
25–26
Veromi, 144
Veterans:
Affairs Medical Center, 42;

of Foreign Wars, 55
ViCAP. *See* Violent Criminal
Apprehension Program
Vidocq Society, 51, 241
Vinson, Sheriff Craig, 11
Violent Criminal Apprehension Program
(ViCAP), 46

Walsh, John, 36, *37*
Walton, R. H., 118, 241
wars:
Civil War, 191–92;
World War I, 28, 193;
World War II, 189, 191
Washburn, Henry S., 191
Wayne County Morgue, 124
Wendland, Arvid, 176
Westmoreland County:
District Attorney's Office, 68;
Home/Poor Farm, 67;
Manor, 67.
See also, coroners; Westmoreland
County Coroner's Office
Williams, Lanell, 6–8
Wilson, Detective Tim, 138
Wolf, Morgan, *88*
World Trade Center, 87, 89, 149, 162

Yavapai County Sheriff's Office,
187–88

About the Author

Silvia Pettem is a researcher, writer, and author, with a passion for cold cases, unidentified remains, and long-term missing persons. She contributed to the identification of the victim of a fifty-five-year-old cold case homicide; she is an associate member of the Vidocq Society and is one of the organization's Medal of Honor recipients. She is also a volunteer in the Detectives Section of the Boulder Police Department and a NamUs instructor in classes sponsored by the Colorado Bureau of Investigation.

In addition, Silvia is a member of Families of Homicide Victims & Missing Persons (FOHVAMP) and The American Investigative Society of Cold Cases (AISOCC). She is the author of more than a dozen books, including *Someone's Daughter: In Search of Justice for Jane Doe*, and *Cold Case Research: Resources for Unidentified, Missing, and Cold Homicide Cases*, and is a contributing author in R.H. Walton's *Practical Cold Case Homicide Investigations Procedural Manual*.

Silvia can be contacted through her website, www.silviapettem.com.